Beauty Shop Politics

WOMEN IN AMERICAN HISTORY

Series Editors
Anne Firor Scott
Susan Armitage
Susan K. Cahn
Deborah Gray White

*A list of books in the series
appears at the end of this book.*

Beauty Shop Politics

African American Women's Activism in the Beauty Industry

TIFFANY M. GILL

UNIVERSITY OF ILLINOIS PRESS
Urbana, Chicago, and Springfield

Publication of this book is supported by a University
Cooperative Society Subvention Grant awarded by the
University of Texas at Austin.

COVER ART: Beautician Vera Pigee discusses voter registration
with a client in Mississippi, 1964. Photograph by Charles Moore.
Used with permission from Black Star.

Library of Congress Cataloging-in-Publication Data
Gill, Tiffany M.
Beauty shop politics : African American women's activism
in the beauty industry / Tiffany M. Gill.
p.   cm. — (Women in American history)
Includes bibliographical references and index.
ISBN 978-0-252-03505-0 (cloth : alk. paper)
ISBN 978-0-252-07696-1 (paper : alk. paper)
1. African American women political activists—History—
20th century. 2. Beauty culture—Political aspects—United
States—History—20th century. 3. Beauty culture—Economic
aspects—United States—History—20th century. 4. African
American beauty operators—Political activity—History—20th
century. 5. Businesswomen—United States—Political activity—
History—20th century. 6. African American business
enterprises—History—20th century. 7. African Americans—
Economic conditions—20th century. 8. African Americans—
Politics and government—20th century. 9. African Americans—
Civil rights—History—20th century. 10. United States—Race
relations—History—20th century.
I. Title.
E185.86.G494   2010
646.7'2092—dc22   2009020148

To my daddy,
George Hilton Gill (1924–1995),
the smartest man I have ever known.

Contents

Acknowledgments

So many have supported me over the years to ensure what first started out as a thought became a seminar paper, then a dissertation, and eventually a book. The words that follow are my humble attempt to express my deepest gratitude.

The seeds of this project and indeed my career as an academic were planted while I was an undergraduate at Georgetown University. I am forever grateful for the mentorship and intervention of Dr. Kim Hall who recognized within me the makings of a scholar while I was still determined to be a lawyer. At Rutgers University I was part of a caring and intellectually engaging community of learners and thinkers. The masterful insights of my advisor, Deborah Gray White, into African American women's history and the historical profession have been invaluable. I would also like to thank Nancy Hewitt for being such a great dissertation committee member and continual champion of my work. This book began as a seminar paper in David Levering Lewis's Seminar in African American History, and I am grateful for his provocative insights in the early stages of this project. I would be remiss if I did not acknowledge the generosity of Clement Alexander Price, Distinguished Service Professor at Rutgers-Newark, who not only guided my scholarly work but also demonstrated in work and in deed the highest ideals of the academic profession. Finally, my graduate student colleagues at Rutgers have remained dear friends and a continued source of support and scholarly wisdom. I especially wish to thank William Jelani Cobb, Justin Hart, Daniel Katz, Peter Lau, Kelena Reid Maxwell, Khalil Muhammad, Amrita Chakrabarti Myers, Aminah Pilgrim, and Stephanie Sims Wright for being amazing thinkers and even better friends.

As a faculty member, I have found the University of Texas at Austin to be a supportive environment in which to thrive intellectually. Colleagues in the Department of History, most notably Toyin Falola, Laurie Green, Frank Guridy, Martin Summers, Alan Tully, Ann Twinam, and Juliet E. K. Walker, have been especially helpful with this project. In addition, my courtesy appointments with the John L. Warfield Center for African and African American Studies (under the directorships of Edmund T. Gordon and Omi Oshun Olomo) and the Center for Women's and Gender Studies (under the directorship of Gretchen Ritter) have connected me to an even wider cadre of scholars and resources. A faculty fellowship from the Humanities Institute provided a much needed course release and stimulating conversation, and I am especially grateful to have received funding and a semester off in the form of a Dean's Fellowship from the College of Liberal Arts.

I have also been amazed at just how much those outside of my home institutions have invested in this project. The American Association of University Women Postdoctoral Fellowship provided financial assistance during the 2005–6 academic year, while fellow panelists and commentators at the Business History Conference, the Association for the Study of Afro-American Life and History, the Berkshire Conference, and the Southern Historical Association offered great suggestions and critiques. Librarians and archivists often went well beyond the call of duty while helping me with this project, especially Wilma Gibb at the Indiana Historical Society, Michael Flug and Beverly Cook at the Carter G. Woodson Regional Branch of the Chicago Public Library, and Kenneth Chandler at the National Archives for Black Women's History. The knowledge, generosity, and enthusiasm of Georgia Robins Sadler, Associate Director of Community Outreach at the University of California–San Diego Moores Cancer Center made the book's final chapter possible. Finally, the University of Illinois Press has been a great place for me to publish my first book. Many thanks to Laurie Matheson for her wisdom and patience and for getting my manuscript into the hands of two careful and insightful readers, Susan Cahn and Lynn Hudson.

In many ways, my greatest debt of gratitude is for those I knew long before I began this book and who will love and support me long after. First, to my family, especially my mom, Helen Gill, my sister, Dorothy Gill, and my nieces and nephews, thank you for being my biggest cheerleaders and reminding me of what is truly important in life. Research trips were always more enjoyable when I knew that I would get to laugh and play with you after a long day in the archives. To my dear friends, Monique Schlichtman and Karen Traylor, you are the smartest women I know; thank you for allowing me to vent when the process seemed too overwhelming and for reminding me to take time to celebrate. Following Jesus Christ while living the life of the mind is often a difficult journey and I am forever indebted to the prayers and support of my various spiritual communities in New York City and Austin. Dear friends at Times Square Church, Promiseland Church, the University of Texas' Christian Faculty Network, and Hope in the City Church provided a respite from the sometimes harsh realities of academia.

Heavenly Father, I look forward to the next milestone of faith we will conquer together.

Introduction

Finding Politics in Unexpected Places:
The Matrix of Beauty, Business, and Activism

In 1957, when Bernice Robinson, a forty-one-year-old Charleston beautician, was asked to become the first teacher for the Highlander Folk School's Citizenship Education Program in the South Carolina Sea Islands, she was surprised for she had neither experience as a teacher nor a college education. This did not present a problem for Myles Horton, founder of the Highlander Folk School; his main concern was that the Sea Islanders would have a teacher they could trust and who would respect them. In fact, for Horton, Robinson's profession was an asset. In his autobiography, he explained the strategic importance of using beauticians as leaders in civil rights initiatives by declaring that "we needed to build around black people who could stand up against white opposition, so black beauticians were very important."[1]

Robinson's activism and Horton's acknowledgment of the strategic importance of beauticians form the basis of my exploration into the ways the black beauty industry since its inception has served as an incubator for black women's political activism and a platform from which to agitate for social and political change. In so doing, I restore economics and entrepreneurship as important variables in black women's activism and community building and argue that the beauty industry played a crucial role in the creation of a modern black female identity and raises larger questions concerning the role of beauty, business, and politics in the lives of African American women. The black beauty industry and particularly beauticians and the institutions they built—namely, the beauty salons they owned and operated and the beauty schools they established—are a fruitful source to explore the ways black women conceived and executed social, political, and economic change during the twentieth and early twenty-first centuries. Often vilified as undermining women's political possibilities and denounced for compromising racial solidarity, the black beauty industry must be understood as providing one of the most important opportunities for black women to assert leadership in their communities and in the larger political arena.

The significant role of beauticians in the African American political tradition has for the most part been ignored by historians, even though their presence was screaming out for recognition from the archives. I first encountered the activist leadership of African American beauticians in the context of the modern black freedom struggle through Bernice Robinson. Thinking that perhaps Horton's observation concerning the importance of black beauticians was limited to the peculiarities of the Citizenship Education Program, I was later astonished to find everyone from Martin Luther King to Ella Baker touting beauticians as key political mobilizers. As I began to step back through the twentieth century, I discovered that beauticians were at the forefront of black internationalism in the 1950s and were undeniably the major financial and physical supporters of Mary McLeod Bethune and her brand of broker politics. Furthermore, some of the most active women in Marcus Garvey's Universal Negro Improvement Association (UNIA) and in the black socialist movements of the 1930s were beauticians. Paradoxically, many of those most active in the early black business and female club movements and those most actively providing a critique to the sexism and elitism of these movements were beauticians. Not only were beauticians, or beauty culturists as they were called for most of the twentieth century, involved in these and other national and grass-roots campaigns, but they were usually represented in large numbers, serving as leaders and mobilizers. Intrigued, I sought out to find out why this was the case and, furthermore, sought to uncover their historical significance. What can we learn by examining the history of beauty and business in black women's lives that we cannot learn elsewhere?

After extensive research, I now posit that beauticians were so politically active because they were among the most economically autonomous members of the black community in the twentieth century. They were at the center of perhaps the only lucrative industry in which all aspects were controlled primarily by black women. Black women served as the manufacturers, practitioners, consumers, and promoters of beauty culture. As a consequence, black beauticians built a livelihood with an economic base independent from and beyond the reproach of those antagonistic to racial uplift and civil rights work, unlike the positions held by other black female laborers and entrepreneurs.

Furthermore, black beauticians had access to a physical space—the beauty salon. At the center of this study is an attempt to understand the historical use of the black beauty shop as one of the most important—albeit unique—institutions within the African American community. Throughout the years covered here, the beauty salon functioned as both a public and private institution, a hidden space where beauty culturists had the economic and physical autonomy to encourage their clientele, as well as other members of their communities, to act on behalf of issues that concerned them. As Robin Kelley has argued, Jim Crow ordinances forced places such as "churches, bars, social clubs, barber shops, beauty salons, even alleys, [to] remain 'black' space." These spaces, Kelley continues, "gave African Americans a place to hide, a place to plan."[2] Of all of the sites he mentions, the beauty shop is the only space that was not only a "black space" but also a "woman's space" owned by black women and a place where they gathered exclusively. I contend that examining beauty shops, beauty organizations, beauty schools, and the women who owned and operated them gives unique insight into black women's resistance strategies and political leadership styles.[3]

Historically, black women in America have had a complicated relationship to beauty standards; not surprisingly, their participation in the beauty culture industry was laden with paradoxes. The women who emerged as producers and consumers of black beauty culture in the early twentieth century were part of a complex cultural and historical lineage. In the eyes of early European traders and slavers, the tightly curled hair texture of Africans was vilified as a marker of difference along with their darker skin color. While in the Americas, African and African American women were confronted with the dilemma of embracing their hair in its natural state or trying to modify it to resemble, though never truly mimic, the hair of whites. As African American women emerged from slavery, the relationship between hair care and black women's social and political identities became even more significant. As beauty culture emerged as an industry in the early twentieth century, black women's hair became an even more contested arena.

Much of the recent scholarship on black beauty culture confronts the conundrum over the relationship of beauty culture and hairstyles to black women's social identities.[4] However, the social, political, and economic importance of beauticians in the African American activist tradition has, for the most part, been overlooked. While this study does not explicitly engage in the politics of hairstyles and adornment, it does address the irony that an industry based on the seemingly apolitical or even counter-political practice of beautification provided a fruitful and important base for black women to launch some of their most significant agitations for social and political change. In fact, I contend that in many ways, black beauticians gained their political strength due in part to the tensions in black hair care over questions of racial authenticity and conformity, assertions of female economic empowerment and adherence to the objectification of women's physical appearance. In many ways these discussions concerning hair and beauty standards merely reflect the debates happening in African American politics concerning the best approaches to confronting racism and its attendant economic disparities. Beauticians, then, were not only well equipped to navigate discussions surrounding black beauty but also served as mediators of political culture for their customers and clients. While the emphasis of this study will be on how the economic foundation and relative security of the black beauty industry impelled black beauty culturists into the political arena, the fact that this base was built upon an industry that promoted the contested terrain of black female beauty will also be interrogated.

In this book I seek to engage the rich historical literature on black women's political activism with the less developed historiography on black women's entrepreneurial developments.[5] Historian Wendy Gamber offers a useful suggestion as to why women in general have been excluded from narratives in business history, explaining that "female entrepreneurs fall between a number of historiographical cracks."[6] Among the historical cracks African American beauticians fall between are the literatures of business and labor history, usually seen as oppositional with different and competing historiographical concerns. This project complicates this binary and hopes to move American history in general beyond this falsely constructed dichotomy. Many black beauticians were businesswomen in the purest sense who owned and operated salons, others were workers in salons, while still others engaged in hair work independently in their own homes or apartments. Yet despite this complexity and even their competing interests, they all shared a common professional identity and considered themselves businesswomen.

This book also problematizes some of the terms used to discuss key concepts and define differing constituencies in business history. As this book demonstrates, there was a great deal of fluidity in the categories of manufacturer, entrepreneur, worker, and consumer in the black beauty industry. Furthermore, the black beauty industry consciously expanded the meaning of the term "entrepreneur" to include large and small salon owners, operators who rented booths, sales agents who peddled and distributed products, as well as highly successful manufacturers of beauty products. In the same vein, a great deal of the black beauty industry's success and appeal lay in the possibility for the lines between producers and consumers to be blurred—even collapsed. Understanding this dynamic not only highlights a unique aspect of the black beauty culture industry but also gives a better understanding of the complexities of these categories in the field of business history in general.

Moreover, restoring economics and entrepreneurship as a factor in political and social activities allows for an examination of the complicated nature of black women's work, class, and status. Beauty culturists in particular had a curious relationship to these variables. While their work was considered unskilled labor by some, they were credentialed and, eventually, licensed professionals. Their class and status in the community fluctuated and was constantly a cause for contestation and uncertainty. Examining beauticians' positions within their communities will undoubtedly provide a more complicated understanding of how these variables operated in black women's lives in general.

*   *   *

Beauty Shop Politics moves chronologically and thematically through the twentieth and early twenty-first centuries. The first two chapters, covering the years from 1900 to 1930, examine the roles of gender and business in discussions of racial uplift by exploring the ideological and rhetorical negotiations made among beauticians and the racial uplift organizations that emerged in this period. Specifically, I explore the ways black beauticians fostered the social, economic, and political networks that bridged the discourses of the black business community, the black female club movement, as well as the New Woman and New Negro movements. These movements, though varied in their ideologies and approaches, relied heavily upon the connections among beauticians and their access to a black female clientele to further their efforts. Consequently, African American beauticians had a great deal of power in shaping political agendas.

Chapter 3 examines the changes in the black beauty industry due to the Great Depression, starting with an assessment of how the Depression era placed black beauticians at the forefront of expanding the nature of business and the role of an entrepreneur. Subsequent government regulations impacted industry practices and enabled black beauticians to play an important role in the changing relationships among African American women, the state, and consumer culture. Chapter 4 describes how black beauticians in the 1940s and 1950s set their sights on expanding their political voice by expanding their social and political influence globally and enshrining themselves as standard-bearers for black beauty throughout the world, while chapter 5 analyzes the crucial role of beauticians in the modern black freedom struggle of the 1950s and 1960s. Finally, chapter 6 includes a detailed analysis of the activism of beauticians in the post–civil rights era. After 1965, there were significant changes in both mainstream black politics and the black beauty industry. In the midst of political and cultural transformations, black beauticians were left to evaluate their industry and their political efficacy.

Combining their economic autonomy with a sense of racial duty, the way black beauticians capitalized on their strategic importance provides insight into the roles economics and entrepreneurship played in black political activism. In African American and women's history, historians, for the most part, have been accustomed to looking to intellectuals, artists, and laborers to find innovative political strategists. Instead, in perhaps one of the most unlikely places, a business enterprise based on something as seemingly frivolous as hairstyling, there emerged a platform through which black women could escape the economic limitations imposed by racism and its enduring legacies and, in turn, build enduring institutions that challenged not only the social discourse of their respective communities but also the larger political arena.

1

Beauty Pioneers

Racial Uplift and Gender in the Creation of a Black Business Community

During his travels throughout the country in the late nineteenth century, Booker T. Washington, prominent race leader and founder of Tuskegee Institute, noticed an interesting phenomenon. Just one generation removed from the shackles of enslavement and battling for their ever-diminishing citizenship rights, African American men and women throughout the nation were embracing the industrial age by owning and operating successful business ventures. While their small-scale enterprises in no way rivaled those of industrial capitalists such as John D. Rockefeller and Andrew Carnegie, who symbolized American business in this age, Washington recognized that African American entrepreneurs had great potential to inspire wealth accumulation within their communities. Washington wanted to organize these "leading and most successful colored men and women in the country who were engaged in business" under his tutelage to link their efforts to his accommodationist and sometimes controversial ideas concerning racial uplift. To that end, in August 1900 he gathered more than three hundred business men and women in Boston, Massachusetts, to establish the National Negro Business League (NNBL).

Washington, however, was not the first or the only black leader who desired to unite and organize the black business community at the turn of the twentieth century. Just one year earlier, the venerable W. E. B. Du Bois, often depicted as Washington's rival in all matters pertaining to black leadership and political rights, also called for African Americans to engage in business enterprises.[1] As correspondence secretary of the Fourth Conference for the Study of the Negro Problems at Atlanta University in 1899, Du Bois was instrumental in choosing the theme of the conference, "The Negro in Business." After conducting a survey to "find in each locality the number and kind of Negro business men," Du Bois gathered some of the era's finest race men and women to chronicle the state of entrepreneurial progress since Reconstruction and posit avenues for future growth. Only a few women spoke at Washington and Du Bois's gatherings, and women's entrepreneurial efforts and accomplishments were marginalized.

At the same time that African American male leaders such as Du Bois and Washington were exploring the meaning of entrepreneurship to the uplift of the race, two black women, Sarah Breedlove and Annie Malone, were struggling for their economic survival. By 1900, Breedlove, who would later become Madam C. J. Walker, was widowed by her first husband, estranged from her second husband, and raising her fifteen-year-old daughter on a washerwoman's meager earnings in St. Louis. Annie Malone was faring slightly better and living in the all-black town of Lovejoy, Illinois, where "in a rear room in a small frame building" she began to manufacture a preparation to stimulate and promote hair growth.[2] It would take Walker, Malone, and the industry they pioneered to move women into the center of the discourse on race and entrepreneurship in the early twentieth century.

Highlighting a major development in early-twentieth-century black life—the rise of a viable black business community—this chapter explores the links between business development and the formation of black womanhood during the early twentieth century. This period, marked by racial violence and disenfranchisement, gave birth to an ideology of racial uplift that had among its victories the "Golden Age of Black Business," an era of unprecedented growth of black business enterprises and the celebration of entrepreneurship as a promising venue for middle-class black men to rise above the economic ravages of segregation. This golden age was marked not only by the expansion of the black business community but also by a connection between entrepreneurship and racial uplift that marginalized black women.[3] Ironically, black businesswomen, particularly those in the beauty industry, not only created and sustained a viable industry based on the female-centered venture of beauty culture but also exploited the connections made in this period between business and identity to legitimate themselves and their industry.

* * *

While the early twentieth century witnessed an intensification of rhetoric and action that sought to bolster black men's business acumen, African American women's engagement in business enterprises dates back to their enslavement. During the colonial and antebellum periods, black women's business activities primarily involved retail and vending enterprises that usually did not garner much by way of profit but allowed black women to control independent enterprises in gender-specific occupations. Black slave and free women often operated in food production, sold goods in open-air markets, worked in dressmaking, and in urban areas hired themselves out as domestic servants and laundresses.[4] While slave and free women appear in the historical record in the colonial and antebellum marketplace engaging in trade and commerce, both legal and extralegal restrictions were used to limit such economic activities. Ordinances in Charleston, South Carolina, for example, restricted blacks from buying, selling, or trading goods without a special ticket or pass. Similarly, in New Orleans, slaves were required to wear special badges and limits were placed on the amount of money they were allowed to earn in any one day. Black women in the marketplaces were often singled out in cities like Charleston and publicly vilified as loose and disorderly in an attempt to delegitimatize their activities. Still, despite legal and social restrictions placed against their participation, black women actively pursued opportunities to have some semblance of economic autonomy through entrepreneurial enterprises.[5]

Ironically, while black women in the colonial and antebellum eras were actively involved in many business ventures, they were slow to get involved in the hair-care industry, an enterprise they would come to dominate in the twentieth century. In the colonial era, white English barbers, wigmakers, and hairdressers cornered the market until after the Seven Years' War, when the enterprise was opened up to the French, who quickly earned the status of being masterful in the hair business. Few blacks participated in this industry at the time, but one Pierre Toussaint, a slave brought to New York from Santo Domingo in 1787, became so successful that he was described as the "most fashionable coiffeur in the city."[6] Toussaint used the money he earned primping New York City's elite families to purchase his freedom and the freedom of other slaves. He eventually became one of the first African American philanthropists, giving much of his money to the then-segregated Catholic Church.[7] Others followed in Toussaint's footsteps and from the late eighteenth century until the 1820s, free black men, primarily from the French West Indies, served wealthy white men and women as wigmakers and hairdressers. However, by the 1820s, as a discourse surrounding black men as sexual predators began to emerge, black men were no longer desirable as hairdressers for white women, particularly in the South.[8]

Just as free black men were being pushed away from dressing white women's hair in the antebellum era, many found an alternative niche in the hair-care industry as barbers. Beginning in the 1820s, they owned and operated elite barbershops for a white clientele. These astute businessmen built upon the role of blacks as personal servants to market their services. The wealth these men accumulated in northern and southern cities allowed them to purchase their family and friends out of slavery as well as make contributions to black churches and other institutions.[9]

In the antebellum period, black women began to enter the hairdressing profession in larger numbers. While slave women had been responsible for caring for white people's personal needs (including hair care) from the beginning of the institution of slavery, the antebellum period saw the emergence of successful black female hairdressers, women who turned hairdressing from a servant's obligation to a business enterprise. Free black women in the North, like their barbering counterparts, served a wealthy white clientele exclusively. For example, the Remond sisters, Celia Remond Babcock, Maritcha Remond, and Caroline Remond Putnam, established not only the largest hairdressing business in Boston, the Ladies Hair Work Salon, but also a wig factory and mail-order hair tonic distribution center.[10] Eliza Potter's autobiography, *A Hairdresser's Experience in the High Life*, describes her activities as a black beautician in service to whites, primarily in Cincinnati, as well as her travels abroad. Published in the 1850s, Potter's work is a departure from the more overtly abolitionist tomes written by her contemporaries and is less an autobiography than a critique of the frivolous lifestyles of her elite white clientele. Still, Potter's recounting of economic and social autonomy demonstrates that even in the antebellum era, hairdressing was a lucrative profession.[11] Black women in the South were also able to earn successful livings as hairdressers. In fact, in her autobiography, Potter describes traveling to New Orleans to train slave women as hairdressers.[12] Marie Laveau, daughter of the famed voodoo queen of the same name (and a voodoo queen in her own right), worked as a hairdresser in New Orleans after the mysterious death of her husband in 1820. Known to be so effective at earning the trust of her wealthy white clients, according to her biographer, Laveau had a virtual monopoly on the profession with the exception of some competition from local slave women.[13]

The end of the brutalizing institution of slavery changed not only the legal designation of African Americans but also their relationship to the economy. Newly freed blacks understood that the power to control their economic destiny was an important way to express their freedom. While blacks primarily sought fair and equitable pay for their labor, many continued to expand the parameters of the business infrastructure they built during the antebellum era. While much has been written about politics in the years following emancipation, economic independence, thrift, and free enterprise were also a large part of the new radical republican ideal.[14] The creation of the Freedman's Savings and Trust Company (more commonly known as the Freedmen's Bank) in March 1865 was, in many ways, the culmination of this economic aspect of freedom. Although a short-lived financial institution that failed during the economic depression of 1873, the bank spurred similar ventures by freedpeople in Virginia, North Carolina, Alabama, and Washington, D.C.[15] These early financial institutions encouraged blacks to start their own businesses and to patronize black merchants.

By the end of the Reconstruction period, black Americans were facing unprecedented changes in their lives. The rise of Jim Crow segregation and the concomitant challenges of racial violence and political disenfranchisement, along with the influx of large immigrant populations into U.S. cities, the quest for empire, industrial growth, and other modern developments, brought about new dilemmas that called for new tactics. Increased violence and hostility toward African Americans led the black community to look internally to create and sustain politically and economically independent families and communities, leading to an expanded role for black women who politicized their roles as mothers and educators and a heightened importance given to a nationalistic economic agenda.[16] In fact, viewed in light of the new ways that politics was defined by blacks, particularly those of the elite and aspiring classes in the age of racial uplift, building up economically viable businesses supported and sustained by black communities constituted a bulwark against black political disenfranchisement.[17] Business and economic empowerment was viewed by black leaders of the day to be one of the more effective challenges to white supremacy and the ravages of second-class citizenship.

In an August 1900 speech, pioneering African American attorney D. Augustus Straker argued that the failures of Reconstruction and the rise of Jim Crow had produced a "crisis of manhood and womanhood development" that could only be remedied by blacks having a "wider engagement in commercial and industrious business and less to do with politics."[18] Black elites united around an ideology of racial uplift to address the crisis Straker outlines but publicly and privately clamored over how to best put the tenets of "self-help, racial solidarity, temperance, thrift, chastity, social purity, patriarchal authority, and the accumulation of wealth" into practice.[19] Nowhere are these battles better articulated than in a discussion of women's roles in the early years of the black business movement. The participation of black women in

Du Bois's "Negro in Business Conference" and the early years of the NNBL illuminate the complexities surrounding the gendered rhetoric of economics and entrepreneurship within the racial uplift ethos. While black women at this time were active in uplift politics and often vociferous in their critique of black men's ability to lead the race, their comments and interventions at the initial conventions and gatherings of the black business movement supported entrepreneurship primarily as a masculine ideal.

Du Bois's 1899 Atlanta University conference included women's voices, albeit in a limited way. Three women spoke at the General Mother's Meeting, with the theme "What shall our children do for a living?" while two other women, Rosa Bass of Atlanta, who "spoke of the wisdom of colored grocers and hucksters," and Hattie G. Escridge, who submitted a paper titled "The Need of Negro Merchants," addressed the entire conference.[20] All the women discussed the need for the black man to "help the race as well as himself" by owning a business enterprise, however, none of them discussed the role of women in the black business community.[21] Instead, they focused on the roles of women as consumers and nurturers of the next generation of young male entrepreneurs. In fact, of all the conference papers collected in Du Bois's study, only one directly addressed the role of women in the black business community. In his discussion of the "Negro Business Men of Columbia, S.C.," H. E. Lindsay observed that with the exception of Matilda Evans, a local physician, the "women of our race . . . are standing aside and allowing the men to monopolize all the professions." This was a surprising statement since black women were boldly at the forefront of so many other contemporary racial uplift activities.[22]

Among the resolutions adopted by the Atlanta University conference was a call for blacks to create an economic infrastructure through an "organization in every town and hamlet where colored people dwell . . . [of] Negro Business Men's Leagues."[23] Ironically, just one year later, it was Booker T. Washington and not Du Bois who brought this dream to fruition when he formed the National Negro Business League.

The first meeting of the NNBL occurred under a cloud of controversy. Booker T. Washington contacted W. E. B. Du Bois and asked for his assistance in compiling a list of Negro businessmen before the Boston meeting, and Du Bois obliged. Yet Washington gave Du Bois little public credit for the idea of a gathering of black businesspeople. And while Du Bois did not openly challenge Washington, clubwoman and civil rights crusader Ida B. Wells-Barnett accused Washington of stealing the idea of a business league from Du Bois. She also derided Washington for trying to divide black America by holding the NNBL gathering so close to a meeting of the National Afro-American Council, the civil rights organization that laid the groundwork for the Niagara movement and the National Association for the Advancement of Colored People. Du Bois was named the coordinator of the council's Negro Business Bureau.[24] In spite, or perhaps because of the warring factions, Washington's gathering was a great success with over 300 delegates in attendance.

The rhetoric of the first NNBL meeting was similar to that of Du Bois's Atlanta conference. The meeting was dominated by men who affirmed to one another and the few women present that entrepreneurial success was necessary for the restoration of the manhood of the race. For example, Gilbert C. Harris of Boston admitted that when he migrated from Virginia to Boston he felt compelled "to do some business to be a man and be recognized among men."[25] He implored young men to "learn some business!" and spoke of the virtues of homeownership.

While most of the male orators spoke directly about the business enterprises in which they were involved, the only female speaker, Alberta Moore Smith, theorized more broadly about "Women's Development in Business." Smith, born in Chicago in 1875, graduated from the Armour Institute of Technology in the Commercial Department and worked as a stenographer for the Afro-American National Republican Bureau and many foreign ambassadors. At an early age, she became involved in clubwork, initially trying to represent black women's issues in mainstream white women's clubs. Personally invited by Washington to address the NNBL at its inaugural convention, Smith delivered a monologue very much in line with the views of the men in attendance, doing little to challenge the placement of men as the center of the black business community. While she made no direct reference to restoring black manhood through involvement in business, she clearly did not see black women upsetting black male leadership in this area but as "taking her place" in a supportive role. Smith's comments were so amenable to the male delegates present that she was elected vice president at the meeting, an "unusual honor to be accorded a woman," and became an organizer of women's business leagues in cities around the country.[26]

Just one year later, at the Chicago convention, Smith gave a more directed speech concerning the need for women to own businesses titled "Negro Women's Business Clubs: A Factor in the Solution of the Vexed Problem." Tempering pride in women's accomplishments with a sense of racial duty, she declared that "Negro women's business clubs do not desire to be known only by their names, but by their good works and the influence they exert in encouraging our women in opening establishments of their own, no matter how small the start may be." She also advocated educating black women so they would be better informed "concerning the mooted questions of the day in which men are deeply interested."[27]

Smith was certainly emboldened by her interaction with the women in the business clubs and leagues that had emerged in cities and towns throughout the country over the last year. By the second convention, she had helped to establish branches of the Colored Women's Business Club in St. Louis, Missouri; St. Paul and Minneapolis, Minnesota; Knoxville, Tennessee; and Greenville, South Carolina. The membership represented a wide range of business and professional interests: bookkeepers, stenographers, nurses, doctors, milliners, seamstresses, dressmakers, journalists, leisure women, modistes, and hairdressers.[28] The combined wealth of the clubs' 250 members was estimated at $55,900. The Chicago club (the club for which there is the most information available) was comprised primarily of women who were college educated or trained in a commercial school.

Among the women Smith encountered in her travels was Dora Miller, the leader of a group of businesswomen in Brooklyn, New York. Miller then joined Smith in addressing the 1901 convention by discussing the organizing activities and accomplishments of "Some Eastern Business Women." She explained to the NNBL that on December 1900 twelve women banded together to organize themselves into the Colored Women's Business Club of Greater New York, which according to Miller was the sole incorporated organization of African American women at the time. The membership was comprised of "seventy-five earnest business women representing twenty-one trades and professions."[29] Building on the momentum from the NNBL's initial meeting, these clubs sought to encourage black women to enter the business world. While the women's clubs espoused a rhetoric similar to that of the NNBL with regard to entrepreneurship, they combined these ideals with the rhetoric of the black female club movement, which was well established by this time.

Indeed, black club women were among the first to discuss economic independence as a key tenet of racial uplift, not just for men but for women as well. In 1895, Josephine St. Pierre Ruffin's gathering of a group of prominent black women in Boston to discuss issues important to black women and to the race in general marked a major moment in the history of black women's political activism. This meeting, considered the genesis of the National Association of Colored Women (NACW), was held over three days in July and was organized so that each day would have a different theme. Ruffin explained that after opening with general meetings, the second and third days would be devoted to the "consideration of vital questions concerning

[the] moral, mental, and physical and financial growth and well-being" of black women.[30]

At this initial meeting, the financial security of the women of the race was raised as a major concern; within a few years the NACW had made economic opportunity for black women a visible part of its agenda. For example, in 1901, the NACW's "departments of organizational work" included typical uplift rubrics like "kindergartens, mother's meetings, domestic science, rescue work, religion, and temperance."[31] But by 1904, the year the organization was incorporated, a department for businesswomen, headed by Mrs. M. L. Crossthwaite of Kansas City, Missouri, was one of five new departments added. In these early years of the organization, the NACW established itself as being concerned not only with the social, moral, religious, and political well-being of black women and children but also with their economic opportunities. A list of specific activities included training Negro girls to be industrious, raising the standard of service among Negro women, and improving the working conditions of black women and girls.[32]

The local Colored Women's Business Clubs that emerged in the early twentieth century straddled the discourses about women's roles articulated by the NACW and conversations about the centrality of business articulated by the NNBL. While these organizations were associated and often shared membership with the NNBL and the NACW, they were separate entities with a distinct agenda. The very name chosen for the women's business clubs illuminates much about what they understood their roles to be. Candace Kanes argues that most white women's business clubs in this era included the word "professional" in their names along with the word "business," denoting the inclusion of working professional women. This was not the case with these early black women's business clubs. For example, Alberta Moore Smith noted in one of her many columns in the *Colored American Magazine* that a "bright Negro youth who was studying sociology" came to her asking questions concerning "Negro working women," and she quickly added businesswomen to the discussion.[33] The use of business without professional was likely deliberate in that they wanted their organizations to be a counterpart to the NNBL and wished to have women directly included in conversations about the importance of entrepreneurship to the uplift of the race.[34]

While one of the goals of the businesswomen's clubs was to secure a wide range of employment for black women who desired it, the overall black female club movement often marginalized poor women. On the other hand, much of the rhetoric of the businesswomen's clubs encouraging black women to enter business did not look down upon laboring women but instead castigated the discriminatory practices that relegated black women to the lowest paying jobs. In a speech to the NNBL that was later reprinted in *Colored American Magazine*, Smith explained that "the strength of many young women [was] being wasted by laborious work in sweat-shops, factories and stores."[35] Women of leisure who did not work and women who worked for selfish reasons, such as "an unsatiable desire for money, [and] fancy clothes," were also chastised for their behavior. These indictments did not absolve black businesswomen's clubs from their elitist practices. As with the larger club movement, much of their rhetoric implied a preference for the "better classes." However, the emphasis on business and entrepreneurship in many ways provided a more level playing field since starting a successful small business was not completely dependent upon prior upbringing, education, or status. It was easier for someone to demonstrate their business success than to demonstrate their moral suitability and elite status, something crucial to being accepted among clubwomen.

Black businesswomen's clubs, though less stringent in accepting women across class and status, were staunch in their policing of ideas about gender and women's roles. Alberta Moore Smith proclaimed at the NNBL convention of 1901: "To the minds of many there is a new woman but in actuality she does not exist. Theories have been put forth to show that she is new, but the only satisfactory evidence or conclusion agreed upon is that she is simply progressing; her natural tendencies having not changed one iota. . . . On the contrary, with all the knowledge gained from free and unconventional education she takes her place in society as a faithful friend, in the business world as a judicious counselor, and in the home as a loving wife and queen."[36] Women in the various branches of the Colored Women's Business Club manipulated turn-of-the-century modes of respectability to include the promotion of business and enterprise. There were constant reminders in speeches and newspaper columns that black businesswomen did not abandon their primary responsibilities of caring for their families and their homes: "No matter what a woman's work or aim might be she can never shake off entirely the responsibilities of the home, for they are joined by inalienable ties." According to turn-of-the-century gender ideals, a woman's primary domestic responsibility was to train her children to be respectable and to represent the race.[37] The clubs encouraged women not only to instruct their children on moral standards but also to train "every Negro child in some profession/ trade or economic science."[38]

Similarly, while women were not told to avoid the business world altogether, they were encouraged to seek refuge in their homes as a way of balancing the demands of the marketplace. The home was described as a sacred place for black women, not just for the duties she needed to perform there on behalf of her family but because the home was perceived as safer than the cold, cruel business world: "The home is the haven of rest to which she flees with exalted thoughts, and tired brain, only too willing to receive the love, peace and quietude which daily awaits her within its sacred walls." For businesswomen home represented both a place they should be pouring their lives into for the sake of their husbands and children and a place of retreat for women from their interaction with the harsh business world. Women were not to avoid the marketplace altogether and remain in their homes exclusively, but they were encouraged to develop their homes as a retreat from the corruption of the business world.

Still, despite the supposed complementarities between home and business, black businesswomen confronted and challenged ideas about femininity since the business world was construed as a male space and the rhetoric of business success for both blacks and whites was expressed in masculine terms. The characteristics that were most honored in the business world were ambition, assertiveness, and competitiveness, traits that were not seen as appropriate for women.[39] Caught between a desire to prove black women's ability to succeed in the business world and the desire to assert their femininity, something they had been denied throughout their history, black businesswomen faced a quandary. On the one hand, they asserted that they were intellectually equal to their black male counterparts. On the other, they calmed fears about women taking over the business pursuits of the race by making it clear that they were not calling all black women to abandon their "proper" stations in life to become businesswomen.

Similarly, Smith and others writing about business practices asserted unequivocally that black women should receive the same wages as their black male counterparts for the same work. Yet these women made clear that they were not seeking political equality with black men. Smith explained that "fair-minded business women do not ask for equal rights in a political sense, but they do ask that they be given an equal showing with the man, with the same freedom to use accessible facilities as those accorded business men." Moreover, while the display of "any of women's weapons of defense, tears, pleadings, etc." was denounced, mother-wit was seen as an attribute in the business world since it provided women with an advantage over men. In all, women guaranteed that success in the business world would not compromise their most positive feminine attributes. The businesswoman, Smith contended, "is as womanly and as gentle as was her grandmother. Contact with the business world does not wear off the fineness which men so much admire in women."[40] The male arena of business, women argued, would only be enhanced by the presence of those who contributed to the business success of the race in socially acceptable female terms.

Still, the link between manhood and entrepreneurship was difficult for club women to overcome. That is not to say that women were not involved with the NNBL or that the black women's business leagues did not try to gain ground for female entrepreneurs during the golden age. However, it took the innovators in the black beauty industry to gain respect and justification for black women in business and make entrepreneurship a viable avenue for black women's activism within the context of racial uplift. Not only would the race celebrate the accomplishments of men in business, but women such as Madam C. J. Walker and Annie Malone would soon become symbols of economic empowerment for the race. In the process, members of the overwhelmingly male black business community and the elite black female club network were forced to reevaluate their understanding of beauty and business, politics and racial uplift.

The Rise of Beauty Pioneers

While Madam C .J. Walker's Walker Manufacturing Company and Annie Malone's Poro Company would become the most successful black beauty enterprises of the early twentieth century, they were not the first to venture into black beauty culture. The late nineteenth century witnessed white-owned companies capitalizing on black women's quest for beauty.[41] Portraying black women as naturally ugly and inferior, many of these companies advertised face bleachers promising to "turn the skin of a black or brown person four or five shades lighter, and a mulatto person perfectly white," and sketches of women with unruly hair were accompanied by promises to fix the "problem." Certainly, it is not shocking that the same culture that was producing violent lynch mobs and segregation would produce advertisements that exploited blacks to earn money. The more puzzling aspect of these early attempts to court the black consumer market with negative depictions was that, initially, the black press was willing to print these advertisements and reap the financial rewards of the advertising revenue. Some newspapers, like the *New York Age* while under the editorial control of both T. Thomas Fortune, a self-proclaimed radical, and Booker T. Washington, who took control of the paper in 1907, published such advertisements without question. *Colored*

American Magazine, a periodical which Washington influenced behind the scenes, initially accepted such advertisements but later stopped.[42]

Indeed, it was black men who first made an attempt to counteract the overtly racist imagery in early beauty product advertisements. Anthony Overton, dissatisfied with the limited professional opportunities for black men, decided to try his luck in the burgeoning pharmaceutical and cosmetics industry. In 1898, Overton established the Overton Hygienic Company, which manufactured baking powder along with its most famous product, the High Brown Face Powder. Unlike white-owned companies, Overton only employed blacks and relied on door-to-door sales to distribute his products. Eventually he gained access to variety stores and drug stores and became the first black manufacturer to get products sold in Woolworth's. Overton used his earnings from the Hygienic Company to become the primary underwriter, between 1916 and 1922, for *Half-Century Magazine,* which became a proponent of the women's club movement. Overton also became actively involved in the NNBL and spoke of his accomplishments at NNBL conventions.[43]

While Overton and even some white-owned companies met success in the early beauty industry, black women such as Annie Malone and Madam C. J. Walker diversified the black beauty industry to include not only the selling of products but also the selling of beauty, independence, and financial success. In many ways, their lives more than their products or beauty education systems reflected the challenges and opportunities that black women faced at the turn of the century and became the basis of their success.

Annie Turnbo (who would be known professionally as Annie Malone) and Sarah Breedlove (who was to become Madam C. J. Walker) were both born during the promise and peril of the Reconstruction era. Walker was born the daughter of freed slaves on a small plot of land in Delta, Louisiana, on December 23, 1867, while Malone was born on a farm in Metropolis, Illinois, on August 9, 1869, to free black parents. Both women were orphaned at young ages and raised by their older siblings. Unlike Walker, who apparently had little formal schooling, Malone completed grade school and attended high school until "poor health obliged her to abandon" her studies.[44]

Malone got her start in the hair-care industry before Walker. As a child, Malone demonstrated a fondness for styling hair and "delighted in dressing the hair of her sisters and associates."[45] She also studied chemistry in school, which led her to create and eventually sell concoctions designed to improve the condition of black women's hair. Her preparations were so successful among the women in her hometown of Lovejoy, Illinois, that she decided to

move to St. Louis in 1902 to expand her business among a larger black population and capitalize on the excitement generated by the upcoming world's
fair in 1904. While in St. Louis, Annie met and married a man who is only
remembered as Mr. Pope. According to Malone, the marriage dissolved because Pope "interfered in her business."

The biggest challenge Malone faced in her St. Louis–based business was
getting word out about her products. By 1903, Malone began to employ agents
who went door to door giving women free scalp treatments. A year later,
she began to advertise in black newspapers. Still, her best advertisements
were her sales agents, who were walking billboards for the effectiveness of
Malone's hair preparations. Malone's best selling product was her "Wonderful
Hair Grower," which she insisted did not dramatically alter the tightly coiled
texture of black women's hair but helped to treat many of the scalp diseases
and conditions that plagued black women in the early twentieth century.[46]
This was only partially true. While Malone's product did not straighten black
women's hair or change the texture to approximate the looser curl pattern of
most white women's hair, the hair grower and the tools that were to be used
with it did temporarily alter black women's hair by stretching and adding
shine to it. The combination of promoting healthy and groomed hair along
with the opportunity to abandon the drudgery of domestic labor by joining
her sales force helped her draw audiences in St. Louis and throughout the
South.[47]

That was exactly the kind of message that resonated with one St. Louis
resident, a single mother by the name of Sarah (Breedlove) McWilliams,
who in just a few years would metamorphose into Madam C. J. Walker,
Malone's greatest rival. Orphaned as a child, married by fourteen, a mother
by eighteen, and widowed by twenty, Walker left her hometown of Delta,
Louisiana, moving first to Vicksburg, Mississippi, and eventually settled in
St. Louis in 1889 with her three-year-old daughter, Lelia.[48] Walker joined her
brothers who were already living in St. Louis and making a decent living as
self-employed barbers. Soon after arriving, she formed a friendship with two
women who were washerwomen and followed them into that line of work,
joining the more than 50 percent of black women in St. Louis who worked
in that field since white immigrant and first-generation American women
dominated the other jobs in domestic service.[49]

Struggling as a washerwoman and dissatisfied with her station in life,
Walker later recounted her frustration and fears to a *New York Times* reporter
in 1917: "I was at my washtubs one morning with a heavy wash before me. As I
bent over the washboard, and looked at my arms buried in soapsuds, I said to

myself: 'What are you going to do when you grow old and your back gets stiff? Who is going to take care of your little girl?' This set me to thinking I couldn't see how I, a poor washerwoman, was going to better my condition."[50] To that end, Walker tried to improve her life and that of her daughter by continuing their education. Saving enough money from her earnings as a washerwoman, she sent her then adolescent daughter Lelia to Knoxville College in Tennessee in the fall of 1902 and enrolled herself in night school shortly thereafter to improve her basic skills.[51] More significant changes also began to occur in Walker's life at this time. She began a relationship with Charles Joseph (C. J.) Walker, a newspaperman who sold subscriptions and advertising for one of St. Louis's three black newspapers. Described as a "boaster, charmer and self-promoter[,] . . . a natural-born salesman . . . [who] loved fine suits and considered well-shined shoes a necessity,"[52] Walker was undoubtedly drawn to C. J.'s ambition and connection to St. Louis' middle-class black community. The two started a relationship and would eventually marry in 1906.

Walker's quest for a better life also drew her to the well-groomed appearance of the women in St. Louis. Perhaps one day, while watching blacks strolling around St. Louis, the sight of black women with healthy groomed hair caught Walker's eye. According to Walker's biographer, A'Lelia Bundles, she most likely suffered from the scalp ailments most common to black women of her generation: dandruff (known then as seborrhea) and psoriasis (known then as tetter). In fact, according to Walker's own testimony, these conditions were so severe that her hair was falling out.[53] Already demonstrating a tenacity and ambition to better her life, she undoubtedly recognized that the condition of her hair marked her as a rural southern migrant. Whether it was by beholding the appearance of neatly coiffed black women on the streets of St. Louis or through hearing Annie Malone's gospel of beauty preached around town by her then small but growing sales force, Walker sought the services of Annie Malone. The exact circumstances of the first meeting of Malone and Walker is not known; Malone would later admit that Walker received her hair treatment services and must have been so satisfied with the results that she became one of her sales agents in 1903.[54]

According to Walker's own accounts, she had already been experimenting with hair preparations before joining Malone's sales force and continued to experiment with her own homemade hair concoctions while working for Malone. By 1905, Walker realized that there were markets of black women untapped by Malone, so she relocated to Denver later that summer to take advantage of the westward migrations of African Americans. Initially, Walker worked as a cook, but she also sold Malone's products part time. She eventually saved enough money to quit her kitchen job and go back to laundry work, which allowed her the flexibility to "work two days a week doing washing" and reserve the rest of her time to providing hair treatments. Armed with business cards and an advertisement in the black Denver-based newspaper, the *Statesman*, Walker promoted the opening of her own hairdressing parlor on Clarkson Street.[55]

By the middle of 1906, she began to distance herself from Malone and emerged in her own right as Madam C. J. Walker. She embraced the term "Madam," which was used primarily by white beauticians to denote their deference to French hairstyling training, and the initials of her husband's name to legitimize her standing within the business community.[56] Soon she began selling her first product, Madam Walker's Wonderful Hair Grower, a direct affront to Malone's own Wonderful Hair Grower. By September 1906, the fierce competition that would mark Malone's and Walker's relationship ensued with Malone publicly accusing Walker of stealing her hair preparations. Company literature later explained that the "demand for [Malone's] 'Wonderful Hair Grower' soon became so great that unscrupulous dealers began to offer imitations to the public under the same name, and it became necessary for the protection of the public as well as for the protection of her business, to place the Preparations under a copyrighted trade-name; so the name 'PORO' was adopted in 1906."[57] Walker was seemingly undeterred by her former employer's denunciation and left Denver with her sights set on exposing more black women to her own products. According to her biographer, she had amassed $3,652 by the time she left Denver, quite an increase from the $1.50 she had arrived with just one year earlier.

Less than ten years after the establishment of the NNBL, both Malone and Walker were emerging as formidable businesswomen. They were pioneering black female ownership of black beauty culture and giving women tangible role models: women succeeding against racial odds and the masculine rhetoric surrounding business in the early twentieth century. They created what they called "hair systems," which included hair-product manufacturing, distribution, and sales throughout the United States and the African diaspora as well as salons and eventually beauty colleges and training programs. The proper use of their products had to be taught to other women, who could then earn a living offering these services in their respective communities. A woman who received a certificate declaring she was trained in one of these systems was bound to use and sell only the products in that particular system, thereby creating a ready-made sales base and ensuring growth.

However, as their respective companies grew, they both had to confront usurpation by their own husbands; both Malone's (Aaron Malone) and Walker's (C. J. Walker) waged failed attempts to take control of their respective companies and disgrace their wives publicly.[58] These women also had to legitimize themselves and their industry to the strong black male business community over which Booker T. Washington reigned. To that end, they earned and, in the case of Madam Walker, demanded recognition from organizations such as the NNBL, connected their industry to the African diaspora, fought to get beauty culture as a course of study in black colleges, and went to great lengths to place their industry squarely within the discourse of racial uplift by openly denying a connection to the controversial and seemingly apolitical actions of hair straightening. While Walker and Malone denied that their products straightened African American women's hair, the development of products that temporarily modified the appearance of black women's hair by minimizing the curl pattern was, as historian Susannah Walker asserts, certainly influenced by white norms that rejected tightly coiled hair as beautiful.[59] The ways black beauty entrepreneurs negotiated these tensions laid the foundation for the political appeals beauticians would make throughout the twentieth century.

By 1912, Madam C. J. Walker believed that she so embodied the principles of the NNBL that she should be allowed to speak at the organization's thirteenth annual convention held in Chicago. Walker by that time had traveled throughout the United States demonstrating her products and training women how to use and sell them, established Lelia Beauty Colleges (named after her daughter) in numerous cities, relocated her business first to Pittsburgh then to Indianapolis to take advantage of that city's central location and proximity to railroads for her growing mail order business, employed a formidable staff of sales agents, attorneys, and business men and women to help her oversee operations, and was establishing herself as a philanthropist. Still, in spite of her credentials, to be given an audience by the NNBL, Walker needed an advocate. She found one in George Knox, publisher of the Indianapolis newspaper the *Freeman*. After a speech by Anthony Overton, owner of the Overton Hygienic Company, whose cosmetic, hair, and toiletry manufacturing company was billed as the largest black-owned enterprise in the country at the time, Knox wanted the audience of the thirteenth annual NNBL convention to hear the story of "a remarkable woman," Madam C. J. Walker. Proudly proclaiming that Walker, hailing from his home state of Indiana, had bestowed a gift of one thousand dollars to Indianapolis's black YMCA, Knox wanted the audience to hear her rags-to-riches story.

Washington ignored Knox's attempts and instead recognized another businessman from Indianapolis whose business and philanthropy paled in comparison to Walker's. Indeed, Walker was ignored until the final day of the convention three days later. After a long lecture by a Texas banker and Washington's favorable response, Walker rose to her feet, looked Washington in the eye, alerted him that she would not be denied, and began a passionate oratory that described her rise from a washerwoman to an established businesswoman as well as her desire to empower other African American women to do the same. "I have made it possible," Walker proudly announced when she finally reached the podium, "for many colored women to abandon the washtub for a more pleasant and profitable occupation." She also pointedly questioned the lack of respect given to those in the beauty business, particularly female entrepreneurs, and added that "the girls and women of our race must not be afraid to take hold of business endeavors and . . . wring success out of a number of business opportunities that lie at their very doors."[60] Walker's speech was a departure from thirteen years of rhetoric that unabashedly celebrated black manhood and entrepreneurship; she spoke boldly of her own accomplishments and for the need for black women to join her in entrepreneurial enterprise.

So many of the conference participants were moved by Walker's speech that at the convention one year later Washington invited her back as the keynote speaker and took great pleasure in introducing Walker as "one of the most progressive and successful businesswomen of our race." Then Walker gave another inspirational speech on her personal entrepreneurial progress and that of the race. Afterward Washington added, "Why, if we don't watch out, the women will excel us!" denoting both his excitement and perhaps his embarrassment over the prospect of women gaining ground in the realm of business.[61] In fact, by 1915, Walker's female-dominated profession was so respected that the NNBL chose the "Beauty Parlor Business" as the theme of the sixteenth annual convention, where Washington made his final convention appearance before his death later that year.[62] Black beauty culture was no longer questioned as a legitimate industry, and more importantly, because of the efforts of Annie Malone and the bold pronouncements of Madam Walker, women were no longer questioned as legitimate entrepreneurs. Both race men and race women could and should engage in business.

However, the nature of Malone and Walker's industry did lend itself to criticism from advocates of racial uplift. Both companies were vilified for straightening and changing the texture of African American women's hair to imitate whites and therefore provoked cries of lack of racial pride. However, advertisements for the Walker and Poro companies avoided reference to hair straightening or skin bleaching, and in truth their respective companies did not advertise such practices until the 1940s, more than twenty years after Walker's death.[63] Still, the Walker and Poro systems did involve an elaborate system of hair manipulation. While shampooing and conditioning were at the center of their respective regimens, they differed on their preferred methods for styling hair. Malone preferred stretching the hair with a puller, a claw-tooth contraption that was heated and then pulled through the hair, while the Walker system used a heated steel comb, referred to commonly as the "hot comb," to release some of the curl pattern. At this stage, heated curling devices were not yet available, so a looser curl was made by wrapping hair around pieces of paper tied at the ends.

Madam Walker, in particular, was vociferous in her insistence that her method had nothing to do with making black women look white. She complained in a letter to her business manager F. B. Ransom in 1918 that despite asking the reporter not to use the words "hair straightener" to depict her hair services in an article printed in the *Post Dispatch*, the words were used. In another newspaper article, Madam stated clearly, "Right here, let me correct the erroneous impression held by some that I claim to straighten the hair. I want the great masses of my people to take a greater pride in their personal appearance and to give their hair proper attention. . . . I dare say that in the next ten years it will be a rare thing to see a kinky head of hair and it will not be straight either."[64] Walker and Malone confronted attacks to their industry based on its seeming contradictory stance to the politics of racial uplift and marked a clear departure from the previous practices of white-owned or male-owned companies that invoked language about hair straightening to sell their products and services. Determined to enshrine her position in the business community, Walker actively pursued coalitions with black educational institutions, a bulwark of racial uplift thought and practice, and traveled to the Caribbean to expand her hair care empire.

In the early years of the twentieth century, most African American women who wished to study beauty culture did so at either Poro College or Lelia Beauty College that were located in cities such as St. Louis, Chicago, Pittsburgh, and New York. However, Madam Walker adopted a new strategy for the training of agents and beauty culturists. She began to appeal to historically black colleges to place her beauty culture course in their curriculum. As early as 1911, a year before she forced her way onto the program of the NNBL conference, she contacted Booker T. Washington about selling her products at Tuskegee Institute and having beauty culture as a part of the industrial education offered to women. In December of that year, she sent him a letter along with a booklet concerning the nature of her business and asked if she could sell her goods on the grounds during the Tuskegee Negro Conference. Washington curtly dismissed her request by explaining that her products would have no place in a "meeting of poor farmers who come . . . for instruction or guidance, and who have very little or no money." He further added that he was "well acquainted" with Madam's business but did not think that a visit to the conference would provide her with the business opportunity she desired.[65] Walker was not discouraged, however, and arrived in Tuskegee to petition Washington again, explaining that she did not want to address the conference merely in an attempt to sell more of her products. Instead, she claimed, "I believe that if they knew of my great struggle from the age of seven years without any parents to . . . six years ago when I entered the business arena . . . and having succeeded in building it up to where my income is now more than $1,000 per month, it would be a great inspiration to them to do likewise." Washington finally acquiesced and allowed her to speak in the Tuskegee chapel for ten minutes, but he did not give her the floor at a regular meeting of the conference. However, those ten minutes made an impact on many in attendance, including Washington himself, since the *Indianapolis World* noted that when Walker was at Tuskegee she gave her hair treatments to eighty-four people, among them Washington and members of his family.[66]

Although she gained some respect, Washington was still reluctant to adopt her beauty course as a part of Tuskegee's curriculum, even after Walker's favorable response at the NNBL's annual convention just one year previous and in spite of the fact that she was already a major financial contributor to Tuskegee, establishing scholarships and giving money for the general operation of the school. Indeed, she used her philanthropy and reputation in the business community as leverage in convincing Washington to allow her to implement her beauty course. As she explained in a letter to Washington, "I think I have demonstrated the fact to you that my business is a legitimate one as well as a lucrative one. Should you see your way clear to reconsider and establish this work in your school, if successful it would mean thousands of dollars to both Tuskegee and myself. You would not only help me, but would help thousands of others who are needy and deserving. Then I could not only give hundreds of dollars to Tuskegee but thousands of dollars."[67] Washington responded to Walker's request by asking her to consider increasing her donations to the school but stated that the trustees and Executive Council of the institute had rejected her proposal. Tuskegee proved to be especially difficult; no matter how much credibility Walker and the beauty industry in general were gaining in black business circles, breaking into the bastion of aspiring-class leadership, the black college system, proved especially difficult.

Shortly before his death in 1915, Washington had a change of heart precipitated by Walker's ever-increasing popularity and perhaps a realization that beauty culture connected with the overall educational goals of his institution, particularly its goals in vocational education and empowering his students with a marketable occupational skill. He may also have been pressured by his wife, Margaret Murray Washington, who recognized that empowering black women with an industrial education proved especially difficult.[68] Madam Walker's beauty culture course helped meet the educational needs of black female students by providing an opportunity for economic independence, something Washington valued greatly. Students would study beauty culture at Tuskegee long after Washington's death in 1915.

With the eventual endorsement of Washington, it is not surprising that other schools soon followed. By 1917 the Walker Beauty Culture Method was being taught at Roger Williams College, Wylie College, Utica Normal and Industrial Institute, Guadalupe College, Arkansas Baptist College, and Mound Bayou Industrial College. Women educational leaders were especially enthusiastic to include beauty work in their curriculum. Mary McLeod Bethune, founder of Daytona Educational and Industrial Training School for Negro Girls, welcomed the addition of beauty culture and personally attested to the effectiveness of Madam Walker's products. She noted in a letter to Walker, "For the past four years my girls and myself have been using your wonderful hair grower. We have proven it to be very beneficial indeed."[69] The educator and the beauty mogul first met at the 1912 National Association of Colored Women's meeting in Hampton, Virginia, and became fast friends, united in their efforts to see black women and girls improve their lives. Another black female educator, Charlotte Hawkins Brown of the Palmer Institute in Sedalia, North Carolina, also gave her students the opportunity to learn Madam Walker's trade. For the most part, schools were interested because they recognized Walker's role as a financial supporter of black education and were eager to form relationships with her and her company. School presidents were quick to remind Walker of her previous generosity in supporting black institutions even as they thanked her for implementing beauty work at their schools. With a promised donation of five hundred dollars to build laboratories, as well as Madam's reputation as a philanthropist who supported black education, and an effort, in her words, to make an agreement that was "beneficial to the school as well as to the agent," only a few schools chose not to accept Walker's offer.[70]

Among the schools that did not welcome the courses were the Florida Baptist Academy's Normal, Industrial, and Preparatory School and Normal Industrial and Agricultural College of Pensacola and Roger Williams College, whose president vaguely explained to Walker in a letter that her desire to include beauty culture in the curriculum would be met "with some opposition."[71] However, N. W. Collier, the principal and treasurer of Florida Baptist Academy, was more forthcoming and noted that his opposition was "because of crowded conditions and lack of facilities" and told her that "should our facilities be enlarged another year, we shall be very glad to open up correspondence" concerning the matter. This was certainly an attempt to get Walker to make a financial contribution to the school to provide the space needed for beauty culture and perhaps the school's other facility-related needs.

According to scholar Leroy Davis, three reasons drove Madam Walker to establish her beauty culture curriculum in black colleges and normal schools. First, it would supply Walker with an adequate supply of agents. Second, it would introduce her products on a world-wide basis and reduce her advertising and traveling costs. And third, public endorsement by black education leaders such as Bethune and Washington would help Walker wipe out her competition.[72] At least one other element was at play here, one that is more difficult to quantify. Walker wanted to add more respectability to the beauty profession and gain more dignity for herself and her causes. She was frank about the initial lack of respect accorded her by Booker T. Washington and others in the National Negro Business League. Walker noted, "I went into a business that is criticized and talked about by everybody—the business of growing hair." She further added: "Now I realize that in the so-called higher walks of life, many were prone to look down upon 'hairdressers' as they called us. They didn't have a very high opinion of our calling, so I had to go down and dignify this work, so much so that many of the best women of our race are now engaged in this line of business."[73]

The addition of beauty culture treatments to college curricula validated the dignity of the profession. Walker understood that most women who would join her profession would not be able to improve their status through large philanthropic gifts or diasporic excursions. However, by placing beauty culture in the curriculum of black colleges, beauticians could claim the status of being college-educated even though a bachelor's degree was not earned. In fact, schools often chose girls from within their institutions who they thought needed beauty training because their social and financial status was particularly uncertain. Mary McLeod Bethune explained to Walker that "the young woman whom we shall send [for the beauty training course] is very much adapted to hair dressing, manicuring, etc., but is totally dependent as far as money is concerned. She is a girl whom we have had in our school for several years, the school being her only home, therefore anything you can do to help her will be graciously appreciated."[74] Walker's presence in various black colleges demonstrates her far-reaching impact on African Americans not solely with regard to beauty culture but also in the realm of education. After conquering black colleges, Walker sought to conquer the black diaspora in the Western Hemisphere.

While Walker and Malone both found success selling their products and entrepreneurial opportunities to black women throughout the Caribbean and South America, earlier travels took them to the region of the United States that boasted of the largest concentration of African Americans—the South.[75] Though Annie Malone never lived in the South, she first turned to southern communities when she was ready to expand her hair treatment business. Company brochures would later boast about her travels, which were seen as the genesis of the company's success.[76] While little record is left of the specifics of her 1906–7 journeys, it is highly likely that Malone pioneered the tactics that Walker used in her own tour of the South just a few years later, employing a strategy of relying on established modes of gathering and communication like churches and club meetings to get news out about their services and products. Under the guise of peddling beauty products, they also brought with them unique ideas about racial uplift and black womanhood. Perhaps more important than anything they carried in their bags, they brought an opportunity for employment outside of domestic service.

For black entrepreneurs to travel throughout the South to sell their products was not unusual. Black beauty pioneers, however, championed a diasporic entrepreneurship, traveling throughout the Caribbean and South and Central America to introduce women of the African diaspora to their products and occupational opportunities. In November 1913, Walker traveled to the Caribbean and Central America with singer Madam Anita Patti Brown and her musicians, who had already traveled to the regions, her niece Anjetta Breedlove, and her chauffeur Otho Patton. They boarded the USS *Oruba* on November 8 and disembarked in Kingston, Jamaica, five days later. They then sailed on to Haiti and Cuba and then back to Jamaica before returning home and making subsequent trips to Costa Rica and Panama.

The trips were a mixture of work and play. Much of the black press coverage of her travels, as well as her own accounts, discusses her leisure and philanthropic activities. She celebrated her forty-sixth birthday and Christmas abroad, and was warmly welcomed by local dignitaries. Walker engaged in a form of empire building; she engaged with the black diaspora acknowledging the connections among African Americans and other African descendant peoples in North and South America all the while embracing her position as a black woman from an imperial power, the United States. America's interventionist foreign policy in the Western Hemisphere, most recently exemplified by the Roosevelt Corollary of 1904, asserted a measure of American control over the region. When Walker encountered peoples of the African diaspora from a standpoint of dominance, she felt empowered to superficially celebrate and unsympathetically critique the lifestyles and customs of the cultures she encountered due to her position as a black woman from the United States.

Through her self-promotion in the black press, she made sure African Americans back in the States were aware of her international activities and observations.[77] Haiti in particular captured her attention. She wrote an article of her observations of the island that was published in the *Indianapolis Freeman* in January 1914. Marveling at the "educational awakening" she witnessed in the country and the "most beautiful women, polite and handsome men" that she met, she also expressed her disgust with the Haitian prisons and the "self satisfied indifference" of the men of the black republic. She went so far as to encourage "the Southern Negro with money" to invest in the uncultivated

Figure 1. Walker Company advertisement, *Crisis,* 19 (November 1919): 359. Used with permission from the Madam C. J. Walker Estate (www.madamcjwalker.com).

soil of Haiti and introduce "progressive American customs and habits." Noticeably absent from her travelogue are discussions of her business ventures on the island, though she did enlist sales agents and demonstrate her products. Instead, her public presentation of the trip focused on her philanthropic activities and how she had a lavish Christmas dinner prepared for Haitian prisoners, even though she was not assured that the food actually reached them.[78] While these trips did help to expand the entrepreneurial reach of the Walker Company, the publicity surrounding them also served to solidify her position within African American entrepreneurial communities.

Black female beauty entrepreneurs during the Golden Age of Black Business faced challenges in legitimizing themselves and their industry within the confines of a black male–dominated business community. They responded by connecting the aims of their industry with the rhetoric of the age concerning economic advancement and racial uplift. In 1918, Madam Walker speculated that "I shall expect to find my agents taking the lead in every locality not only in operating a successful business, but in every movement in the interest of our colored citizenship." Although she died just one year after making that statement, Walker's words were indeed prophetic. Malone and Walker were instrumental in cultivating an industry that not only helped to legitimate themselves in the black business community, but also allowed those who followed in their footsteps to emerge as modern women as the "golden age of black business" connected with other major political and economic developments, namely the Great Migration, the black women's club movement, and the Garvey movement.

2

"Link Up with Us"

Black Beauty Culture, Racial Politics, and the Complexities of Modern Black Womanhood

Adina Stewart, mother of international labor leader Maida Springer Kemp, known best for her work with the International Ladies Garment Worker's Union (ILGWU), realized shortly after immigrating to the United States that there were limited opportunities for black women in the labor force. Born in Panama, Stewart was among the estimated three hundred thousand people from the Caribbean who immigrated to the United States between 1900 and 1930.[1] After she arrived at Ellis Island in 1917 with her husband and seven-year-old daughter, the family settled in Harlem. Not long after, Stewart and her husband separated and Adina was faced with the challenge of raising a daughter on her own. Wanting her daughter to get an education and learn a trade that would eventually allow her to earn a living, Stewart enrolled her in 1923 in the Bordentown Manual Training and Industrial School for Colored Youth in New Jersey, where Maida received a standard industrial education. For girls, this consisted of training in domestic science.

Domestic labor, Stewart soon found out, was also her only option for work. Kemp later recalled that her mother's first job in the United States was as a day worker making $2.10 a day. However, Stewart did not last long due to a confrontational incident with her white employer. While Stewart never returned to day work, she subsequently worked as a laundress and then as a cook at a country club in Connecticut. Frustration with her limited labor prospects led Stewart, like many of her Caribbean counterparts, to pursue a career in the beauty culture industry. While never becoming wealthy, she eventually opened up her own beauty salon and never worked again as a domestic laborer.[2]

Adina Stewart's story was not uncommon. She, like so many other black female migrants from the Caribbean and the southern United States, entered the beauty trade as an alternative to domestic labor. Fueled by a desire for personal independence and financial autonomy, these women arrived in northern and midwestern cities at a crucial moment in the early twentieth century. With the United States' population overall becoming increasingly urban, black women migrants sought to assert a new sense of themselves and demonstrate their ability to function and thrive in these new urban environments.[3] Among the many new aspects of modernity these women embraced when they arrived in these urban spaces was a flourishing black beauty industry with salons ready to help them achieve a modern and urban look as well as schools equipped to train them to become professionals and entrepreneurs. The black beauty industry played a crucial role in providing black urban women with the personal dignity and financial stability they desired and was essential in ushering them into the modern experience by empowering them as consumers and entrepreneurs.[4]

This chapter attempts to further complicate notions of modern black womanhood by moving beyond an analysis of beauty pioneers such as Madam Walker and Annie Malone to focus not only on the economic and social culture that the black beauty industry fostered in cities but also the vibrant political culture created by beauty entrepreneurs. Adina Stewart, the woman with whom I began this chapter, found financial stability in the beauty industry and used the financial autonomy afforded by her profession to support her extensive political work as a supporter of Marcus Garvey's Universal Negro Improvement Association. The unique role that black female beauticians and beauty entrepreneurs played in connecting the racial uplift ideals of the black female club movement, the labor movement, and the race first politics of the UNIA—movements that on the surface seem ideologically opposed to one another and to a business based on hair straightening and styling—illuminate how beauty culturists helped black urban women navigate the complex terrain of black modernity and the paradoxes of class and status in the early twentieth century. The networks created among women in the beauty industry through the club movement and the UNIA fostered a larger political culture within black communities that supported various often competing struggles against racial injustice. These movements, though varied in their ideologies and approaches, relied heavily upon the connections among beauticians as well as their access to their black female clientele.

For black beauticians, these associations served to further legitimate them and their industry in the midst of accusations that the celebration of commercial beauty culture subverted racial uplift and race-first politics. Through a combination of economic opportunity, philanthropy, and institution building, the black beauty industry shaped a broad and inclusive view of black political activism that allowed it to encourage a wide range of black women to get involved in their communities. Black beauticians were especially adept at helping black women navigate the complexities inherent in African American women's transition into modern culture, a shift precipitated in part by the mass exodus of blacks out of the South and the Caribbean to northern and midwestern cities between the two world wars in the period known as the Great Migration.[5]

Most of the black female migrants who arrived in northern cities during the Great Migration were single women, usually between thirteen and thirty years of age, who came in search of independence, financial and otherwise.[6] In these cities, migrant women numerically outnumbered men. This, combined with the ways migrant women boldly embraced the new forms of leisure and amusements available to them, caused white and black social reformers to band together to create institutions to limit the migrants' interactions with their new urban environments. Middle-class reformers' perception that migrating women represented a "problem" was heightened due in part to the perceived inability of black women to be gainfully employed. As early as 1905, white Progressive reformer Frances Kellor, founder of the National League for the Protection of Colored Women, explained that "the problem of the unemployed negro woman in New York City is probably more serious than that of any other class of worker," a seemingly hyperbolic observation that was underscored by the limited employment opportunities for black women, constrained by the totalizing effects of racial and gender discrimination, to find stable employment.[7] Kellor further lamented that African American women, often recruited to work as domestic servants in cities, were often forced into prostitution when domestic labor did not fulfill their economic needs.

One of the recommendations that Kellor made to remedy the migrant girl situation was the creation of training schools and settlement houses that would help "the green helpless negro woman brought up here from the South on promises of easy work, lots of money and good times" adjust to the efficiency required of them in the urban workforce and protect them from the vices of the city.[8] Kellor and many of her contemporaries did not address the employment problems black women encountered as a result of the compounded effect of racial and gender discrimination in the labor market but instead blamed the women themselves for their inability to secure viable and respectable employment. In other words, little attention was given to challenging the economic system; instead, the focus of Kellor and even black reformers such as Jane Edna Hunter and Nannie Helen Burroughs was on the perceived lack of efficiency and poor morals of black women.[9]

Beauty entrepreneurs and the networks of beauty schools they established in northern cities sought to address many of the same issues as Progressive reformers, but instead of fearing the perils of modern urban life, they sought to help black women navigate and even capitalize on the trappings of modern urban life. In 1924, a reporter from the *Saturday Evening Post* commented that "the first thing every negro girl does when she comes from the South is . . . have her hair straightened."[10] Beauty entrepreneurs understood that this phenomenon spoke of black women's desire to embrace some of the trappings of modern life as well as provided an opportunity for black women to gain an economic benefit in the process. They did not try to restrict black women's engagement with modern urban life, particularly consumer culture. Rather, beauty entrepreneurs celebrated and encouraged black women's engagement with commerce through beauty culture. Settlement houses and domestic training schools were designed to protect women from entering into crime and prostitution; beauty colleges, on the other hand, offered a viable financial alternative by providing black women with the marketable skills they needed to keep them from turning to the sex trade or low paying domestic servant work.

As early as 1907, in the nascent stages of the Great Migration, the beauty culture industry was widely recognized as providing economic opportunities for black women who wished to escape domestic labor. In a *Voice of the Negro* article, Katherine Tillman, an essayist and playwright, explained that hairdressing was indeed a worthwhile profession for black women. She explained that "some colored hairdressers earn a good living by giving scalp treatments to colored women's heads and a nice growth of soft healthy hair replaces the short, harsh hair of former days."[11] Madam C. J. Walker declared in a series of lectures given in Washington, D.C., in August 1913 that the time had come for "women of the race to rise above the laundry and the kitchen."[12] Later that summer at the annual meeting of the National Negro Business League, Walker asserted that she was helping black women rise above domestic labor by "employing hundreds of Negro girls and women all over the country" as Walker product sales agents and beauty operators.[13] Maggie Wilson, a Walker Company sales agent from Pittsburgh, lauded Walker for opening economic doors for women like her who were migrants to northern and midwestern cities. In language that echoed the concerns of Progressive reformers, Wilson explained, "You have opened up a trade for hundreds of our colored women to make an honest and profitable living." Wilson continued that African American women appreciated the fact that they could "make as much in one week as a month's salary would bring from any other position a colored woman can secure."[14] With a majority of African American women in northern cities engaged in domestic labor, it is likely that Wilson was comparing the financial opportunities of the beauty industry with the economic limitations of domestic work—the vocation so embraced by Progressive reformers. National statistics bear witness to the increasing appeal of beauty work to black women in the twentieth century.[15]

Walker, herself a former laundress, explicitly compared not only the economic prospects her company provided vis-à-vis domestic labor but also the easier workload: "I feel I have done something for the race by making it possible for so many colored women and girls to make money without working hard."[16] While settlement houses and training schools emphasized hard work as a sign of moral character, beauty schools demonstrated that they better understood the desires of black women migrants, who wanted more free time to engage in the leisure activities of the city. Beauty culture was appealing to black women not only because of its financial dimension but also because it allowed these women to have more control of their free time. While Progressive reformers described their agenda as modern, they minimized the role of commercial leisure activities and commercial beauty culture in helping black women achieve this goal. The black beauty industry merged commercial pursuits with the politics of appearance to promote proper grooming and entrepreneurship as a way for black women to signify their readiness for urban life and define themselves as modern.[17] This was appealing to black women in northern and southern cities alike.

The Modern Woman

In 1916, Mamie Garvin Fields recalled going to a lecture by Mary Church Terrell, president of the NACW, the preeminent black female reform organization, on "The Modern Woman" in Charleston, South Carolina. For Fields, who though living in Charleston had previously migrated to Massachusetts and New York City, it was Terrell's appearance, including her "beautifully done hair," perhaps more than her words, that embodied her speech's title.[18] Fields recalled that Terrell told the black women at the Mt. Zion African Methodist Episcopal (AME) Church that they had their own lives to lead and that as black women they should learn to care for themselves. Terrell encouraged the women in attendance "to go into [their] communities and improve them . . . to go out into the nation and change it. Above all, [to] organize [themselves] as Negro women and work together."[19]

While watching Terrell had a great impact on Fields and the racial uplift work she would later engage in, it is perhaps even more significant that by the time Terrell came to Charleston another "modern woman," Madam C. J. Walker, had already come through town on more than one occasion. Walker proclaimed a similar agenda but added another dimension—financial opportunity. And while Madam Walker, dark-skinned and of humble birth, at first glance bore little resemblance to the lighter hued, refined Terrell, Fields's descriptions of the two women and their messages were strikingly similar. Referring to Walker, Fields noted, "That lady really could inspire you with her lectures. . . . She had a beautiful face, beautiful hair, dressed elegantly. When she stood up to talk, a *go-ahead, up-to-date* black woman was talking, and the women listened to what she had to say."[20] In particular, Field's reference to Walker as a "go-ahead, up-to-date black woman" was reminiscent of the way she described Terrell as the embodiment of the modern woman. However, Walker brought something more than the rhetoric of racial uplift and personal betterment. She also brought a tangible way for black women to obtain economic stability, which enabled black women to change and improve their communities just as Terrell admonished.

Figure 2. Portrait of Madam C. J. Walker. Used with permission from the Indiana Historical Society.

Mamie Garvin Fields's life demonstrates the possibilities for an African American woman who embraced the messages of both of these modern women. Born Mamie Garvin in Charleston, South Carolina, in 1888, Fields was first educated in a one-room schoolhouse and eventually attended Claflin University, where she learned, among other skills, dressmaking, millinery, and pedagogy. Upon graduating from college, she taught in rural schools in South Carolina, but after a few tough years, she migrated to Massachusetts to work as a live-in domestic servant. Disappointed by the lack of free time and low pay, she recalled, "We felt that if we did go out to work, then we ought to make as much money as possible. The money was the point. If we were not doing the best financially, it was time to move."[21] Fields then took a job in a sewing factory, where she made more money than she ever had before. After getting married shortly before the United States entered World War I, Mamie Garvin (now Fields) moved to Charlotte, North Carolina, and New York City before resettling permanently in Charleston.

While Fields's career as a teacher and a clubwoman has been chronicled by historians, her work as a beautician for Annie Malone's Poro Company has not garnered much attention.[22] During her life, Fields started the Modern Priscilla Club and served as a two-term president of the Federation of Women's Clubs, an organization that eventually became affiliated with the NACW. As a teacher, she worked as the head instructor of the Society Corner School on James Island, South Carolina, for almost twenty years. Her traditional Progressive reform work and her beauty work emerged in the same context and were born out of the same sense of duty to the race and desire to be a modern woman. The beauty work, however, also emerged out of financial necessity.

Despite her teaching credentials and experience, Fields found that when she returned to Charleston, "there were more Negro teachers than jobs, even though many children had nobody to teach them." It was at this time that Fields formed a close friendship with another Mamie—Mamie Rodolph, an Avery College graduate. Fields explained that "as young brides and neighbors, we were the kind of pals who would experiment together: read a cookbook one afternoon and then make something we never heard of before, or plan how to copy a design out of a woman's magazine. But the big experiment we did together had nothing to do with cooking or serving. We experimented with 'the Poro System.'"[23] According to Fields, the Poro System came to Charleston via the wife of the Reverend Jesse Beard, a local AME minister who heard Malone speak at denominational meeting "up north somewhere." Mrs. Beard enrolled in Malone's beauty course, which consisted simply of a short demonstration with potential students "working on each other's heads" using "sage rinses, the egg rinses, the pressing oil, the hair-growing pomade, and the special finger movements to make thin hair grow."[24] At the end of this cursory training, the women would receive a certificate of completion and a set of products to get started on heads in their own communities. Once Beard went back home to Charleston, she found an eager group of women anxious to learn the skills she had acquired. Interestingly enough, most of the women who wanted to learn about beauty culture came from within Beard's social circle—well-educated, upwardly mobile, race-conscious women such as Fields and Rodolph. In other words, beauty culture was not just a meaningful economic opportunity for poorer black women who were trapped in domestic labor but also a viable alternative for educated black women who found the more traditional middle-class professions still limited to them despite their credentials.

Historical treatments of Fields's life that overlook her hair work while highlighting her club work are ironic, since the two were inextricably interwoven. Since the only black women who were allowed to teach in Charleston were unmarried women, when Fields decided to return to teaching in 1926, she was sent to a rural school on James Island. While Fields happily taught the three Rs, she was most excited about the other things she was able to bring to her students and their communities. Fields explained that the "black teachers in the country schools served as extension agents, community workers, and a lot else besides: one day I took hairdressing over to my school." And while many of her students were excited to have their hair dressed, some of the mothers of the rural girls were angered and even insulted at Fields's attempt to introduce them to beauty culture. Fields, in her attempt to spread modernity to the young women of South Carolina, encountered resistance from those who saw hairdressing as compromising the values of rural life as well as resentment among the rural poor to those in the burgeoning middle class.

Other women had better luck than Fields in merging race work and beauty culture. Ezella Mathis Carter was both the consummate clubwoman and the successful entrepreneur. Her life provides insight into how these seemingly incongruous worlds of business and social reform intersected. Her 1935 biography, written by Kathryn Johnson, sheds light on this historically obscure yet accomplished woman.[25] Carter was born in Girard, Alabama, and her family moved to Atlanta when she was one month old. Later in life, she earned money by teaching and eventually attended Spelman Seminary, where she specialized in "Teachers' Professional and Missionary Training Courses."[26] She graduated from Spelman in 1907 and subsequently went on to teach at Kowaliga Academic Institute, a school several miles from Booker T. Washington's Tuskegee Institute.

Carter's marriage in September 1909 (Johnson does not give any information concerning her husband) "naturally changed her career." Shortly thereafter, she migrated to Chicago and studied to become a beauty culturist at the Enterprise Institute. Upon graduating, Carter received a certificate and opened up her own beauty shop, where she taught the "art of hairdressing." Like Madam C. J. Walker and Annie Malone, Carter "experimented with various oils for the hair, and was finally successful in compounding her own hair preparations," which were still in demand at the time Johnson's biography was published in 1935. Madam Carter did more than sell beauty products. Carter took advantage of the intimacy of selling beauty products in women's homes to further her involvement in the black club movement. Using a door-to-door sales approach, Carter entered black women's homes and taught them how to care for their hair. Biographer Johnson explains: "She would go into the cabins, which probably had no more than two or three rooms; there she would heat water on the open fireplace, and with what conveniences she could find, shampoo the hair; then with infinite patience, apply the pressing oil, the straightening comb and the presser, and at the end of an hour and half or perhaps, two hours, she would be talking to the woman, giving her a lesson on how to improve her condition and her neighborhood."[27] Madam Carter seized the opportunity offered by entering black women's homes under the nonthreatening guise of selling beauty products to do race work.

Madam Carter clearly understood that the home was a site in which she could advance herself entrepreneurially and act as a social reformer, establishing herself as a true race woman. The NACW took notice of her abilities and named her the chair of the organization's Business Section.[28] In addition, she also sponsored clubs on the local level. After training other women in the beauty trade and in their role as racial uplifters, Carter gathered her sales agents into "Life Boat clubs," appropriately named since the clubs "were designed to save the people in the sections where [the agent] traveled."[29] These clubs were educational, industrial, and benevolent in nature. They collected dues, distributed money to those who were ill, and, in the event of death, provided funeral expenses. The clubs were eventually incorporated under the laws of the state of Illinois and became affiliated (as an associate member) with the National Council of Negro Women (NCNW). In 1927, the club expanded its mission and established a center for rural girls.

The strategy used by Madam Carter, namely, meeting the needs of and administering to the poor within their homes, was a staple strategy of clubwomen in the early decades of the twentieth century. As a part of what they termed the "good" homes project, clubwomen targeted poor black women in their dwellings. Mary Church Terrell, the first president of the National Association of Colored Women, explained in a 1902 essay that it was only through the home "that a people can become really good and great. More homes, better homes, purer homes is the text upon which sermons have and will be preached."[30] Other clubwomen echoed the importance of the black household. "The Negro home," Josephine Bruce said, "is rapidly assuming the position designated for it. It is distinctly becoming the center of social and intellectual life; it is building up strength and righteousness in its sons and daughters, and equipping them for the inevitable battles of life which grow out of the struggle for existence."[31] Madam Carter clearly understood that the home was not only a site in which she could advance herself entrepreneurially but also a place where she could act as a social reformer and establish herself as a true race woman.

Although Fields and, to a greater extent, Carter synergized beauty work and race work, traditional clubwomen, at the forefront of discussions about black womanhood in the early twentieth century, debated the role of the beauty industry in black women's lives. In the very early years of the century, they often led the charge against the burgeoning commercialization of beauty. Cornelia Bowen, one of Tuskegee Institute's first graduates, gave a report to the National Association of Colored Women in 1904 lauding Mt. Meig's Anti Hair Wrapping Clubs, where members pledged "not to wrap their hair in an effort to straighten it." Bowen explained, "It is foolish to try [to] make hair straight, when God saw fit to make it kinky."[32] And while the black beauty industry in this period minimized the connection between the products they sold and the practice of hair straightening, for most in the black community, these products were associated with the practice.[33] In that same year, Nannie Helen Burroughs, a leader of the Women's Auxiliary of the National Baptist Convention and founder and president of the National Training School for Women and Girls, told women that the true way to improve their lives was not through cosmetics and hair treatments but through moral purity, education, and cultural refinement. She argued that improving one's appearance undermined the more important work that a black woman should engage in, namely, improving her "real self." Burroughs continued, noting that "a true woman wouldn't give a cent for a changed appearance of this sort—a superficial nothing. What every woman who bleaches and straightens needs, is not her appearance changed, but her mind. . . . Why doesn't she wish [instead] to improve her real self?" For Burroughs, the rise of beauty culture contradicted ideas of authenticity, and not just racial authenticity but a gendered one as well. Beauty culture, ironically, seemed to disrupt a sense of true womanhood based on the cultivation of moral character.[34]

Still, beauty culturists were able to exploit part of the rhetoric employed by clubwomen to promote their products. The very things Burroughs emphasized—respectability and self-improvement—left room to include physical deportment and good grooming. Indeed, for all of her public lament about the emphasis black women placed on their physical appearance, the young women who participated in Burroughs's National Training School had their hair, body, odor, and clothing checked daily to see if it measured up to Burroughs's high standards.[35] Beauty culturists in these early years also connected their services with good grooming and modernity, arguing that they were not trying to change the appearance of black women. They even went so far to say that there was nothing wrong with black women's natural attributes; they simply sought to enhance the beauty and good characteristics that were lying dormant. A school textbook, *A Complete Course in Hair Straightening and Beauty Culture*, written by Mrs. B. S. Lynk in 1919, went even further. She described the quest for beauty not as a luxury but as a "duty."[36] The purpose of the textbook book was stated in its preface: "If this volume shall be the means of some girl or woman taking hope and gaining information that will lead to success, happiness, and prosperity, these lines would not have been in vain."[37] The rhetoric of uplifting black womanhood, a cause clubwoman saw as their primary goal, was adopted by beauty entrepreneurs who openly connected good grooming practices to moral character and economic advancement.

When ground was broken for the headquarters of Poro College, a black beauty school founded by industry mogul Annie Malone in St. Louis in the fall of 1918, it was heralded as "one of the most unique and most complete institutions in the World."[38] The building, with an estimated worth of more than half a million dollars, was a three-story structure that in addition to housing a beauty parlor and instruction department was equipped with passenger and freight elevators, an auditorium, full-service cafeteria, sewing shop, dormitories, guest rooms, manufacturing laboratories, apartments, and 175 uniformed employees. Malone envisioned the building as more than a testament to the furtherance of her beauty empire, which by that time was considerable, and emphatically declared, "Poro College is consecrated to the uplift of humanity—Race women in particular." Further promotional literature celebrating the ninth anniversary of the College noted that "it may be conservatively stated that PORO COLLEGE is affording a more far-reaching economic opportunity to a greater number of Race women than any other one commercial enterprise."[39]

Certainly it was not shocking for African Americans in 1918 to hear the rhetoric of institution building couched within a highly gendered notion of racial uplift. However, what is striking about the language surrounding the inauguration of Poro College and the building of the black beauty culture industry in general was its economic emphasis and its fluid definition of "race woman." Providing a "far-reaching economic opportunity" was inextricably connected in the Poro Company's literature with more traditional uplift messages of "personal neatness and pride, self-respect, physical and mental cleanliness."[40] Annie Malone and the cadre of beauty entrepreneurs of which she was a part saw beauty work as a more tangible commitment to racial uplift than the social programs of black women's clubs such as the NACW—even if it was not always regarded that way.

Financing the Race

Madam Walker, Malone's main rival, first encountered the ladies of the National Association of Colored Women, the preeminent African American female reform organization of the early twentieth century, at their fourth biennial convention in 1903, while she was living in St. Louis and working as a washerwoman, dabbling in the beauty business and known as Sarah Breedlove. The church Walker attended, St. Paul's African Methodist Episcopal, hosted two hundred NACW delegates representing the "better" women of the race. However, Walker, an unknown washerwoman with high aspirations, was not embraced by the organization's mainly middle-class members.[41] By 1910, once Walker began to experience a modicum of success, she realized that she needed to get out word about her products on the African American convention circuit, especially at meetings where large numbers of black women gathered. She attended the NACW's seventh biennial convention in Louisville, Kentucky, in the summer of 1910, where she was a part of the official delegation from Indiana; however her presence was not noted in any meaningful way.

In 1912, when Walker was formally introduced to the crowd of NACW women who barely knew her just two years earlier, she did not speak of her Wonderful Hair Grower. Instead, she pledged to pay for the travel costs of Mary Church Terrell and two other women to travel to Richmond, Virginia, and appeal to the governor on behalf of Virginia Christian, a seventeen-year-old washerwoman who was set to be executed for killing her white employer. The women of the NACW applauded Walker and praised her for her demonstrated "interest in race progress" by publicly commenting on not just this donation but also her well-known contribution to the YMCA fund in Indianapolis.[42] Walker's popularity with the NACW only grew over the following years: In 1914 Victoria Clay Haley presented a motion endorsing Walker's work for the race, and in 1916 Walker captivated the elite clubwomen by showing pictures of her business establishment and her lavish home.

By the time the NACW met in Denver in 1918, Madam Walker was one of its better-known delegates, even leading a panel discussion on women in business, where she questioned the elitism of clubwomen and expressed what she felt was a moral duty to African Americans migrating from the South. She implored clubwomen, "Shall we who call ourselves Christians sit still and allow them to be swallowed up and lost in the slums of these great cities?" Walker went a step further, not just lamenting the state of the new migrants but also wishing to see them join the ranks of the better classes: "Bring them into your clubs and other organizations where they can feel the spirit and catch the inspiration of higher and better living."[43] Walker, in many ways, earned a platform to make this rebuke because she was known as one of the largest financial contributors to the organization and its causes. After Madam Walker's death in 1919, the NACW memorialized her in their official record, stating that Walker stood out "not so [much] because of her great contribution to improve the personal appearance of her race, as the fact that she realized and provided for honorable employment for developing the manhood and womanhood of the race. The influence of this great woman will never die. Not only in life did she generously aid individuals and institutions, but in death by the provisions of her will, does her generosity still influence almost every phase of our race's life and institutions."[44]

Walker's giving, as the NACW noted, was not limited to the NACW's causes. In 1914, in response to a request from Ella Croker of Indianapolis for a detailed statement of Walker's "gifts, donations, and charitable undertakings," Walker's lawyer and business manager F. B. Ransom recounted a three-page list of her philanthropy, which included everything from giving holiday turkeys to the needy, purchasing a wheelchair for a paralytic man, donating to orphans' homes, maintaining an industrial mission school in South Africa, and donating legal assistance to a "poor boy" serving a life sentence for killing a white man.[45] Not to be outdone, Annie Malone, Walker's primary business competitor and also a member of the NACW, offered financial support to many racial causes, especially the St. Louis Colored Orphan's Home (which was renamed in her honor in 1946), though much of her philanthropy was devoted to religious institutions, especially the AME Church.[46]

Philanthropy was at the center of the way beauty culturists voiced their strength and dignity to the black community. Wanting the financial power of beauticians to be felt beyond their personal philanthropic work, Walker and Malone also established incentives for their employees to engage in supporting the race financially. For example, Poro employees were organized into welfare associations that raised money for benevolent causes. In 1916, Walker began making plans for the organization that would eventually become the Walker Hair Culturists' Union. Walker explained to F. B. Ransom that she wanted to "call a meeting of all the agents and form a National which would be similar to the Women's Federated Clubs."[47] While the union was organized primarily to deal with issues relating to the beauty industry, like learning new hair-care techniques and introducing agents to new products, it was also established to demonstrate the financial and political clout of Walker agents. In a letter to F. B. Ransom, Walker instructed him to "form a letter to be sent to all the agents" appealing to them to donate one dollar each to the Booker T. Washington Memorial Fund. Walker explained, "It will show the world that the Walker Agents are doing something other than making money for themselves. . . . I don't want my agents to fall behind any body of women in this ralley [sic]."[48] Prizes were given to the local clubs of Walker agents that did the most charity work. These actions were noted by journalist George Schuyler who reported in the *Messenger*, "Through these clubs, Madam Walker [has] perpetuated her great spirit of benevolence in every section of the world."[49] This tradition of giving to race causes would continue as a strong part of what was encouraged in beauty college curricula until the 1970s.

The philanthropy of Madam C. J. Walker, while born out of her generosity and sense of duty to her race, was also strategic. Recognizing her power among clubwomen, Walker was quick to make sure her desires were expressed through her philanthropy. She explained in a letter to Ransom, "My lectures in Pittsburgh were a success and the club women are planning to have me stop over on my way South as they want to give a big affair for the Old Folks Home and want me as an attraction and I said that I would, provided they divide the spoils with me for the Old Folks Home of Indianapolis and if it is a success whatever I get I will send it to them."[50] The very woman who was made to feel like an outcast among the ladies of the NACW less than ten years earlier was now powerful enough to demand the terms of her contributions. Indeed, Walker's philanthropy was so renowned that she was inundated with seemingly unending requests from organizations and individuals to provide financial assistance. For example, she instructed Ransom to tell the YWCA to stop pestering her to contribute more money, explaining, "I think I do enough for all of those organizations without them bothering me. I just gave them fifty dollars when I was there in May."[51] Still, despite her frustrations, Walker took full advantage of her position as a philanthropist to gain status for herself and for beauty culturists as a whole. To that end, she encouraged those who worked for her company to be at the forefront of giving in their communities.

While the average beauty culturist was not able to make contributions on par with Malone and Walker, their collective philanthropic achievements made an impact. The authority they gained in their communities through their giving led beauty culturists to see themselves not merely as laborers or even entrepreneurs, but as professionals. In fact, they blurred the distinctions among these categories. With the most prominent club women asserting their identities as professional and college-educated women, beauticians had to find a way to place their chosen field within the newly emerging black professional class.

The Professional Woman

Much of the historical literature on black women in the professions has emphasized teaching and nursing as the most promising avenues for black women to join the professions.[52] However, many women who initially wanted to become nurses or teachers entered the beauty trade after realizing the financial and time commitments necessary to achieve traditional professional status. A beautician from Charlotte, North Carolina, for example, recounted that she always wanted to enroll in nursing school but was discouraged after getting married because her husband believed that the demands would have competed with her responsibilities as a wife and mother. Her husband, however, did not have the same misgivings about beauty school. After the birth of her first child, he encouraged her to enroll in a beauty college, explaining that "it seemed more convenient and easier to do" since it did not take as long as nursing school to complete.[53]

Beauty college was also cheaper than teacher's colleges and nursing schools, and more significantly, it was marketed to black women who otherwise may have seen a professional career as beyond their reach. Walker Company promotional literature explained that "age, family tree, cultural background, professional connection, etc . . . have no bearing on your chance to succeed in Beauty Culture. It is a new day profession, open to all whose ambition leads them to study, prepare themselves properly, and make the sacrifice necessary to succeed."[54] During her travels to Washington, Georgia, in 1916, Madam Walker wrote to her business manager that she "found so many poor people who cannot raise twenty five dollars" that she decided to reduce the price to earn a beauty certificate to ten dollars. Walker added, "I just put them on their honor to pay whenever they can and as soon as they pay it all, we'll give them their contract."[55] For black women desiring a steady income and professional status who did not have the luxury of time and money necessary for extensive professional education, beauty school was a welcome alternative.

Indeed the beauty schools Walker and others created, the majority of which were in northern and midwestern cities, served as key social, political, and economic institutions for black women getting acclimated to urban life. The women who chose to learn the beauty trade were introduced to a vocation, an avenue to entrepreneurship, and a profession. Beauty college curricula instilled in their students the strategic importance of using their position to influence their communities.[56] Graduations were grand events where beauticians showcased their professionalism and proclaimed their importance to their families, friends, and neighbors. Programs from beauty school graduations in places such as Harlem, Detroit, and Indianapolis show pictures of hundreds of perfectly coiffed women dressed in white or in caps and gowns, "their hair and complexion beaming with evidences of care to themselves even as they are prepared to give unto others."[57] These gala events were held in the neighborhoods' most coveted sites, such as the Dunbar Ballroom or prestigious churches such as Harlem's Mother AME Zion. Valedictorians and salutatorians addressed their classmates and diplomas were conferred by the school's president. The graduations were always covered in the black press.[58]

While creating educational institutions complete with elaborate graduations was an important step, beauty culturists understood that one way to help professionalize their career was to create a national organization and therefore formally legitimize themselves as clubwomen.[59] Following the lead of organizations like the National Association of the Colored Graduate Nurses (NACGN), organized in 1909, a group of beauty culturists and hair-care manufacturers convened in October 1919 in Philadelphia. There, Mr. R. V. Randolph organized what was then called the National System Hair Culture League. After merging with many smaller beauty clubs, the name was changed to the National Beauty Culturists' League (NBCL). The organization was incorporated in March 1920 and held its first convention in Philadelphia that same year, electing Madam J. E. Pennick its first president. The first officers, all women except for Randolph, who is credited with being the national organizer, adopted as their national slogan "Link Up with Us."[60]

This organization was not the first gathering of beauty culturists; individual beauty systems like Poro and Walker in previous years organized their agents and operators. In August 1917, Walker convened over two hundred of her sales agents to a meeting in Philadelphia and compelled them to excel not only in business but also in political service to African Americans. After awarding prizes to the agents who earned the most money and recruited the most new agents, Walker gave an inspiring speech outlining the responsibilities that come with love of country. "Patriotic loyalty," she explained, should not "cause us to abate one whit in our protest against wrong and injustice." Her agents took this call seriously and issued a telegram to President Woodrow Wilson expressing their disgust with a recent lynching in Memphis and the recent race riot in East St. Louis just a few months ago. They urged Wilson to "use [his] great influence that congress [*sic*] enact necessary laws to prevent a recurrence of such disgraceful affairs."[61] Undaunted by Wilson's dismal record on civil rights, Walker's agents positioned themselves as women of influence who were willing to use their position as businesswomen to petition on behalf of their customers, patrons, and communities.

Just a few months after the gathering of agents in Philadelphia, Madam C. J. Walker convened a meeting of the leading manufacturers of black hair goods and preparations at her Villa Lewaro mansion in Irvington-on-the-Hudson, New York, under the name National Negro Cosmetic Manufacturer's Association. According to a press release from the Walker Company, "Inasmuch as Bankers, Wholesale and Retail Merchants found it necessary to organize for the purpose of regulating and nearly as possible making uniform their business operations and prices, Walker felt it was equally necessary and urgent that the Hair Growers and Manufacturers of Hair Preparations, organize along such lines." In particular, this organization's stated purpose was to protect black manufacturers and consumers from "the white man who is not interested in Colored Women's Beauty [and] only looks to further his own gains and puts on the market Preparations that are absolutely of no aid whatsoever to the Skin, Scalp, or Hair."[62] Walker's gathering was not limited to one particular manufacturing company, though not surprisingly, Annie Malone, Walker's chief competitor, was notably absent. Still, the gathering was more a response to negative issues in the industry than an attempt to bring beauty culturists together to discuss their role within the black business community and the larger society. The NBCL, on the other hand, had a wider goal and in many ways a longer legacy and more far-reaching impact.

The NBCL is a somewhat forgotten turn-of-the-century organization that merits its own in-depth historical analysis. While this organization was in conversation with the rhetoric of the black clubwomen, it is most illuminating to discuss the organization in tandem with the major white beauticians' organization that emerged as its contemporary in the early twentieth century—the National Hairdresser and Cosmetologists' Association (NHCA). That the black and white beauty industries have different historical trajectories and developed with limited interaction from one another until the 1970s has been analyzed most extensively by Kathy Peiss and Julie Willett.[63] Willet argues convincingly that the black hair-care industry matured earlier than the white industry, especially when one considers the rapid rate at which black women embraced the industry's practices and welcomed it as a profession.[64] Not surprisingly, then, the organizations founded by black and white beauty culturists differed significantly. Their dissimilarities are best reflected in the ways each developed in terms of leadership, scope, and purpose.

The establishment of the NHCA in 1921, two years after the establishment of the NBCL, is yet another indication that in this particular industry, blacks had a more mature understanding of the importance of their trade. The very name of the NHCA, juxtaposed with that of the NBCL, highlights one of the most fundamental differences in the way each organization understood the nature of their work. For black hair-care professionals, as Madam Walker pointed out to those convened at the NNBL's convention in 1912, "hairdresser" was a derogatory term imposed by others. "Now I realize that in the so-called higher walks of life many were prone to look down upon 'hairdressers,' as they called us," Walker explained. "They didn't have a very high opinion of our calling, so I had to go down and dignify this work, so much so that many of the best women of our race are now engaged in this line of business."[65] The term "beauty culturist," as well as the title "Madam," used by those who excelled in the industry further indicates that black beauticians considered their work to be more than "women's service work."[66]

The leadership of each organization also influenced the role the association would play in the larger industry. Although the person who was given credit as the national organizer of the NBCL was a man, neither he nor any other man held any significant office within the organization. In fact, at the eighth annual convention in Memphis, Tennessee, a Mr. Knox, who is also credited as being among the national organizers, was accused of trying to "split the NBCL" by appointing himself president of the newly created and short-lived Cosmetician Society. Vernice Mark, historian of the NBCL for over fifty years, set the record straight about Knox's role in the organization. In the second edition of her history, she explained that "some are under the impression that Mr. Knox was once president of the NBCL," but this was not the case. Madam Estelle Hampton held the presidency during the years in question.[67] In the more than eighty year history of the organization, a man has never held the post of president and very few have even been national officers. This concentration of female leadership was not the case for the NHCA. According to Willett, the leadership of the NHCA in the early twentieth century was decidedly male; indeed, the very tone of the organization "ignored hairdressing's more feminine and homegrown traditions and described the industry's origins in terms of male achievement and scientific development, and not women's work of community concerns."[68]

Whereas in the black hair-care industry, women such as Walker and Malone were heralded as innovators, European men were seen as the originators and leaders of the white hairdressing tradition. While the NHCA was touting men as scientific innovators in hair care, the NBCL considered black women the agents of scientific change and stated that the organization wished "to encourage scientific methods of hair, scalp, and skin treatment."[69] Marjorie Stewart Joyner, who went on to become president of the NBCL in the 1930s, invented and patented the first permanent waving machine in 1928. Joyner recounted in an interview that doing hair "gave her a creative mind." Her cousin, a teacher at a normal school, drew a picture of the model and they, along with another family member, created two or three of the machines but never mass produced them for sale due to lack of money.[70] The black women of the NBCL were just as interested in the technological advances necessary for their industry to thrive and did not see scientific innovation as beyond their grasp.

The two organizations also had very different ideas about professionalism. The NHCA's notion of professionalism was based on "an attempt to disassociate the industry [not only] from women's work but also non-white service work."[71] In other words, in the beauty industry, just as in the medical industry for example, anything black and female was seen as antithetical to an early-twentieth-century notion of professionalism.[72] The trajectory of the black beauty industry differed from that of the white industry in this regard since once black women began to enter into the profession in a significant way, they wielded control and authority and became known as the experts in their field. In the white beauty industry in the first three decades of the twentieth century, women were the primary practitioners in the industry, but the realm of expertise was dominated by men.

The schools and professional organizations founded by beauty entrepreneurs offered more than a moral defense of black womanhood and professional identity—and more than training in grooming hair. They were able to offer black women the chance to become self-employed entrepreneurs and, in many instances, social, economic, and political leaders. Secure in their economic status and professional status, beauty culturists now turned their attention to using their authority and leverage within the African American community to make a political impact.

Beauticians and the New Urban Politics

Lucille Campbell Green, one of the first graduates of Madam C. J. Walker's Lelia College in New York City, was an innovator in using her career as a means to political activism. Described as a light-skinned woman of medium height and build with a head of short cropped hair, Green was born Lucille Campbell in Christiansburg, Virginia, in 1883. She attended Howard University, where she studied to become a schoolteacher, and met and married Joseph Green, who died shortly after the couple moved to New York City. Lucille Green gave up school teaching upon the death of her husband and enrolled in Lelia Beauty College. After graduating, Green "not only started her own salon on 135th Street, but also became a close friend of Madam Walker and a member of the 'society' that grew up around her in Harlem."[73] It was during her trips back and forth to her hair salon on 135th Street and Lenox Avenue (which just happened to be down the corridor from Ernest Welcome, who in 1914 was the head of the Brotherhood of Labor) that Green caught the attention of twenty-five-year-old Asa Philip Randolph. Randolph, the son of a minister and a seamstress, had only arrived in New York City three years earlier and was beginning to connect to the city's activist community but had yet to emerge as the political and labor leader he was to become. Biographer Jervis Anderson describes their subsequent courtship as "brief and unspectacular," stating that Philip took Lucille to stage shows, movies, and, of course, political lectures. Randolph was not very fond of parties or dances, and when Lucille invited him to Madam Walker's soirees, he declined and said that he did not have time to waste on "fly-by-night people."[74]

Even if A. Philip Randolph was not impressed with Madam Walker's parties and her cohort of "successful speculators of recent vintage, community club-women, new urban professionals, and other parvenu varieties," he certainly learned to respect the lucrativeness of the hair-care industry. In fact, it was the marriage of the "socialist and the socialite" on April 15, 1913, that in many ways made A. Philip Randolph's career and political activism possible. The new Mrs. Randolph joined the Socialist Party shortly after the marriage, and as a couple, they committed themselves to political activism, campaigning to elect Socialist Party candidates to local offices.[75]

"I had a good wife. She carried us," A. Philip Randolph noted of Lucille, whose financial backing was crucial to his socialist newspaper, the *Messenger*. Lucille Randolph distributed the paper from her exclusive salon and periodically used her earnings to pay its debts. In 1919, the Justice Department described the *Messenger* as "by long odds the most dangerous of all the Negro publications." When eulogizing Mrs. Randolph, a columnist for the *New York Post* later wrote, "Lucille Greene [*sic*] Randolph seems entitled to the honor of being called the one time second most dangerous Negro in America. The title would certainly have once been official if the agents of the U.S. Justice Department had had the initiative and wit to intercept her postal money orders which helped support A. Philip Randolph's subversive activities."[76] When A. Philip Randolph was asked to organize the Brotherhood of Sleeping Car Porters (BSCP) in 1925, he discussed the job with Lucille, who enthusiastically supported his decision to assist the then-fledgling union. Her financial support became even more crucial while her husband held this post since Philip did not receive a regular salary from the organization until 1936.[77] She also persuaded her friend and colleague, A'Lelia Walker, daughter of Madam Walker and heir to her beauty empire, to donate money to the BSCP and organized other Walker salon operators to contribute money and prizes for the beauty contests the union held.

Mrs. Randolph's support of her husband was not only financial but also social. Through her contacts, he met wealthy African Americans and prominent left-wing whites who added prestige to his political pursuits. She was the one to introduce Philip to Chandler Owen, the person with whom he partnered at the BSCP.[78] Clearly Lucille's relationship to her husband is significant, but her accomplishments as a hairdresser and salon owner in Harlem should be explored in their own right. Jervis Anderson explains: "Lucille became one of the more accomplished and sought after of the Walker students. Her customers ranged from the black elite in Harlem to well-to-do crinkly haired whites from 'downtown.' And one day a week she traveled out to the fashionable Marlborough Blenheim Hotel in Atlantic City to serve a similar white clientele. Her prices seem to have been high, and brought her a considerable income."[79] Anderson argues that as Philip's reputation as a "wild-eyed radical" spread, Lucille's patrons began to shy away, forcing her to abandon her salon in 1927. Yet evidence suggests that Randolph's skills as a beauty culturists were still in high demand at the time she closed her salon. By the late

1920s, Lucille seemed to want to devote more of her time to formal politics, and the demands from the beauty industry may have begun to interfere.[80] Still, her clients may not have been as comfortable with the radical politics advocated by Randolph and others in this period.[81]

Lucille Green Randolph was not the only person involved in the labor movement who started her career in the beauty industry. International labor leader Maida Springer Kemp, known best for her work with the International Ladies Garment Worker's Union, found early on that that there were limited opportunities for black women in the labor force and turned to the beauty culture industry. Kemp's brief foray in the industry came as a result of her mother Adina Stewart, the Panamanian immigrant with whom I opened this chapter.

Stewart wished for her daughter to follow in her footsteps as a beautician, and Maida did eventually earn a certificate from Poro Beauty College in Harlem. Maida worked as a receptionist at Poro College in 1927 but turned down a request from Annie Malone to work as a field representative for the company, in part because of Malone's strict religious beliefs and moral standards. After marrying, Maida (now Springer) left the work force temporarily, since her husband was able to financially support their family, which soon included a son Eric, born in 1929. However the Depression changed the financial situation of the Springer family and in 1932 Maida returned to the work force, not in the beauty industry but as a garment worker.[82]

While both Lucille Green Randolph and Maida Springer Kemp are best known for the work they engaged in after their careers in beauty culture, their exposure to that industry certainly influenced their later political and economic choices. In many ways, the economic activism they eventually dedicated their lives to should be seen as an outgrowth of what was instilled in them in their beauty school training. Furthermore, exposure to the lucrativeness and economic independence of women in the industry provided living examples of the importance of economics to the racial struggle.

Although Maida Springer Kemp's mother could not instill her own enthusiasm for beauty culture in her daughter, she did expose her daughter to political activism. Adina Stewart was an avid supporter of Marcus Garvey's Universal Negro Improvement Association and introduced her daughter to this world of racial pride, pan-Africanism, and economic nationalism. Started during World War I, the UNIA became the largest African American secular organization in history with chapters and membership in the United States, Africa, and the Caribbean. The Jamaican-born Garvey arrived in New York City in 1916 with a distinctly modern political agenda that was economically and racially nationalist.[83]

In all likelihood, Stewart was introduced to Garveyism through her work in beauty culture. According to Barbara Bair, many women who were actively involved in the UNIA earned a living in the beauty culture industry. However, quantifying the numbers of beauty culturists who were involved in the Garvey movement is difficult, due in part to the fact that a person's employment was usually subsumed under their title and position within the UNIA.[84] Still, the organization's emphasis on economic independence and institution building would have made it appealing to women practicing beauty culture. Furthermore, the relationship between Garveyism and beauty culture was cultivated through the *Negro World,* the official publication of the UNIA, which heavily marketed the beauty industry to its readers through its advertisements.

Business and economic development were central to the UNIA's philosophy. In 1919, Garvey and the UNIA founded the Black Star Steamship Line, an international shipping company that was designed to establish "an independent economy, business, industry, and commerce, and to transport our people . . . on business and pleasure."[85] Although selling stocks for the Black Star Line through the mail led to Garvey's imprisonment, his plan for the economic development of blacks around the world had a more far-reaching impact. Greatly informed by the economic policies of Booker T. Washington, Garvey believed in the primacy of economic power in racial struggle.[86] In 1919, the same year as the Black Star Line was launched, Garvey established the Negro Factories Corporation, which manufactured black dolls as well as uniforms for UNIA members and employees. The UNIA also started and encouraged small businesses by creating restaurants, grocery stores, and steam laundries, primarily in Harlem, the organization's headquarters. The organization also attracted many blacks who were already involved in business enterprises. Emory Tolbert's analysis of the Los Angeles local UNIA chapter demonstrates that much of the leadership and many of the rank-and-file were business men and women, who were no doubt attracted to the organization's strong entrepreneurial leanings.[87]

Garvey's belief in a strong independent economic base went beyond sustaining black businesses; it also informed his rejection of white philanthropy for his organization. Unlike Booker T. Washington and even W. E. B. Du Bois, who also advocated the establishment of an indigenous economy under the control of blacks, Garvey refused any financial input from whites, even though it was "white financial institutions [that] held mortgages on UNIA properties."[88] Still, the UNIA attempted to create and encourage an independent black economy that relied upon the black masses and attempted to instill a sense of racial pride based on their financial autonomy.[89]

Ironically, when viewed from the perspective of the many black female beauticians who embraced Garveyism, much of the racial pride upheld in the Garvey movement celebrated and prescribed a narrow view of masculinity.[90] The organization's discourse of firm patriarchal leadership, while always an aspiration, was a contested space among male and female Garveyites. Beauty entrepreneurs, who as guardians of a successful African American enterprise emblematized the UNIA's philosophies of economic nationalism, simultaneously undermined UNIA theories of racial pride and patriarchal order. In many ways, examining Garveyism through the lens of black beauty culture provides insight into the ways that urban African Americans in the early twentieth century navigated through their increasingly complicated political, economic, and social terrain.

When it came to black women as entrepreneurs, women within the Garvey movement were not discouraged from joining the business community because they were thought to be inept but because their involvement in commerce might reflect poorly on the abilities of black men as providers. A *Negro World* article proclaimed this sentiment: "Let us go back to the days of true manhood when women truly revered us. . . . Let us again place our women upon the pedestal from whence they have been forced into the vortex of the seething world of business."[91] Indeed, the very fact that women participated in the workforce was seen as an embarrassment and an indication of black men's inability to provide for and protect their families. However, the organization had to confront the reality that black women actively participated in labor and commerce. For example, a 1924 *Negro World* article described how black women were leaving domestic work to become "barbers, hairdressers, manicurists, and stewardesses," occupations that the article was glad to report "do not have the objectionable features of personal domestic employment."[92]

Despite the limitations imposed on the proper role of black ladies, women in the Garvey movement, particularly under the leadership of Amy Jacques Garvey, journalist and second wife of Marcus Garvey, defied the prescribed norms and used the rhetoric of the movement to their advantage. Nowhere was this contestation over meaning more evident than on the woman's page of the *Negro World*, titled "Our Women and What They Think." Amy Jacques Garvey wanted the woman's page to reflect more than fashion and domestic concerns; in an editorial on one of her women's pages, she paid homage to the "woman of today [who] has a place in nearly all phases of man's life," including business and commerce.[93] In fact, one area of commerce that the *Negro World* was dependent upon was, ironically, the predominately female beauty culture industry.

In many ways, beauty culture fit into the UNIA's conception of black womanhood. Whereas business defined black manhood in Garveyism, beauty in many ways was a cornerstone of black female identity. For example, the UNIA and *Negro World* sponsored beauty contests and fashion shows that celebrated the beauty of black womanhood. Marcus Garvey was even inspired to celebrate the beauty of black woman in poetic verse.[94] However, the UNIA's notion of black beauty depended not on cosmetic artifice but on a supposed natural inner beauty. An article in the January 17, 1925, edition of *Negro World* explained that "real beauty cannot be put on with cosmetics." Another article, printed a year earlier, asserted that "true beauty" was not seen in the face but in the heart and soul of a woman: "A woman's worth is to be estimated by the real goodness of her heart, the greatness of her soul and the purity and sweetness of her character."[95] The changing of African American hair texture to approximate, though never achieve, the straighter hair of most whites would, by these standards, contradict the "true beauty" supposedly valorized in the *Negro World*.

Paradoxically, these discussions of natural black female beauty often shared the page with large advertisements for Madam Mamie Hightower's Golden Brown Beauty Preparations, Madam Rhoda's Twelve Minute Hair Straightener, Pluko's Hair Dressing Treatment, and, of course, the by-then world famous Madam C. J. Walker's Wonderful Hair Grower. Chandler Owen publicly criticized Garveyites for what he saw as a dissonance between rhetoric and practice concerning beauty preparations. In a *Messenger* article published in 1924, Owen explained: "Garveyites and other dark people constantly inveigh against the white man and the Negroes imitating the white man—yet to take this very crowd away from the world would bankrupt Madame Walker, the Poro, Overton, Dr. Palmer's, the Apex, and all other skin whitening and hair straightening systems, in a few weeks."[96] As A. Philip Randolph's close friend and partner in political organizing, Owen benefited directly from Lucille Randolph's financial support; it would have been disingenuous for him to criticize the beauty industry outright since the Walker Company often took out full page ads in the *Messenger*. Owen's assessment was less about railing against the beauty industry and more a critique of the hypocrisy between the UNIA's race first ideologies and its unquestioned acceptance of some beauty culture advertisements that appeared to promote beauty standards that contradicted with a movement based on racial pride. In many ways, the pages of the *Negro World* embodied the tensions of urban African Americans anxious to embrace the beauty of all things "black" yet also wishing to assert a modern consumer identity, which for black women in the early twentieth century was often expressed through beauty preparations. In addition, the *Negro World* and the organizations and ideologies it sought to reflect had to hold to their convictions about the meaning of blackness against the very real acknowledgment that it was the advertising of hair treatments and cosmetic preparations that financially supported the very words they wrote.[97]

An August 1925 article on the woman's page of the *Negro World* asked a pointed question to its readers in the essay's title, "Are We Proud of Our Black Skins and Curly Hair?" The author answers this question with a resounding no and elucidates the lack of pride blacks, particularly women, have in their God-given appearance: "Surely, the Almighty did not make a mistake when he created millions of black men and women. No, instead of being proud of their black skins and curly hair, they despise them rather than build up a great nation with a proper economic basis."[98] Ironically, in another editorial on the woman's page, economics was cited as the reason why blacks straightened their hair and bleached their skin. When asked why blacks would go to such lengths, the writer responded, "To the end that they may be admitted to better jobs, moneyed circles, and in short, share the blessings of the prosperous white race."[99] Blacks were also openly chastised for using modern technology not to advance the race in any significant way but to beautify it: "Negroes use the laboratories, not to discover serums to prevent disease and experiment in chemicals to protect themselves in case of war, but to place on the market grease that stiffens curly hair, irons that press the hair to look like a horse's mane, and face cream that bleaches the skin overnight."[100]

Still, despite such pronouncements, Marcus Garvey and the UNIA's relationship to the beauty industry is best characterized as reciprocal and not antagonistic. Garveyite women worked in the industry, and Marcus Garvey himself actively forged relationships with beauticians and beauty product manufacturing companies. One of Garvey's most loyal supporters was a beautician named Ethel Collins. Collins, like Garvey, was born in Jamaica and immigrated to New York in 1919. A year later, she joined the UNIA and became a stockholder in the Black Star Line. By the late 1920s, she was a featured speaker at UNIA meetings and eventually became the "lady president" of the New York Garvey Club. Collins never married and lived with her siblings while working as a secretary at the UNIA headquarters. Perhaps out of financial necessity or out of sheer desire to do hair, Collins worked as a beautician simultaneously. This was not uncommon.[101] Described as a

"Garvey loyalist," Collins worked with the UNIA for over twenty years as a key player, mainly behind the scenes.[102]

Collins also wrote for the *Negro World*. For Garvey's thirty-ninth birthday, for example, she penned a poignant article chronicling Garvey's contributions to the race: "Thirty nine years ago a babe was born. Little did that mother know that she was contributing the greatest gift to civilization and to her race in that he is the greatest channel which God has used to remove the scales from the eyes of his fellow men." In that same article, Collins expressed enthusiasm for Garvey's economic policies. "If we remain in a consumers' position all the days of our lives," she asserted, "then we will be trampled upon."[103] In 1929, Collins became acting secretary general of the UNIA; after Garvey's death in 1940, Collins continued her close working relationship with Amy Jacques Garvey and was instrumental in the relocation of UNIA headquarters to Cleveland.

Based both on the close relationship that Madam Walker had with Marcus Garvey and the large numbers of women from the Caribbean who attended Lelia College in Harlem, it is not surprising that Collins advertised her services as a Walker-trained beautician operating a salon located at 56 West 135th Street in Harlem.[104] Walker was given credit for contributing "the funds with which he started the *Negro World* and acquired what was later to be known as Liberty Hall."[105] Walker and Garvey also participated together in the short-lived International League of Peoples of the Darker Races, which sought to organize the African American delegates to the Paris Peace Conference of 1919, a gathering of the victorious nations of World War One, into a united platform against Western imperialism in Africa and Asia. While neither Walker nor Garvey reached Paris, their shared support of economic nationalism as a platform for political activism and a way to connect what is now commonly referred to as the African diaspora made them allies until her death.[106]

Even after Walker's death, Garvey's organization continued to celebrate Walker's legacy of entrepreneurial success. Amy Jacques Garvey wanted to encourage other women, especially poor women, to follow in her stead and explained in an 1924 article on shopping: "So many of our women think they need Mme. Walker's wealth to start, but she started with but little money. She had a will and found a way. You can do so. . . ."[107] In 1929, the national supervisor of the Madam C. J. Walker Manufacturing Company, Marjorie Stewart Joyner, was sent as an official delegate from the company to the UNIA convention in Jamaica, the same convention where Collins was named acting secretary general. The theatrically trained Joyner also performed a dramatic recitation at Garvey's birthday celebration at Edelweiss Park. The *Negro World* proudly proclaimed that during her visit, Joyner would "conduct lectures on Beauty Culture at several of the leading department stores in the island that handle the complete line of Mme. Walker preparations."[108] Even the politically cautious F. B. Ransom, who took over the day-to-day operations of the Walker Company after Madam Walker's death, showed his support for Garveyism at a New York meeting of the UNIA where the purchase of Liberty Hall was announced by delivering an address on the viability of black-owned and black-supported enterprises. [109]

The *Negro World* seemed to especially enjoy giving the Walker Company positive publicity. A 1926 article lauded the company for providing all of its employees with a five-hundred-dollar life insurance policy for Christmas, while another article proclaimed that the "extension of Mme. Walker's Business Helps the Race." Walker College graduations were also covered in the newspaper, and Madam C. J. Walker's birthday was posthumously celebrated in its pages.[110] The Walker Company sponsored a "Trip Around the World" contest in 1925 in which people who bought Walker products were encouraged to send proof of their purchases into the company in support of a race leader to win the contest. The UNIA took out full-page ads in the *Negro World* asking for votes for P. L. Burrows, the assistant secretary general of the UNIA. The advertisement explained that "Mr. Burrows' participation in the contest has the sanction of the Hon. Marcus Garvey." Since the only way to vote was through buying products, Garvey was essentially encouraging the purchase of Walker products.[111]

Beauty culturists used economics to bridge the gap between the woman-centered rhetoric of the black woman's era and the masculine discourse of the Garvey movement. Highlighting the opportunities beauty entrepreneurs opened up for black women does not minimize the social and political activity of clubwomen. However, illuminating how they overlooked economic issues explains why by the 1930s black female organizations such as the NACW faced a decline in popularity and in power.[112] The financial difficulties brought by the Depression mandated an approach to racial justice that moved beyond rhetoric on black womanhood, black beauty, or racial authenticity. Beauty culturists were prepared for this shift. Their involvement with clubwomen, labor movements, and popular "race first" groups such as the UNIA allowed them to connect with black women across class lines and develop a multi-pronged strategy to the racial and economic issues confronting black women in the early twentieth century.

Similarly, the 1930s and 1940s also ushered in a new brand of politics for

African Americans. Beauty culturists proved ready for this shift. After navigating the complex social, economic, political terrain of the early twentieth century, black beauticians in the 1930s and 1940s were poised to confront the shifts in their industry and, indeed, in black politics, which now demanded new skills and savvy to engage more explicitly with the state.

3

"This Industry Is Not Typical, but Exceptional"

Redefining Entrepreneurship and Activism in the 1930s and 1940s

In 1936, during what could be considered the height of the Great Depression, sociologist Myrtle Evangeline Pollard made a curious discovery. She observed that within the urban landscape of Depression era Harlem, African Americans had plenty of places to "primp, prance, pray and pass away—judging from the beauty parlors, places of amusement, churches and undertakers' establishments that are seen." Of these establishments, she continued, primping took "first place" based on the abundance of beauty salons.[1] The beauty industry had by the time of the Depression become so deeply entrenched in black communities that not even a global financial crisis could cause its demise.

While beauty shops remained and even flourished in places such as Harlem and indeed throughout the nation during the Great Depression, the same could not be said of other black-owned enterprises. The bakeries, groceries, banks, insurance companies, clothing and hardware stores that emerged alongside black beauty shops during the Golden Age of Black Business were in severe decline after the stock market crash of 1929.[2] When black consumers had even less money to spend due to the financial devastation of the Depression, and black businesses had even less capital at their disposal, more financially secure white-owned businesses took their places.[3] However, the end of the golden age signaled not only an economic downturn but also a decided shift away from, although not a complete abandonment of, the politics of racial uplift and the valorization of entrepreneurship as a viable road toward racial progress. The government's response to the economic crises in the form of New Deal relief programs and state regulations also overshadowed the important, though smaller-scale, philanthropic efforts of black women's clubs. That the core institutions of the black beauty industry, namely, beauty salons and beauty schools, not only survived but thrived under the control of African American women is a testament to the ability of beauty culturists to transform the financial basis of their industry and the nature of their political activism in the 1930s and 1940s.

Inheritors of previous political and philanthropic traditions, the beauty culturists who turned mediating the challenges of the Depression era and World War II into entrepreneurial opportunities asserted their role as beauty activists and were at the forefront of redefining the very nature of business, the role of an entrepreneur, and black women's relationship to the state. This chapter examines the ways black beauticians, who had already won battles to legitimize their industry within African American communities in previous decades, shifted toward beauty education as a way to expand during a time of economic shrinkage as well as engage in discussions concerning the nature of black women's activism in federal and state governments.

While black beauty shops continued to flourish during the Great Depression, beauty product manufacturing, the foundation upon which the entire industry was built, incurred major losses as a result of the Depression. An enterprise that before Black Tuesday seemed invincible was by the 1930s struggling to survive. For example, the Madam C. J. Walker Manufacturing Company reported its highest grossing financial year in 1920, with six hundred thousand dollars in earnings; in 1933, annual sales plummeted to a mere forty-eight thousand dollars. The Poro Company, which moved its headquarters from St. Louis to a massive facility in Chicago at the end of the 1920s, went bankrupt in 1934.[4] In a letter to Poro dealers in 1930, company president Annie Malone urged her sales agents to "concentrate in prayer at 12 o'clock for at least one minute that the conditions be changed, the nation turn back to God and that he will pour out His blessings upon us again."[5]

While the manufacturing sector was in a downward spiral, the situation for other aspects of the industry was more complex and was subject to much debate and scrutiny. Part of a growing national concern with the sustainability of labor during economic crisis, the black beauty industry was examined by the Department of Labor, the Works Progress Administration, and the National Urban League (NUL), in addition to journalists and social scientists.[6] Some, such as Le Roy Jeffries, writing for *Opportunity* magazine, concluded that the entire industry was in decay. His findings were a confirmation of a study of employment conditions in black- and white-owned beauty shops in four cities, conducted by the Department of Labor three years earlier which explained: "Wage reductions and lessened work opportunities in the last few years, resulting in curtailed purchasing power of the Negro Worker, have had a marked effect in reducing the number and activities of Negro shops. Hair pressing, previously indulged by many Negroes, especially by domestic workers, had by 1934 become a luxury to large numbers, even though prices in many shops had been materially reduced."[7] For example, before the Depression, a typical shampoo and hair press rarely cost less than $1.50 and usually was $2.00; by the spring of 1934 these were considered high prices.[8] Historian Jacqueline Jones further argues that during the Depression, a personal beauty regimen had become too expensive for many black working women and beauticians were forced to lower their prices and even barter their services for food and clothing.[9]

However bleak the picture presented by Jeffries and the Department of Labor, there were some glimpses of hope. Pollard's sociological investigation of beauty salons within the context of Harlem's other black-owned business brought her to conclude that "the population of Harlem is very jealous of this profession. It is felt that no other race has a right to one dollar from it."[10] Even though profits declined in shops and the work was often difficult, the little money that was made remained in the hands of black women. In comparison to other enterprises, certain aspects of the beauty industry, even with a significant decline in revenue, remained "depression-proof," which could not be said of most black-owned enterprises, particularly in places like Harlem.[11] In many ways, one's assessment of the industry depended on what aspect of the industry was under investigation. On the shop level, the trade was insulated from white intervention. While whites were interested in getting a share of the profits on the manufacturing side, social segregation kept them from owning and operating black beauty salons. Unlike groceries, retail shops, and eating establishments that became predominately white owned in the wake of the Depression, the specialization and intimacy involved in grooming hair prevented whites from owning salons that served blacks.

Even while profits declined, beauty shops rose to prominence as key leisure sites in this era. A Works Progress Administration interviewer, Vivian Morris, visited various Harlem beauty shops in 1939 as a part of the Federal Writer's Project with an eye toward chronicling the dynamics inside and among these spaces. She classified the salons into four types of shops: those frequented by the "average Harlemite"; the "Hometown shops," frequented by southern migrants; the salons for the "theatrical set," that is, musicians, actors, and dancers; and the upscale salons located in Harlem's famed Sugar Hill, which "cater to the Negro elites."[12] For all of the salons' differences one thing remained—more was happening in the salons than hairstyling. In the wealthier salons, Morris found "well dressed women" discussing "the grave international situation" and "the latest plays." This respectable conversation, however, was interrupted by a man who "darted in the swanky shop with a bag and made his way to the rear" of the shop. Morris explains that the man was "peddling 'hot stuff'" (stolen goods), and the first ones to follow him to the back were the operators, who went single file. However, the operators were not the only ones interested in this illicit commerce, as one of customers asked, "What is he selling?" proceeds to jump out of her chair, "with her beauty treatment half finished" to go, along with other interested customers to examine the lingerie and handbags the man was selling.[13]

In the "hometown shops," so named because these shops drew the "bulk of their patrons from the particular locality from which the operators come from," Harlem's underground gambling economy flourished. Beauty shops were not an uncommon place for such activities to take place. In Chicago at the same time, for example, of the thirty-three places where illegal gambling was know to occur, two were in beauty shops. These establishments ranked third, after shoeshine stands and barbershops, with four and five stations respectively. The beauty shop, in fact, was the only female-dominated space where such activities occurred and perhaps gave black women the opportunity to engage in this activity in a safe and seemingly respectable place.[14] In addition, these hometown shops were also involved in other forms of the informal economy that sustained Harlemites during the Depression. Morris witnessed operators selling tickets to a Beauticians Ball and also saw customers selling tickets to a church supper or rent party.

The 1930s also witnessed unprecedented growth in beauty education. In Harlem alone, there were seven beauty schools in 1936; one year later that number increased threefold.[15] In her ethnographic analysis, Myrtle Pollard suggested that the explosion of beauty schools was a result of beauticians going into beauty education to supplement their incomes during the economic downturn. She explained: "one reason the community has so many schools is because the service the beauty culturist wishes to offer is not always absorbed. Therefore, when income becomes impaired she tries to offset this by teaching."[16] Indeed, increasing beauty education became the primary way the industry sustained itself during the Great Depression. Many of the women who would later become prominent in the industry sustained themselves in the lean years of the Depression by creating beauty schools.

The growth in beauty education happened in places other than Harlem as well. For example, Ruth Matilda Carter, who learned the Walker Hair System in the 1920s, opened an interracial hair salon in a Philadelphia neighbor-hood that was without a beauty shop. Her business thrived until the De-pression came and she was forced abandon her salon due to low profits. As a result, Carter moved to New York in search of employment and worked in a settlement house while taking additional beauty courses. When she returned to Philadelphia to resume work as a beautician, she found that things had improved very little. However, instead of abandoning the beauty industry, she decided instead to shift toward beauty education. In 1933, she founded the Cartier School of Beauty Culture. Within ten years the school had expanded to an adjoining building that also housed independent beauty shops staffed by her graduates.[17] Similarly, the Craig School of Beauty Cul-ture, which merged with the Cartier School in 1967, opened in Philadelphia in 1932 on the "meager sum of $10 and 10 students," and quickly outgrew its space within four years.[18] During the 1930s, when jobs for African American women were already scarce, beauty education offered an additional revenue stream for African American women already in the beauty profession and the opportunity for those new to the trade to learn a marketable skill.

Beauty educators were also in a position to offer something tangible to their communities. At a time when recreational space was difficult for blacks to acquire, Apex Hall, a part of the Apex News and Hair Company head-quarters in Atlantic City, New Jersey, had a dance floor where the likes of Cab Calloway strutted his moves and a basketball court where black players could test their athleticism. The Poro College Building as early as the 1920s housed the headquarters of the National Negro Business League as well as served as a shelter, makeshift feeding center, and hospital for the American Red Cross during the St. Louis tornado of 1927. This continued after the school moved its headquarters to Chicago; the institution's dining room was regularly used for "luncheons where are launched social and charitable undertakings embracing the needs of the great city of St. Louis." Political meetings were also held at Poro College. For example, labor organizer Thelma Wheaton recalled that in 1933, the Poro facilities doubled as "a multipurpose community facility." Walls were removed to create large meeting spaces for both mainstream groups and communists.[19] Furthermore, black citizens were able to pay monthly gas bills and purchase money orders and postage stamps at the building's information booth. The Walker Company's building is also remembered as "the social and civic center of the Indianapolis black community." It has been likened to a "precursor to the modern shopping mall" because it housed various restaurants, retail stores, and places of en-tertainment, including the Walker Theater, the only nonsegregated theater in Indiana, which showed both films and live performances. Its auditorium was a place where blacks could enjoy recitals and theater without the fear of the humiliations of racial segregation.[20]

Indeed, for all of the financial difficulties of the era, the number of black women entering the beauty profession increased throughout this financially difficult decade, from 9,700 in 1920 to 16,300 in 1940.[21] Beauticians in this period, according to social scientist Robert Boyd, were exemplars of the disadvantage theory of economics, which suggests that "disadvantages in the labor market (i.e., unemployment or underemployment) often compels members of oppressed ethnic groups to find an independent means of livelihood." This, Boyd contends, explains the growth in the number of beauticians in the 1940 census.[22] Black women, especially those in northern cities where unemployment rates were highest, continued to be drawn to the beauty culture industry.[23] These "survivalist entrepreneurs" leaned on the beauty trade even during financial uncertainty and signaled a shift in the very idea of entrepreneurship as a way to restore the manhood of the race or promote racial uplift and racial pride. In this period, entrepreneurship was valorized for its ability to help African Americans survive economically, something that beauty culturists going back to Annie Malone and Madam C. J. Walker understood all too well.

This survivalist entrepreneur spirit was manifested in the life of gospel music icon Mahalia Jackson. Born in New Orleans in 1911, Jackson grew up desiring to attend nursing school because, in her words, "the two most inspiring kinds of people I knew—the most a colored girl could hope to get to be—were schoolteachers and nurses." However, she saw those avenues closed off to her due to her family's economic circumstances and instead joined the many black women working as laundresses. Jackson migrated to Chicago in 1927 and was inspired to start a business by the men and women who owned establishments on the South Side. She explained the impression this had on her: "If a Negro man had a business—even if it was no more than a ham-hock joint or hole-in-the-wall beauty shop or an undertaking parlor—it was his. It gave me inspiration to see these things, and while I was riding the elevated trains and busting the washing suds in the white folks' homes, I sometimes thought about someday having my own business."[24] Jackson's mother-in-law owned a cosmetic business in St. Louis and enlisted her to sell the preparations door to door in Chicago. By the early 1930s, she became involved with singing in storefront churches throughout the city and even began earning some money in the music business. Jackson explained, "I was earning enough from my singing to keep me away from the maid's work and the washtubs, but I still never expected to depend on my songs for a living and I wanted to try to have a career in business. I took what money I had and in my spare time I went to the Scott Institute of Beauty Culture to learn to be a hairdresser."[25] In the mid-1930s, during some of the harshest years of the Depression, Jackson opened Mahalia's Beauty Salon, which by 1939 was employing five operators. Before her singing career became so successful that she had little time to manage her shop, Jackson spoke of riding the train on weekends "to sing in churches in St. Louis and Detroit and other cities and then sit up in the day coaches all night to get back to my hairdressing business."[26] In other words, Jackson found two enterprises that were seemingly depression proof for blacks, the beauty and gospel music industries.[27]

Sara Spencer Washington, founder of the Apex Beauty System, relied on an entrepreneurial model similar to the Walker and Poro companies but modified it to meet challenges faced by the industry in the Depression era. Born in Princess Anne County, Virginia, in the late 1800s, Washington joined the migration of blacks to northern cities and headed to Philadelphia in 1911.[28] After trying to open a hair establishment there, she "shifted to the seashore" and instead opened a one-room beauty salon on Arctic Avenue in Atlantic City. Blacks had begun migrating to Atlantic City during the summers as early as the 1870s to work in the then burgeoning New Jersey shore tourism industry. By 1905, 95 percent of the hotel employees were black, and these workers, unlike those who arrived at the end of the nineteenth century, made permanent roots in Atlantic City.[29] Washington's hair-care skills were so much in demand in this black community that she realized that she could not service the residents on her own. She soon expanded her business from a one-room shop and began going throughout Atlantic City and surrounding environs selling hair styling products; she also instructed other black women in her beauty culture system. By 1920, Washington had received a patent for her hair system, Glossatina, and organized the Apex News and Hair Company.

Throughout the 1920s, the Apex News and Hair Company thrived and rivaled the Walker and Poro companies in total revenue and number of sales agents. The Depression did slow down business a bit, but of all the major black hair-care companies, it expanded the most during this period. In fact, Apex advertisements in this era boldly urged black women to enroll in her beauty school and plan for their future by "learning a depression-proof business."[30] Much of Apex's success was due in part to its diverse approach to beauty culture and its ability to be on the cutting edge of political and cultural change. In 1929, Apex launched the inaugural issue of the *Apex News*, the publication arm of Washington's hair-care empire, which ran uninterrupted until 1940. In addition to news germane to those in the industry, the publication also included articles of varied interests. Issues of concern to those in the beauty industry were cast in wider terms. A 1935 article likened the infiltration of white companies in the black beauty industry to "Mussolini's attempted rape of Ethiopia."[31] By 1930, Washington broke into the Harlem market and opened the Apex School of Beauty Culture at 200 West 135th Street. "Just six years later, of the more than 200 beauty shops in Harlem, over 25 percent were shops operated by Apex graduates."[32] Indeed, when most hair-care companies were downsizing and preparing for major financial setbacks, the Apex Company was building laboratories in Atlantic City that "manufactured 75 different kinds of beauty preparations."[33] The company by 1940 had an estimated forty-five thousand agents, and the Apex Schools of Scientific Beauty Culture claimed four thousand graduates a year working in over a dozen U.S. cities, Africa, South America, and the Caribbean.[34]

In 1936, Nannie Helen Burroughs, who voiced a vociferous denouncement of the black beauty industry in 1904, addressed Apex graduates at their commencement exercises. By the 1930s, Burroughs had recognized the industry's ability to provide black women with the skills needed to be gainfully employed, even during the Depression.[35] In direct contradiction to the words she penned in her previous *Voice of the Negro* article, Burroughs proudly proclaimed, to the Apex grads "the beauty industry is ours, and we should keep it as ours." Instead of telling women that they should cultivate their inner beauty and not waste their time on their appearance, as she previously argued, Burroughs asserted that "we must look our best and less than our years at all times in order to hold our husbands if we have one, or our jobs if we haven't."[36] Beauticians had, by the time Burroughs addressed the Apex graduates, become respected as survivalist entrepreneurs who were still creating employment opportunities for black women.[37] Women were willing to make sacrifices to support beauty culture both for the sake of their own beauty regimen and to support one of the few black businesses that remained in the hands of black women in the wake of the Depression.

Regulating Beauty

For all the ways beauty salons and beauty schools sought to bring their communities together and provide economic opportunities, the Depression era highlighted, even exacerbated, intra-industry conflicts. Although the beauty industry had been heralded as an alternative to the drudgery of domestic labor since the end of the nineteenth century, beauty culturists in the Depression-era began to openly express the downsides of their trade. Similarly, the climate of the age brought about increased attention to the beauty industry on a whole as federal and state government agencies began to assess the roles and distinctions between shop owners and beauty operators.[38]

"It's sure no bed of roses," complained a beauty operator in a busy Harlem salon in 1939. "We learned beauty culture to get away from sweating and scrubbing other people's floors and ran into something just as bad—scrubbing people's scalps, straightening and curling their hair with a hot iron all day and smelling frying hair." Another operator in the same salon interjected, "But I think it's a little better than housework—it's cleaner and you don't have no white folks goin' around behind you trying to find a spec of dirt."[39] Despite the continued preference for beauty work over domestic labor, those who did not own their own beauty shops but rented booths in the establishment of another began to see themselves as exploited workers.

The federal government intervened in the cosmetic industry as early as 1906 by adding cosmetic preparations to the list of items to be regulated under the Pure Food and Drug Act. In 1938, Congress passed the Federal Food, Drug, and Cosmetic Act to account for the changes in the production and marketing of food, drugs, and cosmetics. While these laws had an impact on the products beauticians used, they did not have a direct influence on their working conditions.[40] However, by the mid-1930s, the federal government also had started taking an interest in the operating practices of a profession that was known in white beauty industry circles by its more scientific name, cosmetology.

Initially, the average black beauty worker did not seek federal assistance to the degree that white beauty operators did, perhaps because they did not have much confidence in the federal government since there was little evidence of it advocating on behalf of black women in other arenas.[41] Indeed, evidence suggests that blacks in the beauty culture industry were initially leery of the federal government's intervention in their profession. The National Recovery Administration (NRA), a government agency established in 1933 by Franklin Delano Roosevelt to try to stimulate economic growth by establishing more than five hundred codes governing trade, labor practices, and wages, attempted to regulate the beauty trade just as it did many other industries; however a national beauty code was never enacted due in part to the strictly segregated lines that were already drawn between black and white beauticians. The president of a black beauty shop owners association in New York explained that he opposed the idea of a uniform code for black and white beauty culturists since the type of work they engaged in was so different that "it would be disastrous." The letter continued: "We are willing to do our part in the NRA drive but we want conditions that we can prosper by and not suffer by."[42] Black beauty owners and operators understood that their sector of the beauty trade had unique challenges and were not willing to adhere to a generic code that did not address their needs. For example, while restrictions on hours worked was a seemingly positive intervention, domestic workers, the primary client base for black beauty culturists, worked long days, causing government-imposed restrictions to greatly inhibit the ability of beauticians to make money.[43]

In 1938, Edna Emme of the all-white National Hairdressers and Cosmetologists' Association (NHCA) was invited to take part in a conference at the White House convened by Secretary of Labor Frances Perkins to discuss the new areas and industries in which women were now working. According to the NHCA's official history, at that meeting "the national [NHCA] was recognized by the federal government as representative of the profession."[44] This would have certainly been disturbing to both black beauty school owners and operators since, as Julie Willett notes, "the NHCA ignored the African-American beauty-culture industry."[45] This dismissal, according to Willett, was perhaps even more insidious since organizations such as the NHCA not only ignored black beauty culturists but also pushed for increased legislation to separate their work from service work and any association of their status with that of people of color.[46] Still, despite black beauticians not having sufficient representation on the federal level in the debates on regulating the beauty industry, some attention was being paid to black women in the profession, perhaps only because if a federal law were to be enacted both black and white beauticians would have to comply.

For example, when Ethel Erickson set out in December 1933 to compile a report for the Department of Labor Women's Bureau "in response to a request from the NHCA," she visited not only white salons but also black ones. For four months, Erickson analyzed 390 white shops and 75 "Negro shops" in Philadelphia, St. Louis, New Orleans, and Columbus, Ohio, chronicling the average hours worked, weekly earnings, personal history of those engaged in the profession, average size of beauty salon, and type and duration of training. The results were presented in a way that reflected the nature of the profession—in two distinct sections titled "White Shops" and "Negro Beauty Shops."

One of the areas highlighted in Erickson's report was the practice of booth renting. Women who were unable to own their own shops would pay an amount, about $2 or $3 dollars a week according to the study, to rent a space and necessary equipment. African American beauticians were more likely than white beauticians to operate in this way, paying a salon owner a rental fee to conduct business independently. Debates ensued about whether the practice was advantageous. Some argued that it allowed women with little capital to operate as entrepreneurs: "These operators are just as independent as those renting a larger space. They have their own customers and arrange their hours and appointments. Some of the women renting booths reported that they came to their place of business only on certain days."[47]

Indeed, for all of its drawbacks, many beauticians seemed to favor booth renting for the freedom and flexibility it offered them, a luxury for black women in the labor force. One benefit was that booth renting did allow a great deal of fluidity in the distinctions between owner and operator, something that Erickson noted:"[black] beauty shops in their personnel relationships have an atmosphere of independence and on the part of many of the operators there is a spirit of free-lancing that tends to considerable shifting."[48] Still, others contended that this independence came at a cost. LeRoy Jeffries argued that booth renting was harmful since it did not allow beauty operators to benefit from any of the new legislation protecting workers rights, namely, unemployment insurance and the minimum wage law.[49]

In some cases, booth renters, or operators as they were also called, asserted the ultimate independence and eventually owned their own salons. Elizabeth Cardozo Barker, owner of the large Cardozo Sisters Salon in Washington, D.C., explained that "quite a few" of her operators eventually went into business for themselves and "became real (though friendly) competitors." This possibility forced shop owners like Barker to create an amiable work environment in order to retain their employees. Some managers did this in a paternalistic way. In an oral interview, Barker reflected on the different environment in her salon in the 1930s compared to the 1980s when the interview took place: "I don't even know if we could do now what we did then. All workers are more independent [now], and all workers resent anything that looks like—what's the word, paternalism? And that term could probably have applied because we loved each other. They [booth renters] loved us and we [the owners] loved them and I think there are some labor movements which would call that paternalism."[50] While the tension-free environment described by Barker was probably overstated, salon owners understood the need to build relationships with operators so that they would be less inclined to seek employment elsewhere or go out on their own.

Ironically, while beauty operators were not particularly eager to seek the federal government's assistance since it would minimize their autonomy, beauty shop and school *owners* joined forces with state government agencies to try to reform their industry. "Some of the beauticians are anxious for the State to step in and regulate them," Myrtle Pollard explained. "They are, of course, expecting to be in the satisfactory class which passes all the tests and to see thousands of less efficient forbidden to continue work."[51] Beauty school owners and teachers were particularly excited by the prospect of state regulation; beauty competency exams were promoted as a positive step toward the professionalization they so desired. Dorothy Y. Chapman, superintendent of teachers at the Apex Beauty College in New York, explained, "We will profit if the State ruling is passed" since the proposed regulation would not only "benefit the student" but also "protect the public" and rid the trade of itinerant beauticians and those who worked inside their homes. Customers complained that amateur beauty culturists lacked the proper skills and equipment to work on their hair. Those who were working in the industry feared that these "bootleg" beauticians many of whom had no formal training and worked inside their homes cut into their already dwindling profits.

Still, there was never a federal beauty culture code or law enacted.[52] Instead, state legislatures took up the discussion concerning the regulation of the beauty industry. By 1939, all but four states had enacted cosmetology laws and convened boards to enforce and evaluate these laws periodically. Unlike what happened on the federal level, where the NHCA was the lone voice to represent the profession, black beauty culturists organized to get representation on the newly forming state beauty code boards. Indeed, the National Beauty Culturists League's official history lists among its lasting contributions to the beauty culture industry pushing the "fight for better state regulations of beauty culture."

While the NBCL was still the premier national organization of black beauty shop owners and operators, starting in 1930 attention began to shift toward state and local divisions of the organization as the best way to make advances. For example, in 1931 a Cleveland beautician, Mary Beach, organized black beauticians in Ohio because it had been announced that strict regulations and licensing laws were set to go into effect by Ohio law. By 1936 the Ohio Association of Beauticians, Inc., was taking credit for preventing a drastic measure that "would have forbidden the cutting of hair in beauty parlors."[53] Similarly, the North Carolina State Beauticians and Cosmetologists Association, Inc., was organized in 1939 by Helen Starks, the owner of the first black beauty school in North Carolina, as a way for those "practitioners of beauty services" throughout the state to "Link-Up as one and band together for strength" in light of legislative developments in the industry.[54]

Moreover, as important as it was for them to be collectively concerned with legislative matters concerning their professions, they did not see this struggle as isolated from what they saw as an equally important concern: eliminating "segregation because of race on boards of beauty control, state beauty inspectors and examiners."[55] These local chapters of the NBCL petitioned to get black women a place on state boards. They saw the need for individual representation on state beauty boards as a way for them to begin to challenge discrimination in state and local governments more generally. The impact of individual black beauty culturists on state boards was great and not only changed the beauty industry but equipped beauticians with the experience and strategies needed to navigate what Deborah Gray White calls the "practical world of broker politics." White contends that the shift from the "intellectual tradition of the women's era" to broker politics happens in the late 1930s and demanded that black women acquire the ability to successfully negotiate with federal and state agencies.[56]

African American beauticians began engaging with and honing their broker politics skills in the early 1920s. Although most states did not write beauty codes or start licensing beauty culturists until the 1930s, Illinois was an exception. As early as 1924, the state enacted a law governing beauty culture and regulating schools and salons. Even in this early instance, black women were involved. Marjorie Stewart Joyner, who by that time was already the national supervisor of the Walker Beauty Colleges and chief instructor of Walker agents, was one of only three women who collaborated to write Illinois' first beauty code. In 1926, Joyner became the first black woman in the state to become a licensed beautician.[57]

In New Jersey, Christine Moore Howell was making similar strides. Although she did not become a salon owner in Princeton until 1931, by 1935 she was a dominant force on the New Jersey Board of Beauty Culture. Unlike most black beauticians of her day, Howell owned an interracial salon that, according to *Ebony* magazine, had "the coiffure-conscious ladies of the social register beating a limousine pathway to her door."[58] Among her upscale clients were Mrs. Albert Einstein and Mrs. Calvin Coolidge. After studying beauty parlors in London and Paris, Howell published a textbook in 1936 called *Beauty Culture and the Care of the Hair,* which she dedicated to "the many fine women of my race group who have devoted their lives to the advancement of Cosmetology."[59] Based on her textbook and stellar reputation, Howell was appointed as a beauty commissioner to the first New Jersey Board of Beauty Culture Control by Governor Harold G. Hoffman. Cordelia Greene Johnson, who in 1935 organized a group of black beauticians in Newark under the title Modern Beauticians Association of New Jersey, supported Howell's membership by organizing her members to lobby the New Jersey Board of Beauty Culture Control.[60]

Like Howell, Rose Morgan's membership on a state board was also sponsored by a local beauticians' organization, the Manhattan Beauty Shop Owners Association, of which Morgan was a member. Born in Edwards, Mississippi, in 1912, Morgan moved to Shelby with her family when she was two years old, and remained there until she was six. In an interview conducted in 1988, she spoke fondly of her early years in Mississippi, where her father rented land on a cotton plantation and where the family—including her eight siblings—worked as sharecroppers. However when Morgan was six years old, her family migrated north to Chicago, where her father embarked on a career in the hotel business. Morgan admired her father's entrepreneurial acumen and says that he inspired her to begin her first informal business; she made and sold cut paper flowers door to door at age ten.

At age twelve, Morgan began experimenting with the profession that would ultimately bring her success—hairdressing—and began doing hair informally for small wages. Despite admitting that she "never wanted to do anything but hair," Morgan was forced to drop out of school at sixteen and get a job shaking sheets in a laundry. The work was difficult, and young Rose knew immediately that this was not the path she wanted her life to take. She then decided to do hair full time and began working in a salon as an apprentice while also styling hair out of her home. In 1930, Morgan enrolled in Marcy's Beauty Academy to learn the scientific aspects of hair care in order to take the Illinois state board exams, the very exams Joyner had a major part in writing. She began meeting "theater people" and eventually ended up doing actress and singer Ethel Waters's hair. A friend and fellow manicurist then suggested that Morgan move to New York City to advance her cosmetology career. Morgan discussed the prospect with her family and they supported her decision, sending her off to New York with a large party and five hundred dollars in her pocket.[61]

When Rose Morgan arrived in Harlem in 1938, she was "greatly impressed" with the city, saying that its inhabitants were especially "glamorous." Morgan arrived in Harlem at a time when beauty salons were numerous and plentiful. For example, in that year there were seven consecutive beauty salons on Seventh Avenue between 136th and 137th streets alone. An observer noted that "at 136th Street someone opened a dancing school on the main floor of the apartment building on the corner. Otherwise, this would have been a perfect beauty block."[62] Morgan had no problem renting a booth in one of the many beauty salons, a common practice among black beauty operators, especially in

Harlem, where an estimated 65 percent of beauty operators rented booths.[63] A sum was agreed upon by the owner and the booth renter—in the case of Rose Morgan it was ten dollars a month—which allowed her to have access to "a booth, chair, shampoo board, or other equipment, together with light and hot water."[64]

After renting a kitchen from an owner of a dress and hat boutique, Morgan went into business for herself in 1939 and continued owning and operating beauty salons until her death. Harlem's "Sugar Hill" community of black elites proved to be the source of Rose Morgan's success and she remained there for over four decades. In 1946, after a failed partnership with Emmeta Hurley, a sister of the owners of Cardozo Sisters and a performer in the Ziegfeld Follies, Morgan became co-owner of the Rose-Meta House of Beauty, Inc., with Olivia Clarke. The salon boasted a clientele of luminaries, such as dancer Katherine Dunham and Eslanda Robeson, the wife of performer and activist Paul Robeson. Billed by *Ebony* magazine as the "biggest Negro beauty parlor in the world," the salon was located in a five-story brownstone at 148th Street and St. Nicholas Avenue complete with twenty hair operators, three licensed masseurs, a registered nurse, and a full service cafeteria.[65]

New York, with its detailed precedent of poor conditions in beauty salons, waited until the late 1940s to address the inequities in the beauty industry. In 1947, the New York State Department of Labor convened the Beauty Service Minimum Wage Board to make recommendations to the state's industrial commissioner. This board was ground breaking in its attempt to thoroughly examine the beauty industry, and it included Morgan as "the first Negro beauty shop owner to hold membership on a New York State Wage Board." Morgan's place on the Wage Board signaled that the needs of the black beauty shop owners and operators were taken seriously.[66]

Elizabeth Cardozo Barker's appointment on the District of Columbia's Board of Cosmetology was fraught with difficulty. The founder of what would eventually become one of the "most successful and best equipped beauty shops" in Washington D.C., Barker had a family legacy in the black beauty industry. Her grandparents owned adjacent beauty and barber shops in Philadelphia and Atlantic City as early as the 1870s in service of a primarily white clientele. As a child, she and her five sisters (two of whom, Margaret Cardozo Holmes and Catherine Cardozo Lewis, joined her in the business) worked in their grandmother's salon during their vacations. Of her childhood exposure to the family industry, Barker explained, "We were a little like Jewish families, the way they are brought up. If you've ever gone to a Jewish grocery store and noticed that the Jewish children can ring up the cash register at the age of ten. . . . And it's just a way of life to them, to understand about business, all angles of business. And that was the way we were brought up, in the summers at least."[67] However, upon their mother's death in 1911, their father, Francis Lewis Cardozo, a principal of the Deanwood School in Washington, D.C., encouraged the girls to become schoolteachers and sent them to a convent school. Barker says that she and her sisters "married early" after completing high school, thus dashing their father's hopes. However, Barker separated from her husband after just seven years of marriage and was left with two young sons to raise. After working as a typist at Howard University and managing a small branch of a Chicago-based insurance company, Barker was faced with a dilemma. In 1929, both of her sons contracted scarlet fever and she was constantly taking time off from her job to care for them. She asked a friend of hers, "What on earth can I do to earn a living and at the same time be at home with my children?" She continued: "I didn't know how to sew. I couldn't take in washing and ironing. I couldn't think of anything. And all of a sudden, like a thunderbolt, it hit me. Why not hairdressing? . . . And I said this would be something that I could do to take care of my children and make a living as well. And there were no regulations at that time; this was around about 1929. There were no regulations governing working beauty shops in the home. I was perfectly free to entertain the idea."[68]

By 1931, just as the nation was reeling in financial despair, Barker's home-based business was thriving. Often working until midnight, Barker became so successful that she and her sons were able to move out of their small "bachelor apartment" into a large two-room flat. Barker soon had so many customers that her sister Margaret Cardozo Holmes joined her in the business two years later. Holmes recalled that "even though it was in the middle of the Great Depression, we began to prosper and needed larger quarters. So we moved to a larger store and set up a real beauty shop and named it Cardozo Sisters."[69] The larger space also meant that they needed more operators, and Holmes was in charge of training them.

The black beauty shop owners who were appointed to various state boards found that their presence was often met with anger on the part of some whites. For example, when Elizabeth Cardozo Barker was appointed to the D.C. Board of Cosmetology she advocated that an operator should be able to get a shampoo license separately but was met with opposition: "That was fought very bitterly by one of the white members who said what we're trying now is to get away from these kind of people (what she wanted to say was 'poor black people') who were not a credit to the industry. Well, I could see that right away, and so the other black members joined with me and we somehow got this ruling passed."[70]

Despite victories like the one in D.C, black appointees experienced blatant discrimination on beauty boards. Christine Moore Howell, despite having an interracial clientele, also experienced some difficulties. She explained in *Ebony*, "The governor said hundreds fought for positions on the board which only five could fill. The white people were enraged because I, a Negro, had gained the post. Ugly articles appeared in the *Trenton Times*. . . . I was determined to govern the industry to the very best of my ability, and win the respect of those who felt that the color of my skin disqualified me."[71] Despite these challenges, both Barker and Howell spent many years on these state boards, eleven and twelve years respectively.

In Southern states, African American beauticians met even greater opposition. In Texas, as in all states in the Jim Crow South, state beauty commissions only appointed whites, and state beauty examinations were segregated with white examiners administering separate tests. In 1939, J. H. Jemison, owner of the Franklin Beauty School, wrote a letter to Faye Stewart, president of the Texas State Board of Hairdressers and Cosmetologists on behalf of the City-Wide Beautician's Association in Houston asking that "some favorable consideration . . . be given to the idea of a Colored Inspector."[72] Stewart responded just two days later, explaining that it would be too expensive to accommodate their request. Still, the City Wide Beautician's organization, one of the most powerful black beauty groups in the state, continued to work with the state board alerting them to those violating licensing agreements by operating salons out of their homes or renting booths under the license of another person to avoid paying taxes. They were much more successful in this regard as state examiners met to discuss their concerns and decided to go after violators. While the board was not desegregated until 1952, African American beauty shop owners and teachers in Texas continued to use the board to further their professional ends.[73]

The lessons and tactics black beauticians learned through their engagement with state-run beauty boards allowed them to develop boldness when engaging with the state, something that would be tested as the nation prepared for World War II. As the country mobilized at home and abroad, African Americans demonstrated their loyalty to the war effort all the while invoking the language of citizenship rights to confront the all-too-familiar problems of racism and discrimination. Garnering the support of black women for the Double V campaign, a two-pronged battle for democracy and freedom at home and abroad was crucial as African American leaders had to reenvision ways to account for the political, social, and economic changes that were occurring all around them. Access to institutional spaces like beauty salons and beauty schools, as well as their position as arbiters of beauty and consumer culture enabled beauticians to be significant leaders in keeping up the morale of women on the battle and home fronts, organizing mass action protests, and raising money for war bonds.

Black beauticians not only embraced the spirit of the Double V campaign but raised the morale of women on the home front by creating a hairstyle of the same name for their clients.[74] Stylish hairstyles were both a way for women on the home front to demonstrate their support and a way to keep up the morale of women who were directly serving in the war effort. The Women's Army Corps (WACs) enlisted more than four thousand African American women before the war ended, and of those, one battalion, the 688th, was stationed overseas. Of the fifty-one women in the group, three were trained as beauticians, which came in handy since the 688th was provided with straightening combs, marcel irons, and special gas burners and chairs, something not usually provided for the other WAC battalions, so that they would be able to "maintain their personal appearance with little difficulty."[75] An advertisement for DeShazor's Beauty College in Durham, North Carolina, tried to lure more women into the beauty profession by referring to the needs of the women serving the nation: "Calling 500 women—ages 17 to 45. . . . Victory is America's Goal. Keeping our women in the defense program well-gromed [sic] will help to keep up their morale. Our present beauticians cannot serve them all—we need your help."[76] A beauty regimen had become such an integral part of black women's lives that not even the uncertainty of war was enough to harness it.

Beauty culturists also led the way with war bond drives across the nation. Called the "greatest sales operation in history," an estimated eighty-five million Americans purchased $185.7 billion of war bonds during World War II war bonds campaigns. War bonds were initiated as a way for the government to get various constituencies and communities to literally buy into the war effort through economic involvement. African Americans were particularly eager to purchase war bonds. According to Lawrence Samuel, for men such as Walter White of the National Association for the Advancement of Colored People (NAACP) and Roy Wilkins of the National Urban League, buying and endorsing the purchase of war bonds had the inherent complexity of the Double V campaign and demonstrated both a "patriotic duty" and an exertion of African American economic power.[77] While it is difficult to quantify exactly how much money African Americans contributed to the war bonds effort since the federal government chose not to categorize contributions by gender, age, religion, or race, evidence suggests that blacks, especially black women, eagerly supported this aspect of the war effort.[78]

When William Pickens, a field director for the NAACP, was chosen to head the Department of Treasury's Interracial Section and given the leading role in garnering support within the African American community for war bonds, he knew that he needed to tap into already existing social, political, and economic networks. He spent three months in the summer of 1941 gathering lists of viable organizations and concluded that black business leaders such as beauticians "deserved special attention" because they would best

Figure 3. Unidentified beautician with war bonds hairstyle. Used with permission from the Marjorie Stewart Joyner Papers, Vivian Harsh Research Collection, Chicago Public Library.

be able to articulate why the purchase of war bonds would be beneficial to the economic advancement of the race. Beauticians, locally and nationally, were exemplars of Pickens's strategy and actively contributed to bond drives. Through the NBCL, they formed the Beauticians Volunteer Corps, which operated on the national and state level. Under the leadership of Maude Gaston of New York City, beauty culturists "sold over four million dollars in Bonds and Stamps and purchased a 'B' Super Fortress Plane, dedicated to the late Madam C. J. Walker."[79] Beauticians often held rallies at their state and national conventions with the purpose of raising money from the women at the convention. At one such rally in 1943 in Memphis, two hundred beauticians raised over fifty thousand dollars in bonds. Similarly, in Patterson, New Jersey, local beauticians dedicated a day at their annual convention to a bond rally that was attended by William Pickens himself. Surely, he must have been pleased by the $27,900 in cash sales raised and the additional $2,250 promised in pledges.[80] In Philadelphia, for example, beauty salons were the primary place to purchase war bonds.[81] The visibility of beauty culturists caused their endorsement of war bonds to have, according to one historian, "a rippling effect throughout many black communities."[82]

Black troops were sometimes met with contempt when they returned home after their military service. Again beauty culturists' access to space placed them within a position of leadership. In Chicago and in Philadelphia, beauty culturists often offered their schools as servicemen's centers. For example, the Joe Louis Chapter of the Women's Defense Corps of America (Chicago) thanked Marjorie Stewart Joyner for letting them use the Walker School as a meeting place when they "so badly needed one."[83] In 1943, Mayor Edward Kelley asked Joyner and the Walker beauticians to establish a center on the South Side for black servicemen traveling through Chicago. Joyner used her contacts throughout the city to organize local churches and clubs to donate supplies as they established a thriving place for black men to eat, sleep, and partake of entertainment. Pickens lauded Joyner, commenting that "none of us here will ever forget the good work you did in Chicago."[84]

The era of protest politics, when mainstream black political organizations began to work more explicitly with the black working class, was marked by a direct, mass action protest style.[85] Arguably the organization most emblematic of this shift was the Brotherhood of Sleeping Car Porters. Represented by their charismatic leader, A. Philip Randolph, this organization sought to form alliances across class lines to advocate simultaneously for civil and economic rights.[86] Black beauty culturists, already involved in protest politics and already having navigated class tensions within their own industry, not surprisingly emerged as one of the most politically astute groups of black women in this era.

In 1941, Randolph, along with Walter White and other leaders from the BSCP, called for a March on Washington to protest racial discrimination in the defense industries. Looking to amass a broad base of support for the march, Randolph and other BSCP organizers "took to the streets" to promote the march. In Harlem, relying on a tactic introduced to him by his Walker salon owner wife that had served him well in his early years of organizing, Randolph went through the area "talking up the March by word of mouth . . . in all the beauty parlors and taverns, and barber shops." In addition, Randolph and the organizers distributed bulletins to beauty shops that explained the purpose of the march in at least eighteen cities. These tactics were so successful that buses and trains were ready to transport approximately fifty thousand African Americans to Washington, D.C., in the summer of 1941.[87] Beauty shops were proving to be strategic sites as blacks moved toward protest politics. As black female institutions that had a broad-based clientele, they would become instrumental as African Americans shifted their strategies for combating Jim Crow.

Chronicling beauty culturists' experience surviving the Great Depression, the New Deal, and World War II is more than just a reclaiming of their lost contribution. As valuable as it is to uncover the role these women played, it is perhaps more significant to see how beauty culturists, perhaps more than those in any other profession, personified the way that political engagement was being redefined in this era. Weathering major transformations in business and politics, black beauticians were in a unique and admirable position by the end of World War II. With the economic downturn of the Great Depression challenging entrepreneurship as a means to racial uplift, a more expansive role for the black working-class in black politics, and an ability to negotiate with the state and embody patriotism for political ends now the standard for leadership within black communities, black beauticians entered the postwar period with their professional and political identities secure, or so they thought. The Cold War era of the 1950s and 1960s brought new anxieties over racial and class identity that they had to negotiate on a global scale.

4

"We Could Turn the Whole World Over"

The International Presence of African American Beauticians in the Postwar Era

In the spring of 1954, just weeks before the U.S. Supreme Court's landmark *Brown v. Board of Education of Topeka* decision was rendered, members of the United Beauty School Owners and Teachers Association (UBSOTA), a national black beauticians organization, and their corresponding professional sorority, the Alpha Chi Pi Omega (ACPO), embarked on a trip to Europe. One hundred and ninety women along with five men boarded the SS *United States*, and after a prayer for safe travel by Mary McLeod Bethune, founder of Bethune-Cookman College, former member of Franklin Delano Roosevelt's "Black Cabinet," and then president of the National Council of Negro Women, the luxury ship made its way across the Atlantic Ocean. Two years later, the National Beauty Culturists' League, the oldest organization of African American beauticians, incorporated in 1920, went on a similar journey to Europe, visiting ports of call in England, France, Brussels, and Italy.[1]

These journeys took place in the era when people of African descent throughout world were convening in places such as Bandung, Indonesia, to discuss the plight of African, Asian, and Middle Eastern peoples. This was also the period of McCarthyism, Paul Robeson's passport denial, and attempts to silence and discredit Josephine Baker's international journeys.[2] The Cold War's impact on domestic and foreign policy, along with the apex of the modern black freedom struggle against Jim Crow and decolonization movements in Africa, caused issues of race to take on heightened significance within an international context.[3]

African American beauticians, inspired by victories in the 1930s and 1940s that legitimized their industry in the eyes of the state, now sought to secure their position in the black middle class and among white beauty professionals. In this chapter, I wish to explore how travel, particularly international travel, played a crucial role in the formation of black beauticians' professional class identity in the middle of the twentieth century.[4] Moving beyond the boundaries of the United States was not something new for the black beauty industry; turn-of-the-century beauty pioneers such as Madam C. J. Walker and Annie Turnbo Malone traveled throughout the African diaspora promoting their beauty preparations as well as economic opportunities for black women. However, the context of African American postwar prosperity, Cold War repressions, and increased black activism gave their excursions heightened importance. Indeed, these international trips and their extensive coverage in the black press placed beauticians at the center of the discussions concerning the role and status of the African American professionals in the postwar period.

The motivation for these international trips went back to 1932, when Marjorie Stewart Joyner, the dynamic leader of UBSOTA and ACPO, was denied entry into a national beauticians' contest because of her race. More significant was the way that her American citizenship was called into question as a result of her being black. She explained in an oral interview that she was told, "You have to be an American to participate." Joyner retorted, "I am an American, all my people were born here." After she realized that the contest organizers conflated American identity with whiteness, Joyner sought counsel from Mary McLeod Bethune. In a 1993 oral interview, Joyner recounted her memory of Bethune's response: "Dr. Bethune had asked me [well] where did those white ones learn what it is you all are asking them to teach. . . . I said Paris, France. She said well you take them [black beauticians] to Paris, France. I said take 'em to Paris, France? I said Dr. Bethune do you know where that is, she said sure I know, I been there. She said if you buy clothes, car, house, save money and go to Paris."[5] It would be twenty-two years before she had her opportunity to travel to Europe and go where "the white ones learn," but the timing could not have been better. A trip in 1932 might have helped demonstrate that black beauticians possessed the same abilities as white beauticians, but the trip twenty-two years later allowed Joyner and the beauticians to demonstrate that they belonged among postwar middle-class African Americans.[6] Bethune not only inspired the actual trips but also helped Joyner highlight and mold their significance and public narrative in 1954.

Marjorie Stewart Joyner's initial foray into the beauty industry defied its history of segregation.[7] In 1916, she was the first African American to graduate from the predominantly white A. B. Molar Beauty School in Chicago. Later that same year, in a racially mixed neighborhood, Joyner opened a beauty shop that served white customers. After trying to style and groom her mother-in-law's hair and causing her to look, in Joyner's words, "like an accident waiting to happen," Joyner paid $17.50 to enroll in Madam C. J. Walker's beauty training program to learn how to style black women's hair. Within months, Joyner became Walker's chief spokesperson and one of her closest advisers. Before Walker's death, Joyner became the national supervisor of more than two hundred Walker Beauty Colleges, was later named a vice president, and remained on the company's payroll for over fifty years. In 1927, she was instrumental in drafting Illinois' first beauty culture law. Joyner's work supervising Walker agents made her intimately aware of the vast financial and political opportunities afforded by a racially divided beauty system. However, with the regulation of the entire beauty industry as a result of state beauty boards, combined with the new protest and broker politics of the era, black beauticians in the Cold War era began making demands to integrate beauty schools and wanted to have a united political voice to confront state and local governments on policies and regulations that affected their businesses.

These concerns were raised by beauticians and reflected a political shift in general among professional African American women, who were in search of ways to consolidate their own political power as well as make a more concerted effort toward desegregation movements. This shift was evident in the establishment of the National Council of Negro Women in December 1935. The founding of the council and this shift in black female organizing was not without controversy; the creation of the organization essentially marked the demise of the racial uplift era National Association of Colored Women. Mary McLeod Bethune, who served as president of the NACW from 1924 to 1928, was unanimously elected as the first president of the council. Indeed, the vision for the new organization was Bethune's brainchild. Witnessing the growth of black women's national organizations, Bethune found that many of the groups competed for membership and often minimized their effectiveness. To that end, Bethune thought it would be more beneficial to create a central organizing body that would encompass other affiliated professional, religious, sororal, and political groups. Bethune's ultimate goal for the NCNW was to give black women a voice within federal and local government.[8] This focus represented a departure from the woman-centered racial uplift ethos of the early twentieth century.[9] With her finger on the pulse of the changing needs of black women, Bethune brought together black women's organizations to present a united front to state and federal governments.[10]

Among the women Bethune called upon when she established the NCNW was Marjorie Stewart Joyner. Joyner and Bethune were acquainted through their mutual friendship with Madam C. J. Walker, the pioneering beauty product manufacturer and educator. Joyner explained in an oral interview:

> Madam Walker was trying to get groups together in order that she could have people to buy her products for their hair and skin, but especially hair. Madam Walker told Dr. Bethune, "Now Marjorie is on my payroll. You don't have money to pay nobody to go around here to get groups together for you to talk to. Work with Marjorie . . . she's already getting groups together for me so that she can tell them about my products and show them how to get the kinks out of their hair. Then you come right along and tell them about higher education cause everybody don't want to do hair. But maybe they do want to teach school or they want an education even if they don't do anything with it." She said, "so she's got groups and you are welcome to go to any of those groups and talk about your work and it won't cost you nothing because Marjorie . . . is on our payroll."[11]

According to Joyner's account, Walker saw herself and Bethune as having similar goals. As much as Walker espoused beauty culture as a respectable and lucrative profession for black women, she understood that not all black women would desire to enter into the profession. Others may have wished to follow Bethune into higher education. In either case, what both Bethune and Walker wanted was an audience of black women to which to plead their causes. Bethune's relationship with beauticians, especially Joyner, only grew stronger after Madam Walker's death in 1919. Of Joyner, in particular, Bethune proclaimed in 1944, "I have known during the years that I could depend upon you."[12] In fact, Bethune came to rely upon Joyner and the beauticians she organized more than any other group of women. In her capacity as national supervisor of the Madam C. J. Walker Beauty College, and with the initial blessing of F. B. Ransom, general manager of the Walker Company, Joyner solicited funds from Walker agents and beauticians on behalf of Bethune's organizational and educational causes.[13]

In fact, Joyner became so zealous in her work on behalf of Bethune that it got in the way of her business duties at the Walker Company. Violet Davis Reynolds, Ransom's secretary, explained in a letter to Joyner that "while Mr. Ransom did not talk a great deal about the situation (increased spending/ decreased revenue), I gathered that he is greatly disturbed over your increasing outside activities."[14] Bethune, however, was anything but disturbed with Joyner and said of her, "My dear, dear Marjorie. If I had you with me everyday

... we could turn half the world over."[15] In many ways, Bethune's words were not an exaggeration; while not together every day, Joyner remained tireless in her devotion to Mary McLeod Bethune's political and educational projects.

Perhaps Joyner's most meaningful work on behalf of Bethune and the National Council of Negro Women came in 1946 when she established UBSOTA and its sorority, the ACPO. The NCNW, as an "organization of organizations," was only as strong as the groups affiliated with it, and these two organizations were among the NCNW's most active in the postwar period. For example, at the 1947 NCNW convention, the ACPO had the highest number of members (148) of any sorority, surpassing the attendance of even the preeminent black sororities, Delta Sigma Theta and Alpha Kappa Alpha.[16]

While black beauty culturists already had a formidable national organization, the National Beauty Culturists League, Joyner, like Bethune, aptly noted a need for an ideological shift in black women's organizational work in the period after the Great Depression. While the NBCL's primary concern was getting beauty culturists recognized as respectable professionals within the black community by adhering to the gendered politics of racial uplift, UBSOTA sought middle-class legitimacy outside of the confines of racial uplift ethos and began to engage more explicitly with issues concerning citizenship and gaining recognition in the white beauty culture industry. Furthermore, —UBSOTA sought to give voice to those who were the most important players in the black hair-care industry in the postwar period, namely, the teachers and owners of beauty colleges; this group would also often include the owners of beauty salons, since many beauty educators often did both. While the NBCL was moving toward a regional focus, UBSOTA was more concerned with national issues of interest to beauty school owners and black women in general. Still, UBSOTA did not consider itself a competitor to the NBCL, at least not publicly. Joyner explained, "We [UBSOTA] will, of course, attend all the meetings of the National Beauty Culturists' League . . . and cooperate in every way to get our Graduates to join the local chapters of the National Beauty Culturists' League."[17] Indeed, Joyner served as president of the NBCL in the 1930s.

Among its membership, UBSOTA included the beauty culture school owners and teachers of the "chain systems such as Mme. C. J. Walker, Poro, Apex, and all independently owned Beauty Schools throughout America." UBSOTA's first national convention, held February 27–March 2, 1947, at Bethune-Cookman College at the behest of Mary McLeod Bethune, drew 136 members. At that first convention, the organization adopted as one of its primary aims "to aid the construction of a building on Bethune Cookman

College" and to "support Mrs. Bethune in all of her work."[18] UBSOTA and its sorority, ACPO, did just that. In fact, a visitor to Bethune-Cookman College today would find monuments of praise to Joyner and her organizations' work on behalf of the college. Nestled among buildings named for past college presidents and a Supreme Court judge sits Marjorie Stewart Joyner Hall, the only college residence hall named for any beautician, black or white, in the United States—and most likely the world.[19]

Through Joyner's harnessing of African American female political power by means of strategic organizing and philanthropy, black beauty school owners and teachers entered the Cold War era secure in their position as political brokers in their respective communities. However, when they sought to further their status within their communities and increase their visibility and power in the mainstream beauty culture industry and in a larger political arena, they did not focus solely on supporting black institutions such as Bethune-Cookman but instead fixed their eyes upon making a global impact that would pay them local and national dividends in the postwar world. To that end their first stop was not Europe in 1954, but Haiti two years prior.

UBSOTA and ACPO's first international journey took them on a three-day trip to Port-au-Prince, Haiti, as a part of their seventh annual convention, which also included three days of organizational meetings in Miami and a one-day trip to Daytona Beach as the guest of Mary McLeod Bethune at Bethune-Cookman College. Billed as a goodwill trip, the Haitian junket, according to press releases, "marked the organization's first project in building international understanding . . . [and] raising [the] educational standards of its members through travel and intercultural relations."[20] Arriving by special Pan American clipper, the beauticians and their special guests were greeted by the acting ambassador for the United States, Howard Travers, in addition to Haitian president Paul E. Magliore and his wife Yolette Leconte Magliore, who gave them full access to government facilities. Indeed, before the visitors set foot on Haitian soil, Joyner spoke openly of the Haitian government's regular and helpful correspondence in preparing for the trip.

While in Haiti, the beauticians were entertained by government officials at cocktail parties and dances, and they partook of the island's inspirational revolutionary history by placing a wreath at a statue of Touissant L'Overture, the recognized leader of Haiti's battle for independence from French colonial rule. However, the beauticians did not come to Haiti simply to indulge in tourist activities; they came to engage Haitian leaders in discussions concerning gender and economic inequalities in the black republic. To that end, the travelers met with various Haitian women's leagues and social action

Figure 4. United Beauty School Owners and Teachers Association/Alpha Chi Phi Omega (UBSOTA/ACPO) travelers arrive in Haiti, 1954. Used with permission from the Marjorie Stewart Joyner Papers, Vivian Harsh Research Collection, Chicago Public Library.

networks with whom they held a one-day seminar addressing the need for Haitian women to own and operate their own businesses. They also met with the Haitian commerce minister, Jules Domond, concerning the manufacture of cosmetic preparations in Haiti, which would further encourage the establishment of female-owned enterprises. By the end of the trip, the members of UBSOTA had granted twenty-one full scholarships to "deserving Haitian girls for beauty culture training in America."[21] The criteria used to determine the Haitian women's worthiness is unknown. However, this tangible commitment to furthering the economic prospects of the women of Haiti also helped to bolster their own position among black middle-class organizations such as the National Association of Colored People and the *Chicago Defender* newspaper, two powerful voices in African American life and politics that were already actively involved in Haiti.

Increasing tourism and economic development in Haiti were top priorities for the NAACP under the leadership of executive secretary Walter White.[22] In 1947, White, along with Bethune, Eleanor Roosevelt, and other leaders, formed an interracial committee that served as advocates for and advisers to Haiti. By 1950 White had cultivated a relationship with Haitian President Magloire and pledged to get "enlightened and unselfish investment capital to flow through Haiti." White also called for free and democratic elections on the island and vowed to do all he could to increase tourism to the island. However, not just any rank-and-file tourist would do, according to historian Millery Polyne. Rather, "White wanted to attract the 'right type' of American tourist, those with high moral standards and the 'right type of attitude toward race.'"[23] Indeed, tourism to Haiti increased dramatically under Magloire from over seventeen thousand people in 1951 to over sixty-five thousand travelers just five years later. And while White's goal was to increase overall American tourism to Haiti, his greatest sphere of influence was among African Americans, who undoubtedly helped those numbers increase.

Among those with a great interest in Haitian tourism was Venice R. Spraggs, the Washington bureau chief of the *Chicago Defender* who visited Haiti as a part of the "paper's program to stimulate a greater interest in Haiti and other colored republics." Spraggs helped Marjorie Stewart Joyner with the logistics of the 1952 Haiti trip and even accompanied the beauticians on the journey. During the three-day visit with the beauticians, Spraggs spoke to an overflow audience of Haitian leaders about the status of blacks in the United States, openly acknowledging the "shameful segregation and discrimination heaped upon the heads of Negroes" there. However, Spraggs wanted the Haitian leaders to understand that despite the challenges of racial discrimination, African Americans remained "loyal to the concept of democratic government realizing it is their only hope for attaining the full human dignity they seek."[24] In many ways, Spraggs's comments highlight the very real tension African Americans engaged in using foreign travels to meet domestic agenda during the Cold War. African Americans traveling abroad often chose to affirm American democratic ideals even as they were denied the fruit back home. Those who chose otherwise ran the risk of being labeled communists, coming under government surveillance and having their passports revoked.

While African Americans traveling to Haiti were under scrutiny, when the UBSOTA and NBCL decided to visit Western Europe in 1954 and 1956, they knew they had to be even more careful. With the maligning of politically active African Americans as communists at home and with European sentiment increasingly turning against the American government in light of injustices against blacks, a group of African American small-business women on a European "beauty pilgrimage" was latent with meaning and political potential.[25] In other words, the timing of the trips in the context of the Cold War and the early stages of the modern civil rights movement gave them a significance they would not have had back in 1932, when Bethune first suggested the trips to Joyner. Under the charismatic leadership of Joyner, and with the guidance of Bethune, the black beauticians used every opportunity abroad to prove themselves worthy of the benefits of full citizenship, validate their professional skills to white beauticians, and increase their status among African Americans back home.

When paying tribute to "Negro Beauticians as Ambassadors" in her May 15, 1954, *Chicago Defender* column, Bethune explained that "through their travels, they add to their personal stature; but they also give the world a gratifying picture of the Negro Race."[26] This gratifying picture, it seems, was used by the State Department to showcase the beauticians' loyalty to capitalism and the ability of blacks to flourish under the free market system. The American ambassador to France, C. Douglas Dillon, curiously declared that the presence of beauticians in Europe was "a very effective answer to communism."[27]

When preparing for a similar trip in 1960, Joyner asked for an audience with Amory Houghton, who replaced Dillon as U.S. ambassador to France. Joyner explained in her request, "As you know, we are classed as small business people and this is our means of raising our standards, educating our group, and learning foreign techniques that perhaps can be adopted to improve our businesses."[28] Just as they were welcomed by Ambassador Dillon on their first trip to France in 1954, they were embraced by Houghton's diplomatic team six years later. Indeed, for all of the ways the trips served the beauticians' desire for respect, it may have also sought to serve State Department and American embassy officials, who "recognized that African Americans themselves would be most effective in countering negative international opinion" concerning Jim Crow segregation and the mistreatment of African Americans.[29] In other words, a pro-business stance gave beauticians leverage with the State Department, enabling them to travel abroad promoting the goodness of American democracy to African Americans when all the while one of their major goals was to dismantle racism within their industry and pursue a civil rights agenda once they returned home. However, this ideological maneuvering came at a high cost for black leaders since their support for American ideals abroad did little to compel the Truman and Eisenhower administrations to move forward on a civil rights agenda.[30]

While these European beauty pilgrimages did not dramatically alter U.S. foreign or domestic policy, they did give beauticians some leverage when they returned home. The beauticians boasted that "working on French models was not the least bit difficult," demonstrating that their styling expertise went beyond carrying for African American textured hair.[31]

Such a comment seems directed to their white beauty industry counterparts, until one considers that it was published in *Beauty Trade*, the leading black industry publication. In reality, these trips had little impact in breaking down racial barriers in the staunchly segregated industry. Joyner explained that in the wake of UBSOTA's 1954 excursion, "the white schools in the US told [us] afterwards that if they knew [we] had that kind of money they would have let [us] come to [their] school *at night*."[32] In other words, the experiences black beauticians had in Europe learning new and improved beauty techniques, mingling with French hairdressers and British nobility, and spending lots of money did little to gain them respect with whites in the State Department or in their industry.

Figure 5. Marjorie Stewart Joyner (*second from left*) and other members of UBSOTA/ACPO with unidentified French beautician. Used with permission from the Marjorie Stewart Joyner Papers, Vivian Harsh Research Collection, Chicago Public Library.

Indeed, for all of their posturing, black beauticians seemed less concerned with impressing whites and more concerned with establishing their position among the black middle-class, which was undergoing a major restructuring in this period. Not only was the Cold War era a pivotal moment in reconceptualizing African American politics at home and abroad, but the era also coincided with a major redefinition of the black middle class. The postwar period witnessed a growth in African American incomes.[33] As a result, the previous status-based insular group of black elites was being challenged by an emerging middle class who laid claim to middle-class identity through home ownership and consumption practices.[34] African American beauticians, who had always had a dubious relationship to the middle class, became exemplars of this shift and used the publicity surrounding their international journeys to solidify their position within this emerging consumption-based black middle class.

Black beauticians in this period relied upon not only mainstream publications of the black press but also their own publications to publicize their travels. *Beauty Trade* magazine, founded in 1954 by the Calvin News Service, was the premier black beauty publication by mid century. Boasting a readership in Africa and throughout the diaspora, the magazine covered professional issues as well as fashion, health, and business. The publication, however, was not only geared to the beauty professional; it included stories that were appealing to beautician and client alike. For example, Mrs. Joseph N. Grant, "an American Negro teacher who has accompanied her husband on a UNESCO tour of duty to Nigeria," explained that she was "aware of the study tours of individuals and groups as reported in *Beauty Trade*." Grant further explained that she read *Beauty Trade* in her Nigerian beautician's shop.[35] In the pages of *Beauty Trade*, beauticians and their clients learned a great deal about beauticians' travel activities; in addition to the stories of the collective journeys, readers also were treated to reports of women such as sisters Ella Shepherd and Theresa Lockett, who in 1958 visited eight European countries to "study advanced beauty culture techniques."[36] Furthermore, readers learned how to style their hair while on vacation and after they returned with cover stories and photo spreads dedicated, as in the September 1957 issue, to "Back-from-Vacation Coifs."[37]

In addition to the expected coverage in *Beauty Trade*, accounts of these trips were publicized widely in the black press, with *Ebony* magazine, the primary media outlet of the black middle class, leading the way with a four-page spread complete with photographs. The *Ebony* article described the women's attire and gave details concerning the money spent on shopping trips—estimating that some of the women brought as much as three thousand dollars to spend in Europe—and the cost of travel, which was one thousand dollars per traveler. The article went on to describe the impact of African American women spending this money:

> In February [1954], Mrs. Joyner ambled into the offices of the United States Steamship line in Chicago, plunked down $20,000 and announced that this was just a deposit for tickets. The manager gazed at the money in disbelief, then sat down limply.

And while spending money was a means of African American beauticians demonstrating their position in the consumer-driven black middle class, the *Ebony* article also described the women's behavior within the context of the enduring legacy of the politics of respectability, namely that black women who aspired to middle class status had to behave without reproach, "The brown Americans were praised for everything from their mink capes to their good conduct, both of which apparently surprised some Europeans." Described as "dignified American Negroes" in hotel itineraries and in European press coverage, the women were the toast of Europe. However, the article later called into question the morality of the women: "Rumors spread nevertheless, that a few of the female beauticians, who were minus their husbands, behaved naughtily aboard ship and were seen in Paris with 'some of the town's most notorious pimps.'" But the writer gave the ever strategic Marjorie Joyner the last word on the matter: "Joyner scoffed at such reports. . . . Their conduct was on the whole impeccable."[38] Understanding that black women would not be considered middle class no matter how much money they spent if their behavior was questionable, black beauticians in their own public travel diaries and in their interactions with the press highlighted their proper behavior abroad.[39]

If anyone caught a glimpse of the beauticians as they traveled through Europe, one would certainly have a distorted understanding of the severe racial and economic inequalities in American society. Conduct and appearance was often one of the first things commented on by observers. Ambassador Dillon referred to the beauticians as "fur-draped visitors," while Mary McLeod Bethune proclaimed that "it was a glorious sight to see them before they left—all well groomed with perfectly appointed dress and luggage and poised in every way."[40] The travelers themselves were self-conscious of their attire as well. When describing what she chose to wear to begin her transatlantic voyage, Katie Whickham, the vice president of the NBCL, explained, "I chose to travel in a light tweed suit with matching accessories. Even if I say so, I had a business women's look."[41] Chronicling their stylish attire served black beauticians in their attempts to gain status among whites and middle-class blacks as well as supporting the State Department's propaganda of African American success.

That the black press would cover this European trip in such detail was not surprising. In fact, newspapers like the *Chicago Defender* and *Baltimore Afro-American* spent considerable ink chronicling the international travels of its readers. The *Pittsburgh Courier* published a weekly travel column penned by Freddye Henderson, owner of Henderson Travel Services in Atlanta. Henderson and her husband opened their business in 1955 and became the first and one of the most successful African American agencies dedicated to international travel in the postwar period. The column, entitled "Travel by Freddye," which ran from 1957–1963, was at once a place for international travelers to describe their escapades, as well as a forum to provide practical advice on everything from obtaining a passport to purchasing a car overseas. International travel was so popular among African Americans that Henderson observed in a 1962 column that her friend did not want to travel to Europe because "everybody goes there now."[42]

Sociologist E. Franklin Frazier in his critique of the black middle class, *Black Bourgeoisie* published in 1957, described such press coverage as "creating a world of make-believe to satisfy the craving of the black bourgeoisie for recognition." These "fanciful reports," Frazier complained, "are provided for the black bourgeoisie who remain at home."[43] While much has been made of the problems with Frazier's sociological polemic, his observations about the black press's seeming obsession with the travel adventures of the new black middle class combined with the extensive coverage of the beauticians' journeys demonstrates that these travels were a way for the UBSOTA and NBCL to be a part of a postwar conversation about class.

More than the black press was interested in these journeys; leading newspapers in France and England also covered their activities, and French television stations asked their visitors to appear as program guests.[44] Paris bestowed the equivalent of a key to the city on Joyner, while London showed the beauticians Parliament. Lady Astor allowed them to tour her world-renowned gardens, and lavish cocktail parties met them at every port of call.[45] The beauty culturists basked in the preferential treatment they received throughout Europe, knowing that they would find nothing close to it in their country of origin. Historian Tom Borstelmann argues that "for all their colonial practices abroad, the more homogenous Western European nations were typically less racially discriminatory at home than the heterogeneous Americans."[46] African American travelers throughout the twentieth century confirmed this. In 1951, writer Richard Wright called France "a land of refuge" for African Americans, while in 1948, singer and performer Josephine Baker told students at Fisk University that they should visit France to experience the joys of a society without racism.[47] Indeed, the only time the beauty culturists openly confronted racism abroad, according to their accounts, was when they encountered their fellow Americans. Katie Whickham mentions two incidents in her travel journal, one in Florence and the other in Rome, where "a bit of America's segregation lifted its ugly head."[48] Of the hotel in Florence, Whickham explained, "the dining room was exquisite, but a few Americans were there with their poisonous segregational issues."[49] Whickham also recognized that the relationships with the many European stylists they made on their trip would not have been possible in the United States. Of the European stylists they met, she lamented, "they all expressed the desire to be entertained by us should they come to America. How badly I felt when I thought of America's curse, *segregation*."[50] While in Europe, these African American beauticians were able to experience life free from the humiliations of segregation and not only excitedly shared the details with their fellow African Americans when they returned, but also used their experiences with white Europeans to try to shame their white American counterparts in the beauty industry. The former, it seems, was a more productive venture than the latter, as the publicity around these trips served to bolster the image of beauticians in the minds of African Americans and indeed blacks throughout Africa and its diaspora. While they may not have conquered the hearts of Euro-Americans, these trips did help to elevate African American beauticians as the global standard bearers of black beauty and hair care.

The positioning of African American women as the standard bearers, the ones, according to a November 1961 *Beauty Trade* article about the status of black beauticians around the globe, "who [have] set the criterion by which others may follow," was as much about raising their class and status in Africa and the diaspora as among the black middle class in America. *Beauty Trade* magazine boasted of having subscribers around the globe and took great pride in recounting the state of black beauty in various countries. Some, such as Carmen England, owner of Carmen Colonial Hairdressers of London, and Mr. and Mrs. Jose Daniel Garcia, a leading beauty product manufacturer in Havana, Cuba, visited African American beauty schools and shops "to learn more how we [African American beauticians] do things."[51] Just as African American beauticians visited Europe to legitimate their standing in the industry, black women from Africa and the diaspora came to the United States to be validated as stylists and educators in their respective countries. Most came to be educated in African American beauty schools before returning to their respective countries to open their own salons and schools. In 1958, the Apex Beauty College celebrated the graduation of "five attractive women" from Nevis, Jamaica, St. Kitts, Barbados, Virgin Islands, and Grenada who planned to return "to their countries to go into business for themselves."[52] The Madam C. J. Walker College in Washington, D.C., was particularly proud when in 1960, Miss Lucy Haln, daughter of the ambassador of Ghana to the United States enrolled as a student.[53]

Foreign nationals often received their beauty education while in the United States and then returned home to found both beauty shops and beauty schools. Madam Germaine Pierre-Louis, a graduate of Gray's Scientific School in Hempstead, New York, who came to the United States in 1956 presumably through the scholarship program initiated by Joyner in her visit to Haiti in 1952, by the summer of 1960 had opened Haiti's first black beauty school in her native Port-au-Prince. Pierre-Louis got her training in the United States and "sent to the States for her equipment so that Haiti would get a really modern school."[54] Similarly, Dorothy Matthews, owner and headmistress of Dottie's School of Beauty Culture, Bermuda's only beauty school for black women, was trained in New York at the renowned Apex School of Beauty Culture. Matthews returned to Bermuda "determined to make it easier for the many others who wanted to learn beauty culture."[55]

Even when beauty schools were not established, African American women traveled to the Caribbean to showcase and teach their self-proclaimed modern and superior beauty culture techniques. For example, *Beauty Trade* sent a group of African American beauticians to Puerto Rico, who admitted that while the native beauticians (black and white) were "well advanced [and] anxious to learn," they were surprised that the Puerto Rican women grasped the tricks of the trade so quickly."[56] A photo with the caption "Spanish beauty Amparro Suarez, young demonstrator with black hair and green eyes, admires BEAUTY TRADE." signified that even nonblack peoples in the Caribbean appreciated the expertise of black American beauticians, something that stood in stark contrast to the contempt of white American beauty professionals.[57]

As black beauticians throughout West Africa and the black diaspora encountered challenges in the development of their own industry, they looked to African American beauticians for inspiration; a *Beauty Trade* issue dedicated to "how beauticians of color are faring in other countries" went so far as to say that "American Negro Beauticians have brought their profession to rank as one of the finest and largest any American Negro woman can follow—this is the story beauticians in other countries turn to with pride and determination to overcome their difficulties."[58] The wife of the aforementioned UNESCO worker stationed in Lagos, Nigeria, writing on behalf of her Nigerian beautician, perhaps stated it best: "If Europe, as you have said, is the source of beauty culture, then America is the source of the adaptation to this culture to the needs of Africans and African descendants."[59] Beauticians in Africa and the diaspora saw black Americans as the leaders of educational and professional standards, even replicating the practice of closing their shops on Mondays. In many ways in the postwar period, black American beauticians embraced the idea that they were to Africa and its descendants what European hairdressers were to white Americans, the creative and economic innovators and sustainers of a vibrant and independent beauty culture industry.

Still, in spite of their travels, beauty culturists celebrated few victories against segregation at home as a result of their "beauty pilgrimages." They knew that their status would always be compromised if they did not continue to address the racial inequalities within American society as a whole. To that end, they engaged in political activities within their communities that sought to improve their business and status even while improving the lives of others.

5

"Black Beauticians Were Very Important"

Southern Beauty Activists and the Modern Black Freedom Struggle

In 1964, after a sit-in at a Woolworth lunch counter where she had food and drink, not to mention racial epithets, hurled at her, civil rights freedom fighter Anne Moody made a curious sojourn to a place she knew her embattled body and spirit could be refreshed and replenished, a place that stood in stark contrast to the Woolworth counter, a place of safety, refuge, and community support. Her quest did not take her to a local church. As Moody recalls in her canonical memoir, *Coming of Age in Mississippi*, "I stopped in at a beauty shop across the street from the NAACP office. . . . The hairdresser took one look at me and said, 'My land, you were in the sit-in, huh?' 'Yes,' I answered. 'Do you have time to wash my hair and style it?' 'Right away,' she said, and she meant right away. There were other ladies already waiting, but they seemed glad to let me go ahead of them. The hairdresser was real nice. She even took my stockings off and washed my hair while my legs were drying."[1]

Moody's desire to get clean after being doused with ketchup and mustard during the sit-in is not surprising. However, her request to have her hair not only washed but also styled, combined with her description of the gentle pampering by the hairdresser and the deference shown to her by the other clients, highlights that beauty salons functioned as places where black women could rebound from their direct confrontations with Jim Crow segregation. Photographer and scholar Deborah Willis, the daughter of a beautician who spent much of her childhood in her mother's home-based salon, had similar recollections: "Often . . . domestics . . . would leave work and come to our house to be beautiful for church. . . . [They] shared stories about humiliating encounters."[2] Indeed, beauty salons, particularly those in the Jim Crow South, functioned as asylums for black women ravaged by the effects of segregation and served as incubators of black women's leadership and platforms from which to agitate for social and political change.

While activism was already deeply entrenched in the professional culture of beauticians by the 1960s, the political climate of the modern black freedom struggle gave their access to community space and intimate role in black women's lives greater significance. Black beauty culturists in this period were keenly aware of the economic autonomy their profession afforded them, the unique institutional space they controlled, and the access they had to black women within their communities. They were instrumental in developing the political infrastructure for African American women's involvement in the civil rights movement, which was for the most part under black female control and under the radar, hidden from whites unsympathetic to the cause of racial justice.

Beauty Activism in Professional Organizations

Continuing a tradition of political engagement dating back to the organization's founding, the National Beauty Culturists' League should be in the pantheon of civil rights organizations. At the league's 1948 convention in Washington, D.C., President Cordelia Greene Johnson explained that "the time had come for [beauticians] to take an active part in the fight for civil rights." Johnson further exhorted beauty operators to "refrain from the old time practice of gossiping with their customers about petty problems about their neighbors' private lives and rather talk about vital civil rights issues that confront the race."[3] On the one hand, Johnson's comments seem to ignore the long and rich activist history of the organization. However, what is most significant is that Johnson understood that her organization needed to acknowledge and be included in the shift happening in postwar black activism.[4] In 1955, the theme of the NBCL's annual convention was "Beauticians United for New Responsibilities." Maude Gaston, a politically active beautician from New York, led a panel titled "Beauticians United for Political Action," where she and other beauticians already active in political organizing discussed ways for beauticians to harness their political power. That fall, based in large part on deliberations of the 1955 convention, Cordelia Greene Johnson issued a letter to President Dwight D. Eisenhower on behalf of the league expressing their outrage over the murder of Emmett Till in Mississippi. Johnson stated that the NBCL had "supported and cooperated with this administration in every way" but explained that the organization was "deeply concerned about the welfare and civil rights of Negroes in America" and pressed Eisenhower to take bolder steps on behalf of civil rights.

By 1957, beauticians were seen as such a formidable force that Martin Luther King Jr. accepted the invitation to be the keynote speaker at NBCL's convention that summer. King was in high demand that year, receiving three honorary degrees, the NAACP's prestigious Spingarn Medal, and his first ever *Time* magazine cover. His address, "The Role of Beauticians in the Contemporary Struggle for Freedom," was well received and he was awarded the organization's Civil Rights Award.[5] Katie Whickham, who assumed the presidency of the NBCL that year, asked King to address the convention again in 1958. Citing a "long standing commitment in another section of the country," King declined the invitation but went on in a letter to talk about his work in the then-nascent Southern Christian Leadership Conference (SCLC). He asked Whickham if she would instead give veteran civil rights leader Ella Baker a chance to make a statement concerning the voter registration efforts of the SCLC to bring together the "vast wealth of latent potential" that existed among beauticians.[6] Whickham welcomed Baker's involvement, and the two became political allies. Baker, recognizing the NBCL's ability to reach women, later recommended that Whickham become the first female SCLC staff officer. Openly dissatisfied with the lack of women in leadership positions, Baker lobbied extensively to get more on the executive staff. She was successful in 1959, when she proudly announced Whickham's election as assistant secretary: "[I]n keeping with the expressed need to involve more women in the movement, we believe that Mrs. Whickham will bring new strength to our efforts. The National Beauty Culturists' League, Inc. of which she is president, has strong local and state units throughout the South, and voter registration is a major emphasis to its program."[7] However, Whickham's appointment did not have a sustained impact on the SCLC's gender imbalance, as her tenure did not last long, which was common with the organization's female appointees.[8] Although she was only on staff for just over a year, she remained dedicated to political activism throughout her life. Her legacy included an invitation by Vice President Richard Nixon to serve on the President's Committee on Government Contracts, an appointment as a Civil Defense consultant during the Kennedy administration, and an invitation by President Lyndon Baines Johnson to participate in a conference after the passage of the Civil Rights Act of 1964 called "To Fulfill These Rights."[9]

Whickham also was recognized by Louis Martin, a newspaper executive who served as the deputy chairman of the Democratic National Committee from 1961 to 1969, the first African American to hold that post. When trying to figure out a way to extend President Lyndon Baines Johnson's appeal in the 1964 election by "activat[ing] those below the level of the middle-class," he approached Marjorie Stewart Joyner and Katie Whickham to get beauticians in their respective organizations involved in the campaign to elect President Johnson.[10] He found beauticians to be among his most ardent grassroots organizers and explained, "There were some people that were active, some people were interested, some weren't. But where you found a beauty operator who was interested, you really had a jewel."[11] Marjorie Stewart Joyner was certainly one of those jewels and had already been active in political campaigns before she was approached by Martin. Just four years after she led a group of beauticians on their first European excursion, she chose "Your Ballot, Ticket to Freedom" as the theme of the United Beauty School Owners and Teachers Association 1958 national convention. Later that year, after meeting a young senator with presidential aspirations, John F. Kennedy, she articulated UBSOTA's goals: "We aim to make every shop owner and every beautician a missionary to mobilize all the Negro women they come in contact with to make voting next to God and cleanliness."[12] The organization continued to advocate for voting rights, galvanizing black women to vote and support Democratic candidates.[13]

While organizations such as the NBCL and UBSOTA inspired beauticians on the national level, grassroots leaders in state organizations and local beauty shops took Whickham and Joyner's admonitions to heart in unprecedented ways. A flurry of state level organizing emerged in the 1930s and 1940s in response to new state regulation and licensing. Nowhere was this growth in state beauty organizations more evident than in the South.[14] One of the most active of these groups was the Mississippi Independent Beautician Association (MIBA), which started in April 1941 after a local beauty school organized to create an award winning float in the annual Delta Cotton Makers Jubilee parade in Greenville. Seeing the successful float as an indication of the beauticians' latent potential, Clemmie Todd, along with her sister, laid the foundation for the MIBA. In July 1941, eighty beauticians from forty-two cities and towns across the state gathered in Greenville and, according to the association's historian, Evelyn Stegall, "blindly, but enthusiastically set up plans, made laws and by-laws and divided the state into seven districts." In just over a year, the organization boasted more than five hundred members.[15]

By July 1954 the association was formidable enough that their annual convention, held in Clarksdale, garnered front page news coverage in the *Jackson Advocate*, the state's oldest black newspaper. The headline proclaimed, "State

Beauticians Praise Supreme Court Decision; Group Urged to Resist Any Form of Continued Segregation." The Supreme Court decision referenced was the landmark *Brown v. Board of Topeka*, which had declared segregation on account of race in public schools unconstitutional just a few months earlier. White political officials in Mississippi, such as Senator James Eastland, called the decision a "monstrous crime," while Governor Hugh L. White plainly and emphatically stated, "We're not going to pay any attention to the Supreme Court decision. We don't think it would have any effect on us down here at all."[16] Members of MIBA, on the other hand, issued a "Declaration of Principles" that was boldly printed in the *Advocate*:

> We, the members of the Mississippi Independent Beauticians Association in annual convention assembled in Clarksdale, Miss., July 11–14, hereby make the following declaration of principles:
>
> That we go on record as highly endorsing the decision of the United States Supreme Court in outlawing segregation in public schools.
>
> For generations the system of public school provided for Negroes in Mississippi has most assuredly generated a feeling of inferiority as to our status in the community which has a bearing on our hearts and minds.
>
> Now that the United States Supreme Court has declared the practice of segregation in public schools as being unconstitutional we can look forward to our children enjoying in the future the same human rights as children of any other race—the best in public education—hoping they will not have to endure the untold sufferings of their forebears.
>
> We are encouraging the beauticians of Mississippi to cooperate with public school officials when called upon, only to implement the ruling handed down by the high court of the land calling for complete integration, however, under no circumstances will we cooperate with any group which has its objective the perpetuation of segregation in any form—voluntarily or otherwise.[17]

While the members of the MIBA were certainly positioning themselves against whites in their state who were determined to maintain segregation at all costs, a stance that could put their organization, indeed their very lives, in peril, the statement is more accurately understood as an activist call to those within the black community to continue the fight for civil rights. The declaration's publication in the black press, along with African American beauticians' well-established position in black communities, meant that they were not just responding to white supremacy but also were at the forefront of inspiring an activist agenda among the black readers of the *Advocate*. Furthermore, the statement that MIBA would not work with any groups that voluntarily or passively supported segregation is certainly directed toward African Americans who were not willing to engage in the inevitable battle to uphold the Supreme Court's ruling.

In many ways, the different approaches of the national and state organizations reflect Charles Payne's analysis of the community organizing tradition versus the community mobilizing tradition of civil rights activism.[18] While the beautician's organizations on the national level strengthened black women's role in large-scale and national campaigns and events, state organizations focused on activating those within their communities, particularly those who were already a part of local organizations or professional associations, to engage in social change. State organizations were able to speak to the needs and fears of their local communities with accuracy and insight. Beauticians who were organized on the city level in Durham, North Carolina, for example, were perhaps even more in tune with the dynamics in their communities and more vocal about their intolerance for those African Americans who were unwilling to engage in civil rights activism. They reserved their harshest criticism for black male leaders; ministers, seemingly the most praised members of the civil rights community, were often the recipients of their disapproval. Although ministers and beauticians shared an admirable professional position in terms of flexible hours, a stable salary, an all-black clientele, and a nontraditional work environment, beauticians in Durham did not feel as though ministers took advantage of those occupational benefits. When the *Carolina Times* asked its readers if Durham ministers should take a more active part in the civic life of the city, members of the local Cosmetologist Club were among the most vocal critics, contrasting their own activism with the perceived apathy of the ministers.[19]

On the local level, beauticians such as Ruby Parks Blackburn of Atlanta demonstrated the ability to advocate for improvements in their communities while helping their own businesses. Born in Rockdale, Georgia, in 1901, Blackburn received her training at the Apex Beauty School after spending a few years as a domestic worker. In 1932, she opened a beauty shop on Simpson Road in Atlanta and founded the TIC (To Improve Conditions) Club, an all-female organization that over the years of Blackburn's presidency tackled everything from environmental racism to neighborhood beautification. TIC played an important role in getting an additional junior high school for Atlanta's black residents and establishing a day nursery for working mothers.[20]

Although Blackburn became a successful beautician, she never forgot the poor conditions she worked under as a domestic servant.[21] During World

War II she established the Atlanta Cultural League and Training Center for Domestic Workers, an organization whose objective was to make domestic workers more employable. However, beyond simply training better laborers, the organization also had a strong civic and political mission. In the postwar period she tackled issues like political enfranchisement and bus desegregation through the local NAACP which honored her for her efforts in their voter registration drives. In 1951, she formed the Georgia League of Negro Women Voters and worked diligently to overcome obstacles in registering black female voters.[22]

Of all of her efforts, she was best known for her work to get bus service extended to black neighborhoods.[23] In 1953, she and another local business-woman, Irene Sims Hendrix, brought suit against the Dixie Hills Bus Line for not providing "proper and adequate transportation" to black neighborhoods. After being threatened by a boycott, Dixie Hills responded by extending their service and schedule. Blackburn and Hendrix were undoubtedly interested in getting their clients and customers unfettered access to their establishments, but they used this personal agenda to benefit those in their race who were dependent upon public transportation.[24]

While national, state, and local organizations gave beauticians a place to develop their collective leadership, the beauty salon was the site where most of the civil rights activities came to life. The black beauty salon in the Jim Crow South was a unique place, replete with ironies and contradictions. In fact, the paradoxical nature of the beauty shop is what gave it its political power. A salon visit was a personal and intimate experience occurring in the midst of a social context. While the focus is on the client and having her hairstyling needs met, the beautician wields a considerable amount of power as an arbiter of good taste and proper behavior. The grooming that occurs within a salon, which for black women during most of the twentieth century entailed an elaborate process of hair cleansing, conditioning, and oiling of the hair and scalp followed by the pulling of the hair through the teeth of a steel comb heated over an open flame, was at once pampering and torturous. Salons themselves served as places of rest for black female bodies, a luxury for women who often spent their days laboring for white families and their evenings caring for the needs of their own households. Feminist scholar bell hooks remembers the beauty parlors of her youth as places "where one did not need to meet the demands of children or men. It was the one hour some folk would spend 'off their feet,' a soothing, restful time of meditation and silence."[25] However, these same salons were often sites of twelve-hour days of grueling labor for the beauticians who worked there.

Beauty salons, particularly those in the South, conflated homespace and workspace. Linking the rhetoric of the 1950s that emphasized women's domestic duties with the very real financial needs of African American families, beauticians opened salons in their homes so that they could earn a living without disrupting their domestic duties. For example, Coazell Frazier, owner of Cozy's Beauty Nook in St. Helena, South Carolina, opened her salon in her home so that she could care for her ailing mother.[26] Similarly, Bernice Caldwell of Charlotte, North Carolina, "fixed a shop on her sun porch," allowing her to care for her children while earning a living.[27]

Furthermore, a beautician's success was based on her ability to convince her client that her services were not a luxury to be indulged in sporadically but a necessity that required consistent upkeep. Indeed, a trip to the hair salon to receive the standard "press and curl" was a specialized process that required regular visits to the salon. By the 1940s, African Americans became the largest per capita consumers of cosmetic and hair preparations, and this growth increased throughout the civil rights movement.[28] Indeed, in this time of heightened political activity, the practice of straightening or pressing one's hair, linked to white beauty standards in previous decades, had become so deeply entrenched in black women's lives that there was little discussion over its meaning. Older public debates over whether straightened hair detracted from racial consciousness had largely been abandoned. Indeed, by the 1950s, beauticians were well known and respected for supporting causes to dismantle racism and used their activism to minimize discussions concerning the conflation of hair straightening with a white beauty aesthetic.

However, by the early 1960s, there were changes in the services offered in salons. Beauty culturists who were accustomed to doing a press and curl as their standard repertoire were now faced with learning how to use chemical straighteners and even learning to style wigs. Rose Morgan openly discussed having to shift with the times when, in 1962, the wig craze took off. Morgan opened a wig salon and explained that her operators were now trained to administer "both the older thermal, or 'heat' method of straightening hair and the newer chemical hair relaxing processes." She also diversified her line of services by offering manicuring, make-up application, and massage therapy. In addition, she added a charm school for children and adults on the premises.[29]

In the 1950s and 1960s, hair that was styled to release or straighten the curl pattern was the only acceptable way for African American women to wear their hair. For whites to see black women with their hair in its natural state was considered feeding into negative stereotypes of black women as unruly and undeserving of respectable treatment. As Maxine Leeds Craig points out, "Grooming was a weapon in the battle to defeat racist depictions of blacks."[30] Photographs of those who engaged in the early civil rights movement depict well-groomed women with fashionably straightened and styled hair.[31] The instructions given to Vivian Malone and James Hood to "dress modestly, neatly . . . as if you were going to church" when they attempted to register for classes at the previously segregated University of Alabama in 1963 would have meant for Malone, at least, that her hair be freshly pressed.[32] A legacy of the era of racial uplift in which notions of respectability governed the actions and presentation of black bodies, African Americans in the modern civil rights movement linked grooming to racial progress and political acceptance. Beauty product manufacturers such as the Madam C. J. Walker Company, which once had avoided any reference to hair straightening and advertised their products by invoking racial pride and economic opportunity, now openly advocated straightened hair as the only acceptable way for a black woman to wear her hair.[33]

Beauticians, therefore, had to walk a fine line in salons: they had to create a relaxing environment in the midst of smoking hot combs, chemical creams, and pulled hair; they had to create a sense of community in the midst of gossip and rigid beauty standards; they had to sustain a politicized environment in the midst of the frivolity of hair care. To that end, they relied heavily upon their roles as counselors and confidants. Many beauticians, such as Christiana Pitts of Raleigh, North Carolina, felt this was a natural outgrowth of her personality and explained, "I always did love people. . . . So I was just at hand being a counselor too. Not in an aggressive way, not trying to make anybody do anything, but ending up 'cause they wanted to ask me, not just for hair but kind of counseling on living."[34] Others, such as Margaret Williams Neal of Wilmington, North Carolina, understood that her clients not only visited her for physical beautification but also desired, perhaps even expected, her to care about their nonbeauty needs. She remembered that hairstyling was not the only reason women came to her Wilmington, North Carolina, salon, noting that "women would come by just to chat—an elderly woman would sit there to feel better since she lived alone."[35] A beautician, she further explains, "is the one that you are there with them and you sit in there and they can talk to you and you'll listen and that's what they want."[36] African American women in the Jim Crow era visited beauty salons for more than grooming; they looked to these sites as places of safety and empowerment. It is no surprise, then, that black women and those wishing to reach them would look to their beauty shops as key institutions in the fight against segregation.

Cora McLeod, a Durham beautician and member of the Cosmetologists' Club, "remembered that the NAACP often visited her shop during the 1950s and 1960s with fliers urging people to become involved in civil rights activity."[37] Similarly, organizers who wanted to get information out about the election of Lyndon Baines Johnson in 1964 also turned to beauty shops to distribute campaign literature to blacks. Louis Martin, who expanded the work he did with beauticians' organizations to include local beauty shops, explained that "the most significant thing about the 1964 vote thing was we had to figure out how to reach the rank-and-file blacks without necessarily paying dues to local wheels that wanted money. You had to bribe them to give out your literature." He said that he stumbled upon an "inspired idea" when in five states he put materials in "every beauty shop. . . . The material was there. They didn't have to pass it out. It was just sitting there and the people would come in and see it. The politicians couldn't figure out what happened. . . . But we shipped it in and that really worked. We got out a bigger vote in the states in which that operated."[38] These efforts on the part of the NAACP and the Democratic National Committee were not dependent upon a savvy beautician, but the mere availability of a space frequented by a varied group of African American women that was hidden from those with a competing agenda. In other words, the black beauty salon was considered an important political institution for those interested in the furtherance of black civil rights.

However, not all beauty salons were involved in politically subversive activities. Still, even those salons that did not explicitly engage in political activities served as vital community institutions. For example, in Tippah County, Mississippi, Hazel Foster, a beautician, earned such a good living that she became the first person in the county (white or black) to own a telephone and was literally the center of the town's communication.[39] Communication often led to gossip and community divisions. Harriet Vail Wade, a beautician from New Bern, North Carolina, recounted the story of a woman in another salon who shampooed a client, put her under the hood dryer, and proceeded to talk about her on the phone. To the beautician's chagrin, the client heard every word and an argument ensued.[40] Wade noted that the best way to understand her salon was that it was a meeting place "for information like a newspaper is now or like television. People spoke of their accomplishments, bragged on their children, talked about how hard times were." Margaret

Williams Neal says that while overtly political conversations did not take place in her salon, she did see beauticians having a role in their clients' lives beyond just spreading gossip: "We listen, we give advice. I guess you have to tell your problems to someone, and a beautician is the one that you are there with them and you sit in there and they can talk to you and you'll listen and that's what they want."[41] So whether functioning as a safe space or a contested space, it was a location that was unique in its ability to sustain community. For African American women in the Jim Crow era, excluded from the male-dominated spaces of the black church and the white-dominated spaces of formal political networks, the ability to gather in a place of pampering and self-care led to community activism.

The Consummate Beauty Activist

Of all of the civil rights programs initiated in the South, the one where beauticians were the most visible was in the Highlander Folk School's Citizenship Schools Program. Committed to interracial education and political action since the 1930s, the Highlander Folk School emerged at the "forefront of the drive to end racial segregation in the South, during the 1950s."[42] Starting in 1953, the Tennessee-based group led by Myles Horton began to turn its attention toward racial discrimination with a workshop titled "The Supreme Court's Decisions and the Public Schools." Highlander held workshops throughout the 1950s that drew those who would become movement figures, but the school's greatest contribution to the civil rights movement was the Citizenship Education Program it started in 1957.

In 1954, Esau Jenkins, the owner of a small bus line that transported people on the South Carolina Sea Islands to their jobs in Charleston, attended his first Highlander workshop and shared his experiences as a native of Johns Island, South Carolina. The South Carolina Sea Islands at the time had a population of four thousand people, 67 percent of whom were black, 90 percent of whom were illiterate. To complicate matters further, Sea Islanders primarily spoke a Gullah dialect and therefore had difficulty finding employment beyond the most menial jobs. Jenkins came to Highlander and described the local people's desire to vote as well as their extreme poverty and illiteracy. Septima Clark, a Charleston schoolteacher, also happened to be attending a workshop at Highlander in 1954, and she, Jenkins, and Horton began brainstorming about bringing workshops like the ones being held at Highlander to the people of the Sea Islands. Highlander staff began making trips to Johns Island in November of that year.[43]

The following year, Septima Clark invited her cousin, Bernice Robinson, to attend a Highlander workshop with her in Tennessee that sought to connect local economic concerns to global developments. Robinson, a forty-one-year-old Charleston beautician, was struck most by the interracial living arrangement at the school, something she was not accustomed to in her hometown. Before she left the workshop, Robinson told her cousin that she would do anything to help the organization fulfill its mission. It is a promise Clark would ask her to make good on in just a few months, when she invited her to become the first teacher for Highlander's Citizenship Schools.

Bernice Robinson's life experiences prepared her for the role she was to play in the Citizenship Education Program. Born in Charleston, South Carolina, on February 7, 1914, during "the first time that they had had snow in maybe one hundred years," Robinson had a happy childhood. Although her family was not rich, her father, a bricklayer and tile setter, refused to say that they were poor.[44] Her soft-spoken mother was primarily a homemaker who took in sewing to supplement the family's income. While Robinson noted that white people were not talked about much in her home, she recounted that both her mother and father were adamant about preventing their children from working for whites: "The only thing that was ever discussed in my family in reference to the whites was that my mother said, 'Well, I don't ever want any girl of mine to do any domestic work or work in these white folk's kitchen.'" As a child, Robinson was raised to value economic self-sufficiency.

Early in her childhood, Robinson showed promise as a musician. After graduating from high school, her older sister, who had migrated to New York City, planned to enroll her in the prestigious Boston Conservatory of Music. Robinson went to New York City in the summer of 1931 to work with her sister in the garment industry and save money for school. Unfortunately, her sister became very ill and was forced to quit her job, so Robinson's plans for college were thwarted. Concerned for her future, Robinson returned to Charleston and sought financial security in a short marriage that brought her a daughter, Jacquelyn, but little else. Left with a child and little money, Robinson took a job as a maid at a hunting resort on one of the Sea Islands. "My mother cried when I did it," Robinson explained, "because she had never wanted any of her kids to work in a white person's place like that, but I was always a realist, and I knew that when you've got to do it, you do it and get it over with."[45] Though she defied her mother's wishes, Robinson understood domestic work was one of the few reliable ways for a black woman to make a living in the South.

After her failed marriage and her dead-end job as a maid, Robinson became increasingly frustrated with her lack of employment prospects, so in 1936, she, like so many others, migrated north to New York City. She began working again in a garment factory during the day and, in her own words, "at nights I went to school to learn beauty culture, and then on weekends I would work at beauty shops to get some experience."[46] Robinson found beauty work to be more consistent than laboring in a garment factory. She explains: "I made good money there—about thirty-five to forty-five dollars a week— and I probably would have stayed in that work, but the problem with that was that in a garment factory that salary was not *steady*. It was only steady for a period of time. . . . That's when I said, 'I need to get into something that's steady,' and I began to take courses in beauty work. And it really *was* steady." Beauty work proved for Robinson and other black women to be not only an escape from domestic labor but also a better labor alternative than the seasonal and volatile industrial labor since black women were often the last hired and the first fired in factories.[47]

Still, while beauty culture paid well and was steady, it was laborious. Robinson often had to work eighteen-hour days, causing family members in Charleston to be concerned about her health. The long hours seemed to get to Robinson as well. Soon after the start of World War II, she decided to move to Philadelphia, where her sister was living, and take the civil service examination. She qualified to work with the Philadelphia Signal Corps but did not like Philadelphia and subsequently returned to New York City. She again took the civil service examination and was sent to work with the Internal Revenue Service and subsequently the Veteran's Administration. In 1947, just as she was about to begin work with the Treasury Department making seventy-five dollars a week, she had to return to Charleston to care for her sick mother. She did not have plans to remain in Charleston for more than a few days, but her mother's condition worsened, and Robinson remained in Charleston until her own death.

Charleston, Robinson soon realized, did not present her with employment opportunities comparable to the ones she had in New York and Philadelphia. She was unable to get civil service work despite her experience and qualifications. The best she could get in Charleston was a job "working six days a week for an upholstery man making cushions for fifteen dollars a week." Robinson was not just appalled by the low wages in Charleston but also disturbed that she was unable to register to vote there, since that was something she was accustomed to in New York and Philadelphia. In New York City, as early as 1944, she even helped a black assemblyman mail cards and letters to his constituents. Indeed, the intersection of her economic necessity and political disappointments fueled the groundbreaking path that her life was soon to take.[48]

In 1950, Robinson returned to the profession that served her well in New York City during the Great Depression. She learned what many other black women trained in beauty work understood: Beauty work was not only depression proof but also migration proof and Jim Crow proof. In other words, it was something that a black woman could depend upon for a steady income whether she was in a Madam Walker salon on 145th Street in Harlem or in a back room off a kitchen in Charleston. Robinson explained that after her father died, her brothers built her a beauty shop in her Charleston home, where, she says, "I started making it all right."[49]

Robinson's economic self-sufficiency in turn fueled her political career in Charleston. Although Robinson had been a member of the Charleston branch of the NAACP since she returned to the city in 1947, it was in 1951 that the branch and even Robinson herself became a force to be reckoned with in the black freedom struggle. In fact, Robinson was instrumental in getting the number of NAACP members up from three hundred to over a thousand; she opened up her beauty shop as a meeting place to strategize about voter registration drives as well as to distribute NAACP literature. In the words of her interviewer, Elliot Wigginton, her salon became a "center for all sorts of subversive activity."[50] Robinson says of her involvement in voter registration, "It got to the point where we were working so hard getting people to register to vote, that I would leave people under the dryer to take others down to the registration office to get them registered. I would say, 'If you get too hot under there, just cut her off and come out!'" According to Robinson, she realized the importance of voter registration based on her experience in New York. "When I lived in New York I was able to vote . . . and then when I came home I couldn't vote," she explained. "So as soon as the decision was handed down then I was ready, gung ho, to get out there and help other people get registered."[51]

Robinson also attributed her extensive involvement with voting rights and other civil rights campaigns directly to the economic autonomy she enjoyed as a beautician: "I didn't have to worry about losing my job or anything because I wasn't a schoolteacher or a case worker with the Department of Social Services or connected with anything I might be fired from." Robinson knew about this firsthand since her cousin Septima Clark was a schoolteacher who failed to have her contract renewed just before she was scheduled to retire and subsequently lost all her pension benefits due to her civil rights involvement.[52] Clark was not alone. In 1955, in response to the *Brown* decision, the

South Carolina legislature passed a law making it illegal for city and state employees to belong to the NAACP. The South Carolina state NAACP, of which Robinson served as a branch secretary, saw its membership drop as a result of these pressures. In 1954, there were 7,889 card carrying members; by 1957, the number had dropped to 2,202.[53] Robinson noted that the measures taken by the legislature had created "quite a lot of fear among teachers and other public employees whom we have depended upon for years."[54] She further lamented that "that's the way it was all over the South. The whites would chop you down in a minute if you were dependent on them for a job." But Robinson explained her own situation: "I had my own business, supplied by black supply houses, so I didn't have to worry. Many people did."[55] She felt so beyond reproach that she told her customers, many of whom were teachers, nurses, and domestic workers, to have their NAACP membership cards sent to her house so that their white mailman would not see them and subsequently tell their employers. However, once Robinson became involved with Highlander's Citizenship Schools, she did lose friends who feared reprisals for associating with her. When an article was published about the Citizenship Schools in a white Charleston paper, Robinson was ostracized from her card group and ignored by neighborhood friends who thought her activities were too radical.[56]

By the end of 1956, Robinson's civil rights work was so impressive that Septima Clark suggested to Myles Horton that Robinson was best qualified to be the first teacher for Highlander's Citizenship School. After two decades working primarily in the labor movement, in 1953 the Highlander staff launched a series of workshops that focused on community desegregation. With the assistance of Clark and Esau Jenkins, a Citizenship Schools project developed on the South Carolina Sea Islands. The ultimate goal was to teach black adults to read and write and to prepare them to register to vote. After finding a location, they needed to find a suitable teacher. Black schoolteachers were eliminated immediately, even though, as Katherine Mellen Charron notes, Clark herself, a lifelong educator, saw the Citizenship Education Program as an extension of the work black schoolteachers had been doing since the turn of the century. Still, Clark's difficulties trying to mobilize and organize teachers who were dependent upon the state for their livelihood, in addition to her concern that formal educators would be too curriculum driven and too far removed from the lives of their illiterate Johns Island pupils, led Clark to her cousin, Bernice Robinson. The ever-stubborn Myles Horton eventually concurred.[57]

On January 7, 1957, Robinson stood before her first class of eleven women and three men at the Johns Island Citizenship School in an old dilapidated school building purchased by Highlander. Even though Clark, the seasoned educator, was involved in the selection process for a teacher, it was Robinson who, in the words of Horton, "developed the [educational] methods used by the Citizenship Schools."[58] Robinson established a pedagogical approach based on the needs of the students and told them on the first day, "I'm really not going to be your teacher. We're going to work together and teach each other." She also engaged them as active participants in the learning process, asking them what they wanted to accomplish in the class. The students, the majority of whom were completely illiterate and the remainder only partially literate, explained that they wanted to write their names, read the Bible, fill out a money order, and fill out blanks when ordering from a catalog. In addition, Robinson mimeographed sections of the South Carolina election laws, and many of the students mastered the text and learned basic literacy skills over the two month session. By February of the next year, eight of the fourteen students with at least five months of classes were able to read the required paragraph in the state constitution and sign their names in order to receive their voter registration certificates.[59]

Witnessing the success of the Johns Island School, others were soon added in neighboring regions. Beautician and activist Marylee Davis of North Charleston, who had also attended workshops at Highlander, asked for help in starting a school in her neighborhood and offered her beauty parlor as a meeting place.[60] Robinson served as the teacher for the twelve women enrolled in the school, most of whom were domestic workers. Davis, an integral part of the North Charleston community, was intimately acquainted with the conditions plaguing her neighborhood and wanted the students to not only learn to read the required passage for voter registration but also learn how to navigate local political hierarchies to get better roads and other community improvements.

Based on the success in South Carolina, Horton, Clark, and Robinson sought to expand the program to Tennessee, Alabama, and Georgia and realized that beauticians were best equipped to further Highlander's Citizenship Schools' goals. In December 1960, Clark, who had assumed the role of director of education, convened a meeting specifically for "members of the beauticians' profession only" at Highlander's headquarters in Monteagle, Tennessee, to be held January 15–16, 1961. The workshop, "New Leadership Responsibilities," was convened, according to Clark, because the "Highlander

Figure 6. Bernice Robinson (*standing left*) and Septima Clark (*standing right*) facilitate a teacher training workshop. Used with permission from the Wisconsin Historical Society (WHi-41508).

Folk School has been impressed with the leadership possibilities among beauticians." She continued in an appeal letter sent to beauticians in the three states: "This is one of the professions which offer to its members great freedom for leadership in community action. We also see it as offering opportunities especially suitable for *professional* women who also want to be active in the struggle for justice in the South."[61]

While Clark understood that women like teachers in the typical middle-class professions were not the best option for Citizenship Schools teachers, she knew that she had to appeal to the professional identity of beauticians to encourage their participation. In his autobiography, Myles Horton explained the strategic importance of gathering beauticians as leaders in civil rights initiatives due to their unique status in their communities. "A black beautician, unlike a white beautician, was at that time a person of some status in the community," he explained. "They were entrepreneurs, they were small business women, you know, respected, they were usually better educated than other people, and most of all they were independent."[62] While beauticians had an elevated status, were small-business women, and were usually better educated, they, unlike teachers, did not have a separation from or a patronizing relationship to the black masses. Because of segregation, they were indebted to the black community for a client base and were never far removed from their respective communities.

Moreover, black female beauticians had a degree of independence relative to other blacks—especially black women—whose occupations were usually under the watchful eye of whites. Throughout the Jim Crow years, black women worked primarily as domestics, doing work that was often isolating and constantly supervised, clearly not offering a site to organize collective resistance. Even black professional women, like schoolteachers within segregated school systems, faced constraints due to their dependence upon white-run school boards and city councils. Beauticians worked within black female–owned establishments, were supplied by black manufacturers, and were patronized by black female clients within segregated communities.

On January 15, 1961, fifty-two beauticians from several counties in Tennessee and Alabama met for two days at Highlander's headquarters.[63] Many were given scholarships to attend and carpooled to Monteagle. While on the two-hundred-acre farm nestled in the Cumberland Mountains, they participated in workshops led by Horton, Robinson, and a beauty shop owner named Johnnie Mae Fowler, who was already active in her community in Winchester, Tennessee. Fowler's presentation, "The Beauty Salon: A Center of Communication and Influence," delineated key areas where beauticians could be an asset to the civil rights movement. She envisioned beauticians providing leadership in efforts to see that the *Browder v. Gayle* decision to desegregate buses and train stations was a reality in their communities. "We think the beautician should step out front and our people will see us doing this [*sic*] things without fear," she stated. What beauticians should be doing, Fowler said, was "sitting on buses on a first come first served basis." She also explained that beauticians "can help a lot by discussing this [desegregation of public transportation] in their salons." Beauty salons, according to Fowler, should be the primary place for the community to gather and obtain information. She encouraged the beauticians to not only open their businesses for civic meetings, PTA groups, and other social organizations but also to keep abreast of local happenings, like the schedule for school board meetings, so that they could share the information with their clients.

The meetings inspired the beauticians in attendance to act immediately to impact their communities. Just one day after the adjournment of the gathering, the women, under the leadership of Eva Bowman, former state inspector and examiner for the Tennessee Cosmetology Board and main contact person for the Highlander meeting, announced the formation a board of directors, who would be responsible for implementing what was to be called the Volunteer Health Center in Fayette County, Tennessee. The board was comprised solely of beauticians who attended the workshops. The center was to benefit twenty sharecropping families evicted by white landowners in retaliation for a series of events that started in 1959 with the conviction by an all-white jury of a black man who was accused of killing a white man. Local black leaders filed a suit under the Civil Rights Act of 1957, citing their omission from jury pools based on being prevented from registering to vote. The African Americans won their case, and led by gas station owner John McFerren and his beautician wife, Viola, they organized voter registration drives in the county. Despite widespread intimidation tactics and an escalation of tension in Fayette County, more than twelve hundred African Americans voted in the November 1960 elections. As a result, white landowners evicted black sharecroppers en masse, and those with no where else to go were invited to set up tents on the property of an independent black landowner, Sheppard Towles, forming what residents called "Tent City."[64]

The inhabitants of Tent City had many needs, including food, clothing, and security. Inspired by their recent trip to Highlander, beauticians thought they were best able to tend to the health of Tent City's inhabitants. The beauticians demonstrated a complex understanding of citizenship rights and education; while they were brought to Highlander under the auspices of the traditional Citizenship Education Program, they forced Highlander to expand the meaning of citizenship to addressing issues concerning the immediate needs of their communities such as health care. Clark and Robinson supported these efforts even in their capacities as director of education and field director, respectively, but the onus was on Bowman and the beauticians on the board of directors to execute the plans for the center.

At their initial meeting held in January 1961, the beauticians outlined a comprehensive plan: They were to purchase a tent and floor along with heating and lighting facilities, propose a trip to Tent City for the state beauticians' organizations from Alabama and Tennessee to view the needs up close and enlist them in fundraising efforts, and contact doctors and nurses to establish the medical program. That nurses and doctors were not the ones to initiate this program demonstrated just how much more beauticians were connected to the needs of the poor and those who were living out the often difficult backlash of exercising citizenship rights.[65]

Things were promising—at first. In February, beauticians met at Highlander for a second time and agreed to place donation boxes for Tent City in their shops, donate the money earned from one client's hairdo each week, and encourage those within their professional networks to do the same. In March, more than three hundred beauticians from Chattanooga pledged their support and donated money to the center, and plans were made to break ground on an actual building in late April. This shift from putting up a tent to erecting a building for the center led to confusion and greatly undermined the project. Clark, the seasoned leader and pragmatist, directed Bowman in a letter to "buy a tent and get to work on the things needed in the community now. Then later push the county to get a building and maintain a clinic or integrate the one they have."[66] Unfortunately, the beauticians' dreams for a health center were never fully realized, and after living in tents for over two years, the residents of Tent City began moving into new, affordable homes.[67]

Despite the failure of beauticians to provide a health facility for the residents of Tent City, the Highlander Folk School continued to partner with beauticians. In the midst of the Tent City debacle, another "New Leadership Responsibilities" workshop exclusively for beauticians was held at Highlander in late October 1962. An announcement explained that the purpose of the meeting was "to find the things which need to be done in a community that cannot be done by City, State, or Federal employees." The flier also addressed the question "Why beauticians?" by affirming, "Beauticians can speak out openly and can publicly promote the cause for justice and equality in the South," in ways that others could not.[68] In March 1963, beauticians attended a demonstration at Highlander on "How to Use a Voting Machine," so that they could share the information with their clients when they returned home.

Beauticians and beauty shops proved to be so effective in part because they were so hidden. It took whites in the Charleston area a while to find out about the schools Bernice Robinson had started. Otis Perkins, a reporter from the *Charleston News and Courier,* was surprised that schools had been conducted for three years before the white community discovered anything about them.[69] Similarly, Robinson, despite being an essential part of Highlander, was not well known among those who were trying to destroy its operations. In 1961, Highlander's Tennessee facility was raided by the Grundy county police department, and everyone on site was charged with possession of whisky. While most of the charges did not stick, Horton's deed to the property was declared void at the circuit court. The case went up to the Tennessee Supreme Court, which upheld the decision and revoked Highlander's tax exempt status. As a result, by the summer of 1961, Highlander was beginning a process of ending its involvement with the Citizenship Schools and handing its administration over to the Southern Christian Leadership Conference. Still, anyone with ties to Highlander was closely watched by the Tennessee authorities. For example, the *Chattanooga Free Press* ran an article in May 1961 vilifying Septima Clark for taking the Peace Corps examination in Chattanooga. The "second Negro woman" who accompanied Clark was unknown to reporters, but based on a photograph printed in the newspaper, she was Robinson. In fact, the reporter was surprised that they knew so little about "the second Negro woman," especially since she gave the Highlander Folk School as her address.[70] Despite Robinson's activism, she and indeed all the beauticians in the movement always seemed to operate below the radar, exactly where Horton and other movement leaders thought they were most useful to the cause.

When administration of the Citizenship Education Program was handed over to SCLC, the project's leaders, including Andrew Young, continued to rely upon the independence of beauticians, though Young marginalized their input—and indeed women's input in general.[71] Young explained that when he could not locate a black leader within the community, he and his team would go to the beauty parlor in addition to male-owned barbershops and funeral homes to find economically independent black leaders.[72] While beauticians were not targeted exclusively under SCLC's administration of the program as they were with Highlander, one emerged as a leader in the Citizenship Schools in the volatile region of Clarksdale, Mississippi. Clarksdale had an active NAACP that mounted a successful boycott against white-owned businesses for their discriminatory hiring practices, poor service, and segregated practices. However, the town also had a particularly repressive chief of police who attempted to suppress black resistance through violence and intimidation. The law also turned a blind eye toward violence inflicted upon African Americans by racist whites. For example, Vera Pigee, a beautician who had served her local NAACP as branch secretary and youth branch organizer, was beaten by a gas station attendant in 1963 when she attempted to use the whites-only bathroom. As with most of the violence inflicted upon African Americans, the police turned a blind eye to the white assailants and even joined them in the terrorizing of black communities.

In spite of, or perhaps because of, such difficulties, African Americans in Clarksdale were eager for Citizenship Schools, and Pigee was eager to be involved with establishing the program.[73] Pigee, known for wearing hats and encouraging her clients to engage in the freedom struggle from the beauty shop she operated attached to her home, attended a Citizenship Education Workshop in 1961 and impressed the staff so much that they pegged her to be a supervisor of the schools in her region. Just four years later, she could boast of twenty Citizenship Schools, and in 1965 alone, of registering more than one hundred voters, no small task in such a volatile region. Andrew Young admitted that while male leaders were at the forefront of the movement, it was women like Pigee who really "ran the operations."[74] Her economic independence was crucial in a repressive place like Clarksdale, and while that did not prevent her getting beaten, she never had to fear losing her job.

In fact, Clarksdale's chief of police, Ben C. Collins, interrogated both Vera Pigee and her husband Paul concerning their civil rights activities at their respective places of employment. When Collins questioned Paul Pigee, a laborer at North Delta Compress, a cotton compression and warehouse facility, he asked him, "Do you want this job?" and spoke to his foreman about Pigee's work hours and performance. After Paul refused to denounce the civil rights activities of his family, the chief turned to his manager and stated, "I know you are going to fire him." When the manager replied that he had no cause to terminate Pigee, Collins replied, "Cause? Don't you know that his wife is the most aggressive leader of the NAACP in Clarksdale?" But the manager stood his ground and asserted Pigee's exemplary work performance.[75] When Collins confronted Vera Pigee, there was no manager or foreman with whom to deal. Instead, he asked about her customers, and Vera refused to divulge their names, explaining, "I pay city, county, and state taxes to operate a legitimate business. You have moved in with *your* secretary and made your office in *my* beauty shop. Now I am asking both of you to leave. If I ever need your service I will call you." While neither Paul nor Vera Pigee lost their jobs as a result of Collins's actions, Collin's use of workplace intimidation is telling. Vera Pigee felt empowered enough to withhold her clients' names and expel the staunch segregationist from her salon because she held ownership of her labor. Her husband was perhaps equally willing to stand up to Collins, but his economic stability was dependent upon a thankfully supportive employer.

Conclusion

When remembering the Highlander Folk School, Myles Horton marveled at the role of beauticians in the Citizenship Education Program: "They thought that I was bringing these beauticians together to talk about straightening hair or whatever . . . they do, [but] I was just using them because they were community leaders and they were independent. . . . We used beauticians' shops all over the South to distribute Highlander literature on integration."[76]

In many ways, Horton's statement illuminates the key issues surrounding the unique ways beauticians merged their profession with the politics of the civil rights movement. They were, for the most part, highly regarded in their communities and strove to be among the best women of the race. However, because of segregation and their indebtedness to the black community for a client base, beauty culturists were never far removed from their respective communities.

While women like Ruby Blackburn, Bernice Robinson, and Vera Pigee were undoubtedly activists, they were still businesswomen. Septima Clark said of a beautician who was involved in the Highlander Folk School's Citizenship Schools Program that "she wished to see her street and that section improved in order to preserve and advance her economic investment." Still, Clark was quick to add that the beautician was ultimately "more interested in doing something for the people who were suffering" than in advancing her own business.[77] Beauticians demonstrated that they could look after their own economic needs and the needs of their communities simultaneously, perhaps better than any other group of black businesspeople.

Moreover, beauticians had a degree of independence relative to other blacks—especially black women—whose occupations were usually under the watchful eye of whites. During the years of the freedom struggle, Southern black women worked primarily as domestics, doing work that was often isolating and constantly supervised, clearly not offering a site to organize collective resistance. Even black professional women, such as schoolteachers within segregated school systems, faced constraints due to their dependence upon white-run school boards and city councils. Beauticians worked within black female–owned establishments, were supplied by black manufacturers, and were patronized by black female clients within segregated communities. They took advantage of the benefits of their economic independence and the heightened political activity of the 1950s and 60s to take risks without fears of reprisals, something they had done for most of the twentieth century.

6

"Among the Things That Used to Be"

Beauticians, Health Activism, and the Politics of Dignity in the Post–Civil Rights Era

After deciding to stop straightening her hair in the post–civil rights era, writer Alice Walker reflected in a 1987 Founder's Day speech at Spelman College, "I remembered years of enduring hairdressers . . . doing missionary work on my hair. They dominated, suppressed, controlled."[1] For Walker, embracing her hair in its natural state was both a political and spiritual liberation. She was not alone. By the late 1960s, black women who had been socialized with the idea that straightened hair was synonymous with good grooming began celebrating and embracing notions of racial pride and self-expression that were exhibited in one's physical appearance as well as in tangible expressions of black protest.

Reminiscent of the turn of the twentieth century, when hair straightening was seen as contradicting racial uplift, the late 1960s saw a resurgence in arguments against hair straightening. Although black beauty shops were often sites where black women organized for resistance, younger African American women began to reject the grooming practices that typically went on in these salons. Black beauticians were no longer esteemed members of the black community but were remembered as being complicit in black women's oppression.

The post–civil rights period witnessed major changes in the black beauty industry and in the relationship between beauty and black womanhood. While most analyses of black beauty culture and politics in the post–civil rights era focuses on the rise and fall of the popularity of the Afro, this chapter seeks to widen that discussion by examining the impact of changing black aesthetics, global corporate interests in black hair product manufacturing, and the end of legal segregation on the political activism of black beauticians.[2] Moving beyond the declension narrative of post–civil rights African American history, this chapter explores the vibrant political culture that still exists in black beauty shops today.[3] While much of the political leadership of black beauticians in the Jim Crow era came as a result of their economic independence and access to a space where black women could hide and plan, the post–civil rights era finds black beauticians explicitly engaging in what I call the politics of dignity. They demonstrate that seemingly frivolous acts like care of the body, hairstyling, and personal adornment help form platforms for black women's resistance, particularly in the realm of health activism in the late twentieth and early twenty-first centuries.

A New Black Aesthetic

In the late 1960s, the aesthetics of black hair underwent a dramatic transformation. For decades straightened hair, that is, hair that was pressed with an iron comb and curled with hot rollers or, by the 1940s, hair that was chemically straightened, was unquestionably the standard of beauty for black women—for both the activist and the apathetic. However, by 1968, among those such as Gloria Wade-Gayle, who came of age during the black freedom struggle, "an activist with straight hair was a contradiction, a lie, a joke really."[4] Echoing shifts in the larger realm of black politics of the late 1960s, when younger activists rejected many of the integrationist, nonviolent direct action protest tactics of mainstream civil rights groups, organizations dominated by college-aged blacks moved toward a more nationalistic political agenda that demanded that race pride not only be expressed through activism but also be embodied in one's personal style and appearance. The Afro, or natural as it was also called, in many ways, came to exemplify the spirit of this culture.[5]

As many black women started to reflect on what was gained and what was lost in their new assertions of black identity, they also described missing the intimate communal experience of a visit to the beauty salon. Even though, according to Willi Coleman's poem "Among the Things That Used to Be," the new aesthetics of racial pride empowered black women to "walk / heads high / naps full of pride / with not a backward glance / at some of the beauty which / use to be," she lamented about the absence of beauty shop culture in her life. She explains: "Use to be / Ya could learn a whole lot of stuff / sitting in them / beauty shop chairs / Lots more got taken care of / than hair / Cause in our mutual obvious dislike / for nappiness / we came together / under the hot comb / to share / and share /and share / and share."[6] She continues, "cause with a natural / there is no natural place / for us to congregate / to mull over / our mutual discontent." Those sporting the natural were not alone in missing out on the female bonding in beauty shops; beauticians missed their patronage and were determined to make their services desirable, even necessary, for those who no longer wished to straighten their hair.

While women such as Willi Coleman lamented the loss of a place for women to congregate, lost profit was foremost in the minds of beauticians. A June 1969 *Ebony* magazine article gave voice to their plight: "While the 'natural' has found its way into the classroom and cocktail party, as well as the strongholds of militance, an adverse reaction has been noticeable among those who fear it the most—the Negro hairdressers. Many of them readily predict its quick demise, perhaps through wishful thinking. They see it as a passing fad that just might diminish their volume of business while it runs is course."[7] A beautician, identified in the article only as "an irate Midwestern stylist," explained that those embracing these natural styles as a sign of black power are damaging a long tradition of black entrepreneurship: "People do all this talking about black power and going 'natural,' but they don't stop to think that it might backfire. . . . Money is so much of where it is all at and they haven't considered that the big Bs have been the backbone of Negro business in this country—the beauty shop, barber shop, bar and barbeque joint. If they go all the way with this thing, they'll just be putting people out of work."[8] The stylist's words were not complete hyperbole. Beautician Margaret Williams Neal remembered in an oral interview that "afros hurt black beauty shops a lot" because the style was, in her estimation, "a lazy man's hairdo." Indeed, the National Beauty Culturists' League conducted a study in 1970 that found a 20 percent decline in beauty shop revenue.

Linking a trip to the beauty shop to black economic nationalism was one of the many ways black beauticians tried to market the necessity of their services. In addition, according to Susannah Walker, they combated the notion that the style was a "lazy man's hairdo" by publicly declaring that a proper Afro must be professionally styled and maintained.[9] They asserted that the Afro was simply a style among other styles for black women, all of which required the deft hands of a trained beautician. What began as a political statement was soon embraced by beauticians who wished to capitalize on its popularity. Beauticians weathered a brief time of diminished profits and rebounded as a plethora of new products and services soon became available to black women in the hair-care industry.

By the 1980s, ideas about what constituted a beautiful and stylish black woman expanded to include chemically straightened and natural styles. Although women who choose to wear their hair unstraightened or braided have encountered discrimination in the workplace, there seems to be a growing acceptance of African American hair that has not been straightened. Natural hair-care and braiding salons designed to style black women's hair without chemicals are now commonplace in urban areas. Simultaneously, there has been a proliferation of styles that use hair extensions and weaves to lengthen one's hair, which some argue is indicative of a desire to emulate white women. While it is highly unlikely that there will ever be a consensus on the meaning of beauty in black women's lives, one thing is without question: Black beauty is big business. Whatever the changing aesthetics and political implications, black beauticians continue making themselves and their services relevant and necessary.

The same cannot be said for black hair-product manufacturers. By 1953, all of the pioneering black manufacturing moguls—Madame C. J. Walker, Annie Turnbo Malone, and Sara Spencer Washington—were dead, as were their successful "systems" linking product manufacturing and beauty education. The decline of the system method marked a significant change in the beauty industry. Without the vertical integration of beauty product manufacturing and education, black women lost much of their presence and power not only in the industry but also in their respective communities. While the Walker Company continued its involvement in beauty education well into the 1970s, the company was never able to rebound in its sales for hair preparations after the Great Depression. By the time the company was sold in 1985, it was losing money and was a far cry from its former glory.[10]

A few black-owned companies, most notably Johnson Products, founded in 1954 by George H. Johnson, were successful in the 1960s and 1970s, but by 1980 Johnson's market share had dropped 20 percent due to major incursions from white-owned companies.[11] In 1986, Irving Bottner, president of Revlon's professional products division, stated in an interview with *Newsweek* that "in the next couple of years, the black owned [beauty product manufacturing] businesses will disappear. They'll all be sold to the white companies."[12] While the comments inspired much criticism and even a boycott, it unfortunately proved to be prophetic.[13] L'Oreal purchased black-owned Soft Sheen and Carson Products in 2000, enabling it to obtain over 20 percent of the market share of the $1.2 billion a year "ethnic hair care industry," while Alberto-Culver and Procter and Gamble combine to hold another 47 percent of the industry.[14] In addition, successful beauty companies such as Aveda and

Paul Mitchell now market race-neutral products that have made significant inroads into black hair care. The distribution and manufacturing aspects of the industry are not the only ones which have witnessed the declining control of black female entrepreneurs. Other ethnic and immigrant groups have begun to offer services that were previously under the sole purview of black women. Asian and Asian American–owned nail salons have replaced the black manicurist who traditionally had a booth in the neighborhood beauty salon.[15] Similarly, Korean Americans dominate black beauty-product distribution and maintain that control by publishing industry materials and order sheets only in Korean.[16]

Various factors converged in the post–civil rights era to change the nature of beauty education as well. With the end of legalized segregation and with white-collar work and college education a feasible option for an unprecedented number of African American women, beauty schools in this period struggled to market their services as a meaningful path to a professional career for the best women of the race. State beauty regulations, introduced to the profession in the late 1920s, became even stricter in the period after 1965. Combined with the exponential growth and, in the South, the desegregation of colleges and universities, African American beauty schools were forced into a different, sometimes obsolete role as community colleges and vocational schools began preparing women for the state examinations.[17]

African American beauty schools and beauty educators welcomed the changes to the industry. No longer concerned with providing a relatively quick and easy means to a professional status, African American beauty schools embraced the new move toward technical training. "Beauty culturists" and "beauticians," the preferred term of African American women who practiced the beauty trade for most of the twentieth century, now became "cosmetologists" or "hair stylists," terms that minimize status and emphasize technical expertise. Beauty work for African American women was no longer a profession but a vocation, and the black beauty schools that remained in this period emphasized this distinction.

Initially excited about the prospect of working with community colleges, black beauty educators soon found themselves having to compete with community colleges and technical schools for students. Beauty schools began to market their services in unprecedented ways, breaking down the racial barriers that previously defined the industry and, for African Americans, became a springboard for political solidarity. An advertisement for the black-owned Franklin Beauty School in Houston targeted those finishing high school in 1971, explaining, "Brown, Black or White Beauty Comes Only Through a Visit to Us." In 1973, longtime beauty educator Marjorie Stewart Joyner explained that "all persons in the beauty culture field should learn how to dress the hair and skin of black, white, yellow, brown or Chicano customers."[18]

With the majority of women in the beauty industry being trained in community colleges and technical schools, not in independently owned and racially segregated beauty schools as in previous decades, the status of African American beauticians within their communities, as well as the role of beauticians in political activism has changed. While the beauty industry has always attracted women who looked for financial advancement, the profit motive is now unabashedly promoted. Deniece Henry, cosmetology instructor with Sheridan Technical Center for Cosmetology, stated recently, "I don't teach black hair care. I teach them it's a business and after they are educated they see where the money really is."[19] When interviewed in 1993, Harriet Wade, a Durham, North Carolina, beautician, lamented what she perceived as a difference in the way she was trained in beauty culture in the Jim Crow era and the ways that beauty schools now educated students. She explained, "The school I went to taught you self-reliance, reliability. It was more than just doing hair, but I think now they are not learning anything . . . [no] self pride or anything. They're just doing hair. . . . So many [younger beauticians] are embarrassing now and it's just not a profession anymore."[20]

Part of Wade's lament may have also been based on modern stylists eschewing participation in professional organizations such as the National Beauty Culturists' League. While the league and its state and local affiliates still exist, membership is in severe decline and most cosmetologists trained in the last twenty years have never even heard of the organization. Katie Catalon, current president of the NBCL, is trying to remedy the lack of interest by inspiring members to reflect on the organization's long history and recruit others. She encourages members to "persevere" in spite of criticism from those who find the organization irrelevant. "It is amazing to others that find it unrealistic that there are still those of us that remember and cherish what our Pioneers related to in beginning this wonderful organization," she notes.[21] In fact, even when younger women join these organizations, they are hesitant to get overly involved. Retired San Diego beautician Tommie Flanagan expressed her frustration in getting younger beauticians to assume leadership positions in a local professional organization: "We need a president, a young president, and secretaries and all that stuff. They'll [younger beauticians] come for a minute, but they don't stay."[22]

However, the current generation of stylists have not completely abandoned gathering for professional purposes. Instead, the aspiring-class sensibilities and camaraderie of the NBCL have been replaced by the theatrics and competition of hair shows. The Bronner Brothers hair show, billed as the "greatest hair show on earth," takes place annually in Atlanta, Georgia, and is hosted by Bronner Brothers Enterprises, one of the few remaining black-owned hair product manufacturing companies. While the Bronner Brothers trade shows date back to the company's inception in the late 1940s, in 1993 the company and the shows entered into a new phase with the annual hair show taking center stage. The 2008 event, which took place at the Georgia World Congress Center, one of the largest convention facilities in the nation, featured product exhibits and hairstyling classes, but the attention-getting events were more entertainment than education and included the Hollywood hair gossip forums, exotic hair exhibits, a Fire and Ice "grown and sexy party," and a comedy show. The centerpiece and climax of the Bronner show are the five hair competitions in which stylists compete with one another for fame and bragging rights.[23]

While the Bronner Brothers show attracts a large audience, no hair show is as electrifying as the Detroit-based "Hair Wars." Described as a "three-hours-plus extravaganza of blooming, towering, blinking, spinning, smoking, cartoon-like hair creations," participating stylists and salons spend months preparing their over-the-top hair creations for the annual contest. The competition is fierce and is dominated by men, many of whom came to hairstyling after the postindustrial meltdown and auto manufacturing layoffs in the Motor City. Hair Wars promoter David Humphries explains that "the only thing that could replace that [employment with the Big Three Automakers] was the hair business, because it was so lucrative. So guys started going to beauty school." Tickets to the event cost twenty dollars per person, and the one-thousand-person audience is filled with stylists and nonstylists, most of whom are there for the entertainment, because, as the announcer, retired stylist LaToya Pearson, exclaims, the "hair business is nothin' but show business!"[24] Since 1994, the shows have toured throughout the United States and have been seen by more than one hundred million people. Humphries has been approached by E! Entertainment and the Fox television network to present Hair Wars as a reality television show, but he has turned them down. "I don't want them to try to make fools out of these hair people," he explains. "They wanted backstage to be chaotic and out of order and people fighting, and that's not what happens." While Humphries has rejected the prospect of a reality show, the media, fashion and arts communities have embraced this mixture of business, artistry, and entertainment.[25]

Still, such theatrics and frivolity has not prevented professionalism or even politics from being a major part of the industry, and black beauticians have emerged at the forefront of the black women's health movement. While dismantling the blatant forms of segregation and discrimination were the primary goals of black beauticians during the freedom struggle, the post–civil rights period has forced black women to confront issues surrounding more subtle effects of racism. To that end, the 1980s saw the birth of the black women's health movement.[26] With black women more likely to die from cardiovascular disease and breast cancer than white women, making up close to 60 percent of the HIV/AIDS cases among women, and having a lower life expectancy than white women by five years, the very survival of African American women is at stake.[27] Nowhere are the health crises of black women more evident than in states of the former Jim Crow South. Of the twenty-two counties targeted by the National Black Leadership Initiative on Cancer (NBLIC) as "high prevalence cancer communities," more than 36 percent were in the South, 9 percent above the next highest region, the Midwest.[28] Still racial disparities in health care are a national phenomenon.

Even though African American women's involvement in health activism dates back at least to the 1890s, when African American sororal groups, midwives, and public health nurses addressed racial disparities in health care, the creation of the National Black Women's Health Project (BWHP) signaled a new wave of black women's health advocacy. In the summer of 1983, on the campus of Spelman College, Byllye Avery convened a national conference of more than sixteen hundred health educators, health-care providers, and concerned lay people. Gathered under the theme "I'm Sick and Tired of Being Sick and Tired," paying homage to the words of civil rights activist and freedom fighter Fannie Lou Hamer, the three days of workshops, exhibits, films, speeches, and demonstrations culminated in a keynote address by June Jackson Christmas of the School of Bio-Medical Education at the City University of New York. Christmas implored those gathered to "do more to learn and understand the causes of our being sick; the reasons for our having been tired. Black women face the triple jeopardy of being black, female, and poor in a racist, sexist and class structured society."[29] The best attended workshop, "Black and Female: What Is the Reality?" which was held three times to overflow crowds, was exclusively for black women and sought to confront the myth of the black superwoman, the black woman as the pillar of strength. Women shared their experiences of trying to live up to unreasonable expectations, often to the peril of their health, and the need to establish safe zones within their communities to continue these discussions.

Beauticians, ever aware of the issues confronting black women have proven especially helpful in health activism for the same reasons they were central in previous types of activism. In fact, beauty shops in the contemporary period best exemplify the community safe zones proposed by the National Black Women's Health Project. In cities all across the South, initiatives such as the Madam C. J. Walker Health Empowerment Project, Stay Beautiful, Stay Alive, and Beauty and the Breast train beauticians to serve as health educators and referral agents concerning breast and cervical cancer prevention. The beauticians who participate agree to use their salons as health awareness sites and to encourage their clients to eat right and visit their doctors for yearly mammograms and Pap smears. Beauty salons, where touch and care of the body are high priorities, provide a place for black women's bodies to be dignified and find a safe place for care and exploration.

After losing an aunt to breast cancer in 1988, Anderson, South Carolina, salon owner Mary Louise Fant joined the Beauty and the Breast campaign, which was supported in part by a grant from the Susan G. Komen Breast Cancer Foundation. According to Fant, the real tragedy in her aunt's death was that she had not seen a doctor in more than fifteen years before her cancer diagnosis. Echoing the lament over the superwoman burden expressed at the BWHP conference, Fant attributed her aunt's severely delayed doctor visit to the fact that "we [black women] don't take care of ourselves because we're taking care of everybody else." The beauty salon, perhaps the one place where black women do not feel guilty about taking care of themselves, proved to be a great place for women to learn about the importance of self-exams and yearly mammograms. Fant filled her salon with pamphlets and posters, and armed with information she learned in the Beauty and the Breast training program, she rattles off the dismal statistics concerning black women and breast cancer as she scrubs a client's head in the sink. For Fant, such education and advocacy was a natural outgrowth of her role as a beautician. She explained, "The relationship that a beautician has with her clients is the right atmosphere. We talk about any and everything. It's just easy to talk." Originally, the Beauty and the Breast program challenged the hair stylists to talk to fifty clients about breast cancer over the course of a year; Fant made her fifty-person quota in just two weeks.[30]

One of the most successful models in utilizing beauticians and salons in health advocacy is the Black Beauticians Health Promotion Program, a partnership between the University of California–San Diego Moores Cancer Center and local beauticians. Started in 1994 as the brainchild of Georgia Robins Sadler, the associate director of outreach at the center, the program received a grant of three hundred thousand dollars from the Bristol-Myers

Squibb Foundation in 1997. Originally, Sadler thought that black churches were best equipped to promote healthy behaviors among African American women, but she was disappointed due to low turnout and realized that among the few who showed up to meetings were those who already had adequate information and just wanted more. These were not the people Sadler wanted to reach. After talking to a black colleague who had a "great hairdo" and hearing about the amount of time black women spent in salons getting their hair styled, Sadler then began targeting beauticians and beauty salons for her outreach efforts. Salons proved to be the ideal atmosphere. Unlike churches, where discussions of the body are often taboo, Sadler explained,

Figure 7. Tessie Bonner, beautician and health educator.
Photo by Marc Tule, courtesy of University of California at
San Diego Publications.

"You literally and figuratively let your hair down in a salon."[31] Clergy and female leadership in the churches helped her identify "civic-minded cosmetologists." Eight enrolled in the pilot study, with twenty signing on within three years.[32]

Once committed stylists were chosen, they met periodically with Sadler and her staff. The stylists agreed to allow a research assistant to come to the salon on a variety of days to conduct a survey on health issues confronting African American women. The survey included questions designed to assess the client's knowledge of four key diseases: diabetes, cancer, cardiovascular disease, and heart disease. Employing the "Health Promotion Model," which asserts that cognition of a particular disease "is presumed to affect actions, and environmental events are proposed as operating interactively in determining behavior," the survey asked the women to list the top four most serious health threats facing African American women and inquired as to whether they participated in health-screening activities (mammograms, eye exams, physical examination, sugar/diabetes test screening). Finally the survey asked about their ability to affect their own health outcomes as well as their source for health information. The findings of the survey of 1,055 women were published in the *Diabetes Educator* in the summer of 2004 and the *Journal of the National Medical Association* in January 2005. One of the major conclusions of the research was that for those who did not have an ongoing relationship with a medical professional, it was important to find nontraditional ways to provide them with information and inspire them to take action concerning health screenings and healthy behaviors. The stylists who offered their salons for the surveys also offered their services as health educators.

While the stylists were eager to participate in the program, some thought it would be more difficult to get their clients involved in the program. Sylvia Bennett of Hairitage Salon thought the surveys would be viewed as an intrusion into the pampering that they sought in the salon: "Sometimes people just want to relax. They don't want to be interviewed or anything when they come to the salon." Suspicion over how the information would be used by University of California also raised concern among clients, and Bennett explained that her clients often asked whether Georgia Sadler was black or white. "That was the first question. And she [Georgia Sadler] wasn't [black] . . . People are skeptical [when] they learn you trying to do studies on black people."[33] Bennett assuaged her clients' doubts by personally vouching for Sadler's integrity and even putting clients in touch with Sadler if they had questions she could not answer personally. The Beauticians' Health Promotion Project demonstrated the role stylists can play in building trust for institutions that are viewed as having adversarial relationships to black communities. In the end, only 13 percent of those approached to be a part of the study declined participation.[34]

While the success of the Beauty and the Breast and the Beauticians' Health Promotion project relied upon dynamic stylists such as Mary Louise Fant and Sylvia Bennett, the Stay Beautiful/Stay Alive program focused its efforts on the potential for beauty salons to serve as safe and inviting spaces. In cities such as Atlanta, Birmingham, and Houston, beauticians not only conveyed the message of health advocacy but also, with the help of the NBLIC, transformed their actual salons into breast and cervical cancer screening sites.[35] In other words, instead of waiting for black women to visit a doctor, the doctor and the cancer screening equipment went to the one place African American women were willing to pay attention to their bodies on a regular basis—the beauty salon.

Partnerships among public health advocates, social service agencies, and beauticians have proven particularly successful in confronting health crises of a more intimate, perhaps even taboo, nature—namely, HIV/AIDS and other sexually transmitted diseases as well as domestic violence and sexual assault. Based on the success of a South Carolina beautician who turned her salon into a repository for condoms and HIV/AIDS prevention literature and whose story is chronicled in the 1990 documentary *DiAna's Hair Ego*, HIV and AIDS education, as well as condom distribution and safe sex parties, are also taking place in beauty salons across the country.[36] In 1997, the California AIDS Prevention Campaign initiated "Protecting Your Customers, Protecting Your Friends," a program that encourages salon owners to show a ten-minute video concerning the importance of getting tested for the disease and make a scratch-off card that contain quizzes about HIV and AIDS available to their clients.

The campaign at beauty salons was more successful than a similar program attempted at local churches and represented a departure from an earlier tradition in which the church was the primary institution to disseminate crucial community information, according to Vera Ray, the project's coordinator. "Historically, when black people have needed to organize or get the word out, they've used the churches. But some churches don't want to hear our message; they think we are promoting sex."[37] Still, even within the safe confines of the beauty salon, Ray acknowledged that though she had "some good talks with the beauticians and their clientele," it "takes a couple of trips before someone will ask, 'So where can I get tested?' It takes that long." Thankfully stylists have an enduring relationship with their clients and can be a part of a long-term process.

Furthermore, law enforcement and social service agencies are now working with black beauticians, training them to be on the alert for signs of domestic abuse in their clients. SafePlace, a sexual and domestic violence prevention and advocacy organization in Austin, Texas, initiated the Help Cut Out Sexual Assault (HCOSA) campaign in 2007 targeting African American salons as places to disseminate information concerning their services to rape and sexual assault victims. Taking into account the extensive underreporting of sexual violence, a study conducted in 2000 found that 19 percent of African American women had reported being raped.[38] Other studies have found that African American women were less likely than their white counterparts to disclose their sexual abuse and assault.[39] SafePlace's earlier attempts to connect with African American female sexual assault survivors through churches were not very successful. However, within six months of distributing brochures and posters as well as training stylists in how to discuss sexual assault in their salons, clients have been disclosing sexual assault and have begun the process to rebuild their dignity and their lives.

*   *   *

No events in the early years of the twenty-first century have unearthed the complexities of race, class, and gender in contemporary America more than the aftermath of Hurricane Katrina and the 2008 Democratic Presidential Primary. On the one hand, the response to Hurricane Katrina in the summer of 2005 exposed an American betrayal; the needs of African Americans on the Gulf Coast, particularly black women and their children, were essentially ignored. However, in the early months of the 2008 Democratic presidential primaries, particularly in the weeks leading up to the January 26 South Carolina primary, African American women were a coveted demographic. Overly simplistic, even insulting discussions as to whether black women would vote based on their gender connection with Hilary Rodham Clinton or their racial solidarity with Barack Obama filled the news media and consumed the political strategies of both candidates. Whether forgotten or courted, the rapport African American beauticians had with black women as well as the notion of the beauty salon as a comfort zone made them key factors in bridging twenty-first-century economic and political divides.

The devastation Hurricane Katrina wrought on the lives of the Gulf Coast's dispersed African American population is unfortunately still evident. In the storm's immediate aftermath, one of the first requests to come out of the convention centers, arenas, and gymnasiums where many were temporarily housed was for ethnically appropriate hair-care products for survivors who were frustrated with the shampoos, conditioners, and styling aids offered in the standard Red Cross packs. Indeed, while the Red Cross quickly reached its limit in accepting clothing for the evacuees in Austin, Texas, requests for black hair-care products, along with hair-care product drives, continued for weeks. Similar calls for hair-care products abounded from Houston to Cape Cod as the relocated evacuees sought to rebuild their lives. For those who already had experienced so many indignities, not being able to care for their hair in the manner they were accustomed added further insult.

Beauty salons and beauticians were among the first to recognize how important hairstyling and grooming were to the Katrina evacuees. In Austin and Houston, local black beauticians offered their styling and grooming services to the evacuees free of charge either on site or by providing shuttle services to local salons. In Nashville, Tennessee, owners of the Essence Day Spa were among the first to supplement the efforts of the local Red Cross, which found itself inadequate to understand and serve the needs of the sixty-five hundred Katrina evacuees in its midst. They opened their salon to provide, according to an observer, "a little humanity . . . a hug, a sympathetic ear, favorite hymn tune and, just maybe, some hair relaxer." Evacuees appreciated these gestures, which brought "a measure of normality amid chaos." Colleen Zakrewsky, director of the Nashville Area Red Cross, took note of the beauticians' efforts, recognizing the importance of these simple acts of compassion, and vowed to change her chapter's operating procedure to include ethnically sensitive hair grooming services.[40]

Futhermore, Willie Morrow, a California hair-care manufacturer known best for introducing the afro pic in America in the 1960s and for developing the infamous "curl" formula so popular in the 1980s, donated more than one hundred thousand hair and skin care products from his SOS Jam Line along with "salon chairs, professional sinks, blow dryers, curling irons, and clippers"—not to the rank-and-file evacuees of the Austin Convention Center or Houston's Superdome but specifically to African American beauticians from the Gulf Coast whose businesses had been destroyed. Morrow, one of the few remaining African American hair-care manufacturers, explained, "The black hair care business has always been strong in our community and now a great number of them have been wiped out of business. I'm working to get these people back into business."[41]

While certainly the demands of shelter, food, water, clothing and employment should be top priorities as the evacuees rebuild their lives in Houston, Baton Rouge, Atlanta, or the numerous other cities where they now reside, the discussions surrounding hair care and the economic stability of the beauty

industry highlight some major issues that the aftermath of Hurricane Katrina hopefully will bring out into the national debate. For African American
women, a key way to reclaim one's dignity in the wake of physical trauma
and deprivation remains hairstyling. Willie Morrow's reaching out to beauticians as being key to rebuilding the black economy for the dispersed is, in
my estimation, a wise move. His attempt to "hurricane proof" this vibrant
industry, one of the few industries that were depression proof in the 1930s,
is compelling. Even in a political economy that disenfranchises so many
African Americans, the beauty industry, at the beginning of the twenty-first
century, represents much of what it did to black women in the early years
of the twentieth century; it remains one of the few places where African
American women can reclaim their personal and economic dignity.

The early months of the very long Democratic primary season focused
on the black female vote. Entering the list of media-contrived demographics
after 1992's and 1996's soccer moms and the Nascar dads of 2004, the summer of 2007 introduced the beauty shop voter into the political vernacular.
Referring to black women who were considered for a few months at least to
be a key constituency, the "beauty shop vote" was seen as crucial to winning
states such as South Carolina, which have a large African American population. The two Democratic frontrunners, Senators Hilary Rodham Clinton
and Barack Obama, aggressively pursued black women in what one South
Carolina voter called her "comfort zone," the local beauty salon. Lisha Yd-
stie explained, "We [black women] make our choices a lot of times based on
people who come into our comfort zones."[42] Clinton and Obama courted
beauticians and their clients and sent their staffers with campaign materials
into key comfort zones.

Hilary Rodham Clinton approached beauty industry leaders such as Katie
Catalon, president of the National Beauty Culturist League, and even addressed the organization at its eighty-eighth annual convention in Fairfax,
Virginia, in July 2007. During her well-received address, she ran through a
slideshow of her hairstyles over the years: a short bob and a long bob, bouf-
fants and sleek looks. She included images of these hairdos on the hundreds
of cardboard flyers she sent to beauty parlors across the state.

Obama's campaign employed a more grass-roots approach to reaching African Americans. It initiated what it called the B&B (Beauty Shop and Barber
Shop) strategy, dispersing groups of young volunteers across the state. For
example, Ashley Baia, a twenty-three-year-old volunteer in Horry County,
traveled to various salons on Thursdays, Fridays, and Saturdays developing
relationships with stylists and clients, answering questions about Obama's

record, and distributing campaign pamphlets. A volunteer's blog on Obama's official campaign site summarized the rationale behind the B&B strategy: "We have to bring the discussion to the places people gather, in the little leisure time they have left. They can't always come to us and our meetings and house parties. . . . Work your local B&B shops with confidence."[43] Barack Obama went on to win the South Carolina primary based in part on his ability to get his message out to African Americans who voted for him in record numbers.[44]

While much has changed in the black beauty industry and in black women's political lives over the course of the twentieth century, these examples demonstrate that beauty salons remain places where black women feel safe to deal with intimate issues that are for the most part ignored in the larger society. They are one of the few places where black women can still gather and have their dignity restored, a political act in and of itself. Similarly, beauticians are still viewed as trustworthy enough for clients to share the most intimate details of their lives and respected enough to help them make important political decisions. In perhaps one of the most unlikely places, a business enterprise based on something as frivolous as hairstyling, has emerged a platform for black women to heal from and challenge the limitations imposed by the intersecting challenges of sexism, racism, and economic disenfranchisement.

Notes

Introduction

1. Myles Horton, *The Long Haul: An Autobiography* (New York: Doubleday Books, 1990), 102.

2. Robin D. G. Kelley, "We Are Not What We Seem: The Politics and Pleasures of Community," *Race Rebels: Culture, Politics, and the Black Working Class* (New York: Free Press, 1994), 44.

3. Sara M. Evans and Harry C. Boyte's notion of free spaces as "public places in the community . . . in which people are able to learn a new self-respect, a deeper and more assertive group identity, public skills and values of cooperation and civic virtue . . . settings between private lives and large scale institutions . . . with a relatively open and participatory character" is also useful. *Free Spaces: The Sources of Democratic Change in America* (Chicago: University of Chicago Press, 1992), ix.

4. Kathy Peiss, *Hope in a Jar: The Making of America's Beauty Culture* (New York: Metropolitan Books, 1998) is the most comprehensive work on the role of beauty culture in forming black and white women's modern identities. A number of works have looked specifically at the role of beauty culture in black women's lives, most notably Ayanna Byrd and Lori Tharps, *Hair Story: Untangling the Roots of Black Hair in America* (New York: St. Martin Press, 2001); Maxine Leeds Craig, *Ain't I a Beauty Queen: Black Women, Beauty, and the Politics of Race* (New York: Oxford University Press, 2002); Ima Ebong, ed., *Black Hair: Art, Style, and Culture* (New York: Universe Publishing, 2001); Susannah Walker, "Black Is Profitable: The Commodification of the Afro, 1960–1975," in *Beauty and Business and Style and Substance: Selling Beauty to African American Women, 1920–1975*, ed. Philip Scranton (Lexington: University of Kentucky Press, 2007); Juliette Harris and Pamela Johnson, eds., *Tenderheaded: A Comb-Bending Collection of Hair Stories* (New York: Pocket Books, 2001); and

Noliwe Rooks, *Hair Raising: Beauty, Culture, and African American Women* (New Brunswick, N.J.: Rutgers University Press, 1996). Julia Kirk Blackwelder's *Stylin Jim Crow: African American Beauty Training During Segregation* (College Station: Texas A&M Press, 2003) looks exclusively at black beauty education, while Julie Ann Willet's *Permanent Waves: The Making of the American Beauty Shop* (New York: New York University Press, 2000) examines black and white beauty shops as labor sites. There have also been recent biographies of Madam C. J. Walker, most notably A' Lelia Bundles, *On Her Own Ground: The Life and Times of Madam C. J. Walker* (New York: Scribner Books, 2001).

5. Notable exceptions are Juliet E. K. Walker, *The History of Black Business in America: Capitalism, Race, and Entrepreneurship* (New York: Macmillian Reference Library, 1998); Robert Olwell, "'Loose, Idle, and Disorderly': Slave Women in the Eighteenth-Century Charleston Marketplace," in *More Than Chattel: Black Women and Slavery in the Americas*, ed. David Barry Gaspar and Darlene Clark Hine (Bloomington: Indiana University Press, 1996), 97–110; Lynn Hudson, *The Making of "Mammy Pleasant": A Black Entrepreneur in Nineteenth-Century San Francisco* (Urbana: University of Illinois Press, 2003); Elsa Barkley Brown, "Womanist Consciousness: Maggie Lena Walker and the Independent Order of St. Luke," *Signs* 14 (Spring 1989): 610–633; Bundles, *On Her Own Ground*; Peiss, *Hope in a Jar*.

6. Wendy Gamber, "A Gendered Enterprise: Placing Nineteenth Century Business-women in History," *Business History Review* 72 (Summer 1998): 192.

Chapter 1. Racial Uplift and Gender in the Creation of a Black Business Community

1. For more information on Booker T. Washington and W. E. B. Du Bois's differences of opinions on black politics, see Louis Harlan, *Booker T. Washington: The Making of a Leader* (New York: Oxford University Press, 1972); and David Levering Lewis, *W. E. B. Du Bois: Biography of a Race, 1868–1919* (New York: Henry Holt, 1993).

2. "Annie M. Turnbo Malone," *Who's Who in Black America* (New York: Who's Who in Black America, 1927).

3. Walker, *History of Black Business in America*, coined the phrase "golden age of black business" to describe the "emergence of leading black capitalists who acquired millionaire status and established million dollar enterprises" and includes a substantial discussion of the period in chapter 7. I would also add that this golden age is not just reflected in the economic wealth of these enterprises, but also includes the organizing of smaller black business men and women into business leagues.

4. For more information on the enterprises of enslaved black women, see Walker, *History of Black Business in America*; and Olwell, "Loose, Idle, and Disorderly," 97–110.

5. For a larger discussion of the entrepreneurial pursuits of free black women in the antebellum period, see Wilma King, *The Essence of Liberty: Free Black Women*

During the Slave Era (Colombia: University of Missouri Press, 2006); Jessica Millward, "'A Choice Parcel of Country Born': African-Americans and the Transition to Freedom in Maryland, 1770–1840" (Ph.D. diss., University of California, Los Angeles, 2003); and Amrita Chakrabarti Myers, "Negotiating Women: Black Women and the Politics of Freedom in Charleston, South Carolina, 1790–1860" (Ph.D. diss., Rutgers University, 2004).

6. Quoted in Walker, *History of Black Business in America,* 44.

7. For more information on Pierre Toussaint, see Arthur Jones, *Pierre Toussaint* (New York: Doubleday Books, 2003).

8. While the image of black men as sexual predators really comes to fruition during Reconstruction, sexual mores began to dictate a separation between black men and white women in the antebellum period in the slaveholding South. See Doug Bristol, "The Victory of Black Barbers Over Reform in Ohio, 1902–1913," *Essays in Economic and Business History* (1998): 251–260. It is important to note that black men as "hairdressers" show up in probate records in Boston into the 1860s; see "African-Americans in Antebellum Boston," www.primaryresearch.org/bh/probate.php/ (accessed May 15, 2009).

9. For more information on black barbers in the antebellum period, see Doug Bristol, "From Outposts to Enclaves: A Social History of Black Barbers, 1750–1915" (Ph.D diss., University of Maryland, 2002); Quincy T. Mills, "Color-Line Barbers and the Emergence of a Black Public Space: A Social and Political History of Black Barbers and Barber Shops, 1830–1970" (Ph.D. diss., University of Chicago, 2006); and Walker, *History of Black Business in America,* 107–109.

10. King, *Essence of Liberty,* 73–75; Walker, *History of Black Business in America,* 141–143.

11. Eliza Potter, *A Hairdresser's Experience in the High Life* (1859; reprint, New York: Oxford University Press, 1988). For a larger discussion of the significance of Potter's work, particularly with regard to her labor and entrepreneurship, see Xiomara Santamarina, "Black Hairdresser and Social Critic: Eliza Potter and the Labors of Femininity," *American Literature* 77 (March 2005): 151–177.

12. Potter, *Hairdresser's Experience,* chap. 2.

13. Martha Ward, *Voodoo Queen: The Spirited Lives of Marie Laveau* (Jackson: University Press of Mississippi, 2004), 80–83.

14. For a larger discussion of the political and economic dimensions of Reconstruction, see Eric Foner, *Free Soil, Free Labor, Free Men: The Ideology of the Republican Party before the Civil War* (New York: Oxford University Press, 1970); Eric Foner, *Reconstruction: America's Unfinished Revolution* (New York: Harper and Row, 1998); W. E. B. Du Bois, *Black Reconstruction: An Essay Toward a History of the Part Which Black Folk Played in the Attempt to Reconstruct Democracy in America, 1860–1880* (New York: Harcourt, Brace, [c. 1935]); Thomas Holt, *Black Over White: Negro Political Leadership in South Carolina During Reconstruction* (Urbana: University of Illinois Press, 1977); Sharon Ann Holt, "Making Freedom Pay: Freedpeople Working for

Themselves, North Carolina, 1865–1900," *Journal of Southern History* 60 (May 1994): 239–262; and Julie Saville, *The Work of Reconstruction: From Slave to Wage Laborer in South Carolina, 1860–1870* (Cambridge: Cambridge University Press, 1994).

15. Joe William Trotter, *The African American Experience,* vol. 2 (Boston: Houghton Mifflin, 2001), 317.

16. Elsa Barkley Brown, in her discussion of the Blacks in post–Civil War Richmond, explains that as "formal political gains, initially secured, began to recede and economic promise became less certain and less surely tied to political advancement, the political struggles over relationships between the working class and the newly emergent middle class, [and] between men and women . . . increasingly became issues." "Negotiating and Transforming the Public Sphere: African American Political Life in the Transition from Slavery to Freedom," *Public Culture* 7 (1994): 117.

17. Here I am invoking Michele Mitchell's use of the term "aspiring class," which she defines as "cohort of ambitious activists" who had "an abiding concern with propriety—not to mention a belief that morality, thrift, and hard work were essential to black progress." Michele Mitchell, *Righteous Discontent: African Americans and the Politics of Racial Destiny after Reconstruction* (Chapel Hill: University of North Carolina Press, 2004), 10.

18. D. Augustus Straker, "Manhood and Womanhood Development," *Colored American Magazine* 2 (February 1901): 312.

19. Kevin K. Gaines, *Uplifting the Race: Black Leadership, Politics, and Culture in the Twentieth Century* (Chapel Hill: University of North Carolina Press, 1996), 2.

20. W. E. B. Du Bois, ed., *The Negro in Business* (Atlanta: Atlanta University Press, 1899), 49.

21. Hattie G. Escridge, "The Need of Negro Merchants," in Du Bois, *Negro in Business,* 61.

22. H. E. Lindsay, "Negro Business Men of Columbia, S.C.," in Du Bois, *Negro in Business,* 63.

23. Du Bois, *Negro in Business,* 50.

24. For information on the NNBL's early controversies, see John H. Burrows, *The Necessity of Myth: A History of the National Negro Business League, 1900–1945* (Auburn, Ala.: Hickory Hill Press, 1998), 38–39.

25. Gilbert C. Harris, "Work in Hair," in *Proceedings of the National Negro Business League,* First Annual Meeting (Boston: J.R. Ham Publisher, 1900), 77.

26. Biographical information on Alberta Moore Smith's life is found in "Editorial and Publisher's Announcements," *Colored American Magazine* 2 (November 1900), 73–75; and in Candace Kanes, "American Business Women, 1890–1930: Creating an Identity" (Ph.D. diss., University of New Hampshire, 1997).

27. Alberta Moore Smith, "Negro Women's Business Clubs: A Factor in the Solution of the Vexed Problem," in *Proceedings of the National Negro Business League,* Second Annual Meeting (Frederick, Md.: University Publications of America), 62.

28. For more information on the members of the colored women's business clubs,

see ibid.; and Dora A. Miller, "Some Eastern Business Women," *Proceedings of the National Negro Business League,* Second Annual Meeting, 58–62.

29. Miller, "Some Eastern Business Women," 62.

30. Elizabeth Lindsay Davis, *Lifting as They Climb* (Washington, D.C.: National Association of Colored Women, 1933), 16; emphasis added.

31. Deborah Gray White, *Too Heavy a Load: Black Women in Defense of Themselves* (New York: W. W. Norton, 1998), 34–35.

32. Davis, *Lifting as They Climb,* 87–88.

33. Alberta Moore Smith, "Why?" *Colored American Magazine* 3 (October 1901): 467.

34. For the distinction between "business women" and "women in business," see Kanes, "American Business Women," 3; Smith, "Why?" 467–470.

35. Alberta Moore Smith, "Women's Development in Business," *Colored American Magazine* 4 (March 1902): 325.

36. Alberta Moore Smith, "Women's Development in Business," *Minutes of the National Negro Business League,* 132.

37. See Gaines, *Uplifting the Race,* especially chapters 4–6, for a discussion of the patriarchal family norms that were emblematic of the racial uplift ethos; and Mitchell, *Righteous Propagation,* especially chapters 2–5.

38. Smith, "Woman's Development in Business," *Colored American Magazine,* 326.

39. Gamber, "Gendered Enterprise," 189.

40. Smith, "Woman's Development in Business," 324.

41. See Bundles, *On Her Own Ground*; Peiss, *Hope in a Jar*; and Rooks, *Hair Raising.*

42. For an account of how the paradox of T. Thomas Fortune's militancy and acceptance of these beauty ads invited ridicule from the *New York Times,* see Bundles, *On Her Own Ground,* 67.

43. See Bundles, *On Her Own Ground,* 133–134.

44. *Poro College in Pictures with a Short History of Its Development* (St. Louis: Poro College, 1926), 4.

45. Ibid.

46. Bundles, *On Her Own Ground,* 65.

47. Cincinnati Poro Dealers, A *Brief History of the Rise and Development of Beauty Culture,* pamphlet from Cincinnati Convention, June 27–29, 1948.

48. Walker was widowed in unknown circumstances in 1888. This was not unusual since 20 to 25 percent of black women in southern cities became widows between 1880 and 1910—a much higher proportion than in the white population due to higher death rates among black men. See Jacqueline Jones, *Labor of Love, Labor of Sorrow: Black Women, Work, and the Family from Slavery to the Present* (New York: Basic Books, 1985), 114.

49. For a larger discussion of the employment practices of black women in St.

Louis, see Lawrence Oland Christenen, "Black St. Louis: A Study in Race Relations, 1865–1916" (Ph.D. diss., University of Missouri, 1972); and Bundles, *On Her Own Ground*, 45.

50. "Wealthiest Negro Woman's Suburban Mansion," *New York Times Magazine*, November 4, 1917.

51. Bundles, *On Her Own Ground*, 58.

52. Ibid., 57.

53. Ibid., 64.

54. Ibid., 65.

55. Ibid., 83.

56. Other black business women would eventually use the term "Madam," but it remained almost exclusively a term for black beauty culturists.

57. *Poro College in Pictures*.

58. For more information on Walker and Malone's troubles with their husbands, see Bundles, *On Her Own Ground*, 90, 124–6, 163, 237.

59. Susannah Walker, *Style and Status: Selling Beauty to African American Women, 1920–1975* (Lexington: University of Kentucky Press, 2007), 45.

60. A'Lelia Bundles, *Madam C. J. Walker* (New York: Chelsea, 1994), 13.

61. Ibid., 17.

62. For more information on the life and activism of Madam C. J. Walker, see Bundles, *On Her Own Ground*; Darlene Clark Hine, "Booker T. Washington and Madam C. J Walker," in *Speak Truth to Power: Black Professional Class in United States History*, by Darlene Clark Hine (Brooklyn, N.Y.: Carlson, 1996), 95–104. Leroy Davis, "Madam C. J. Walker: A Woman of Her Time," in *The African Experience in Community Development: The Continuing Struggle in Africa and the Americas*, vol. 2, ed. Edward W. Crosby, Leroy Davis, and Anne Adams Graves (Needham Heights, Mass.; 1980), 37–60; Beverly Lowry, *Her Dream of Dreams: The Rise and Triumph of Madam C. J. Walker* (New York: Knopf, 2003), and Peiss, *Hope in a Jar*.

63. According to Noliwe Rooks, "Hair straightening and threats of inferiority were not the primary basis on which these women argued for use of their products" and instead advocated standards of beauty that "were not predicated on negative racial ideologies." See *Hair Raising*, 47–48.

64. Bundles, *Madam C. J. Walker*, 67.

65. Madam C. J. Walker to Booker T. Washington, 2 December 1911, and Booker T. Washington to Madam C. J. Walker, 6 December 1911, in Louis Harlan and Raymond Smock, eds., *The Booker T. Washington Papers* (Urbana: University of Illinois Press, 1972) (hereafter cited as *Booker T. Washington Papers*), 384 and 398.

66. Walker to Washington, 17 January 1912, in *Booker T. Washington Papers*, 456–457.

67. Ibid., 456.

68. Mrs. Booker T. Washington, "What Girls Are Taught and How," in *Tuskegee*

and Its People: Their Ideals and Achievements, ed. Booker T. Washington, (New York: D. Appleton and Co., 1905), 68–86.

69. Mary McLeod Bethune to Madam Walker, 5 April 1917, Box 1, Folder 4, Madam C. J. Walker Papers, Indiana Historical Society, Indianapolis (hereafter cited as MCJW, IHS).

70. Madam Walker to F. B. Ransom, 15 December 1916, Box 1, Folder 6, MCJW, IHS.

71. A. M. Townsend to Madam Walker, 12 May 1916, Box 1, Folder 4, MCJW, IHS.

72. These three reasons were offered by Davis, "Madam C. J. Walker," 37–60.

73. Minutes of the Thirteenth Annual Convention of the National Negro Business League, Chicago, 1912.

74. Bethune to Walker, 5 April 1917.

75. According to census data, in 1910 over 90 percent of African Americans lived in what would be considered the South. See *Statistical Abstract of the United States, 2003*.

76. *Poro College in Pictures.*

77. For press coverage of her international travels, see "Madam Walker Sails for Cuba," *Chicago Defender*, November 29, 1913; "Mme. Walker Returns Home," *Indianapolis Freeman*, January 17, 1914; "Madam C. J. Walker Seeing the Islands of the Southern Seas," *Indianapolis Freeman*, 17 January 1914; "Good News from Madam Walker," *Chicago Broad Ax*, January 24, 1914.

78. "Madam C. J. Walker Seeing the Islands."

Chapter 2. Black Beauty Culture, Racial Politics, and the Complexities of Modern Black Womanhood

1. For more information on Caribbean migration to the United States in the early twentieth century, see Irma Watkins-Owens, *Blood Relations: Caribbean Immigrants and the Harlem Community, 1900–1930* (Bloomington: University of Indiana Press, 1996); and Joyce Moore Turner, *Caribbean Crusaders and the Harlem Renaissance* (Urbana: University of Illinois Press, 2005), chapters 1 and 2.

2. Information on the life of Adina Stewart can be found in Yvette Richards, *Maida Springer Kemp: Pan-Africanist and International Labor Leader* (Pittsburgh: University of Pittsburgh Press, 2000), 13–35; and Maida Springer Kemp, interview by Elizabeth Balanoff, in *The Black Women Oral History Project: The Arthur and Elizabeth Schlesinger Library on the History of Women in America*, ed. Ruth Edmonds Hill (Westport, Conn.: Meckler Press, 1991).

3. In many ways, black beauticians could be seen as operating at the intersection of the discourses on the New Woman and the New Negro. For more on the discourses on the "New Woman," see Judith M. McArthur, *Creating the New Woman: The Rise of Southern Women's Progressive Culture in Texas, 1893–1918* (Urbana: University of Illinois Press, 1998); Joanne J. Meyerowitz, *Women Adrift: Independent Wage Earners*

in Chicago, 1880–1930 (Chicago: University of Chicago Press, 1988); Peiss, *Hope in a Jar*; Kathy Peiss, *Cheap Amusements: Working Women and Leisure in Turn-of-the-Century New York* (Philadelphia: Temple University Press, 1986); and Stephanie J. Shaw, *What a Woman Ought to Be and to Do: Black Professional Women Workers during the Jim Crow Era* (Chicago: University of Chicago Press, 1996). For a discussion of the "New Negro," see Alain Locke, ed., *The New Negro* (1925; reprint, New York: Touchstone Books, 1991); David Levering Lewis, *When Harlem Was in Vogue* (New York: Oxford University Press, 1979); Jervis Anderson, *This Was Harlem: A Cultural Portrait* (New York: Ferrar, Strauss, and Giroux, 1981); and Davarian Baldwin, *Chicago's New Negroes: Modernity, the Great Migration, and Black Urban Life* (Chapel Hill: University of North Carolina, 2007).

4. This argument is at the center of the work on beauty culture by Peiss, *Hope in a Jar*; Bundles, *On Her Own Ground*; Rooks, *Hair Raising*; Walker, *Style and Status*.

5. For a larger discussion of the period known as the Great Migration, see Joe William Trotter, ed., *The Great Migration in Historical Perspective: New Dimensions of Race, Class, and Gender* (Bloomington: Indiana University Press, 1991); Carole Marks, *Farewell, We're Good and Gone: The Great Black Migration* (Bloomington: Indiana University Press, 1989); Beverly Bunch-Lyons, *Contested Terrain: African American Women Migrate from the South to Cincinnati, Ohio, 1900–1950* (New York: Routledge Press, 2002); Milton Sernett, *Bound for the Promised Land: African American Religion and the Great Migration* (Durham, N.C.: Duke University Press, 1997); and Victoria Wolcott, *Remaking Respectability: African American Women in Interwar Detroit* (Chapel Hill: University of North Carolina Press, 2001).

6. For more information on the demographics of the women who journeyed to northern cities, see Sharon Harley, "For the Good of Family and Race: Gender, Work, and Domestic Roles in the Black Community," *Signs* 15 (Winter 1990). For a discussion of the reasons black women migrated north, see Darlene Clark Hine, "Black Migration to the Urban Midwest: The Gender Dimension, 1915–1930," in Trotter, *Great Migration in Historical Perspective*, 127–146; Victoria Wolcott, *Remaking Respectability*; Bunch-Lyons, *Contested Terrain*.

7. Frances Kellor, "Southern Colored Girls in the North," *Charities*, 18 March 1905. For more information on Kellor's life, see John J. Miller, "Miss Americanizer: Frances Kellor," *Policy Review: the Journal of American Citizenship* 83 (May–June 1997): 64–65.

8. Kellor, "Southern Colored Girls in the North."

9. Hazel Carby, "Policing the Black Woman's Body in an Urban Context," *Critical Inquiry* 18 (Summer 1992): 741.

10. Quoted in Peiss, *Hope in a Jar*, 231.

11. Katherine Tillman, "Paying Professions for Colored Girls," *Voice of the Negro* (January and February 1907): 55.

12. "The Negro Woman in Business," *Indianapolis Freeman*, 20 September 1913.

13. Minutes of the Fourteenth Annual Convention of the National Negro Business League, 211.

14. Maggie Wilson to Madam C. J. Walker, 1 October 1913, in *Walker's Hair Parlor and Lelia College Brochure*, quoted in Bundles, *On Her Own Ground*, 179.

15. There are slight discrepancies between the census record and the statistics compiled in Bundles, *On Her Own Ground*, 353. While the numbers differ, both sets show at least fourfold growth in the number of black beauticians from 1900 to 1920. It must be remembered that these statistics do not indicate the number of women doing hair work in their homes or in informal settings. While I am focusing on beauty culture in northern cities, it is important to note that by the 1930s, beauty culture became an important part of life even in the rural South. See Hortense Powdermaker, *After Freedom: A Cultural Study in the Deep South* (1939; reprint, New York: Russell & Russell, 1966), 180.

16. *New York Age*, n.d., Hampton Institute Archives, quoted in Bundles, *On Her Own Ground*, 180.

17. Use of the word "straighten" to describe the styles and grooming practices advocated by Madam Walker and her agents is problematic since it was a word that Walker never used herself or in any of the promotional materials distributed by the company during her lifetime. Still, this is perhaps the best known word to describe the popular grooming practices of the day. For more on this, see Rooks, *Hair Raising*.

18. For a description of Fields's impressions of Mary Church Terrell, see the opening pages of White, *Too Heavy a Load*, 21–23.

19. Mamie Garvin Fields with Karen Fields, *Lemon Swamp and Other Places: A Carolina Memoir* (New York: Free Press, 1983), 189–190.

20. Ibid., 187–188.

21. Ibid., 151.

22. For example, in two biographical summaries of her life, one by Karen Fields in "Mamie Elizabeth Garvin Fields," in *Black Women in America: An Historical Encyclopedia*, ed. Darlene Clark Hine, Rosalyn Terborg-Penn, and Elsa Barkley Brown (Bloomington: Indiana University Press, 1993), 426–428, and the other by Shaw, *What a Woman Ought to Be*, there is no mention of Fields' profession as a Poro beauty culturist.

23. Fields, *Lemon Swamp*, 187.

24. Ibid., 188.

25. Kathryn Johnson, *What a Spelman Graduate Accomplished: Ezella Mathis Carter—A Biography and an Appeal* (Chicago, 1935). Johnson actually accompanied Carter on her southern journeys.

26. Ibid., 12.

27. Ibid., 14.

28. Ibid., 23.

29. Ibid., 32.

30. Terrell is quoted in Paula Giddings, *When and Where I Enter: The Impact of Black Women on Race and Sex in America* (New York: Bantam, 1984), 99.

31. Bruce is quoted in Giddings, *When and Where I Enter*, 100. Originally from Josephine Bruce, "What Has Education Done for Colored Women," *Voice of the Negro*, July 1905, 296.

32. Quoted in Bundles, *On Her Own Ground*, 77.

33. For a larger discussion of the connection between beauty products and hair straightening, see Rooks, *Hair Raising*; and Walker, *Style and Status*.

34. Nannie Helen Burroughs, "Not Color but Character," *Voice of the Negro*, July 1904. See the distinctions Peiss makes in *Hope in a Jar*, chapter 2, between make-up and cosmetics.

35. See Rooks, *Hair Raising*; and Evelyn Brooks Higginbotham, *Righteous Discontent: The Women's Movement in the Black Baptist Church, 1880–1920* (Cambridge: Harvard University Press, 1993).

36. See Mrs. B. S. Lynk, *A Complete Course in Hair Straightening and Beauty Culture* (Memphis: 20th Century Art, 1919), 7.

37. Ibid., 6.

38. *Poro College in Pictures.*

39. *"Poro College 9th Anniversary Celebration Program,"* Box 1, Robert O. French Papers, Vivian G. Harsh Collection, Carter G. Woodson Regional Library, Chicago Public Library (hereinafter cited as VGHC).

40. *Poro College in Pictures.*

41. Bundles, *On Her Own Ground*, 75.

42. For a recounting of Walker's appearance at the NACW's eighth biennial, see Bundles, *On Her Own Ground*, 129.

43. This speech to the NACW convention in Denver 1918 is recounted in Bundles, *On Her Own Ground*, 227–228.

44. Davis, *Lifting as They Climb*, 263.

45. F. B. Ransom to Ella Crocker, 19 November 1914, Box 9, Folder 1, MCJW, IHS.

46. For more information on Annie Malone's philanthropy, see Gwendolyn Keita Robinson, "Class, Race, and Gender: A Transcultural Theoretical and Sociohistorical Analysis of Cosmetic Institutions and Practices to 1920" (Ph.D. diss., University of Chicago, 1984).

47. Madam Walker to F. B. Ransom, 17 April 1917, Box 1, Folder 4, MCJW, IHS.

48. Ibid.

49. George Schuyler, "Madam C. J. Walker: Pioneer Big Business Woman of America," *Messenger*, August 1924, 264.

50. Madam Walker to F. B. Ransom, 22 February 1916, Box 1, Folder 3, MCJW, IHS.

51. Madam Walker to F. B. Ransom, 18 September 1916, Box 1 Folder 5, MCJW, IHS.

52. See Darlene Clark Hine, *Black Women in White: Racial Conflict and Cooperation in the Nursing Profession, 1890–1950* (Bloomington: Indiana University Press, 1989), xv.

53. Almetto Alexander, interview by Karen Ferguson, 11 June 1993, Behind the Veil Collection, John Hope Franklin Research Center for African and African American Documentation, Duke University, Durham, N.C. (hereafter cited as BTV).

54. Walker Beauty Colleges, MCJW, IHS.

55. Madam Walker to F. B. Ransom, 26 September 1916, Box 1, Folder 5, MCJW, IHS.

56. See Blackwelder, *Stylin' Jim Crow*. Although she deals primarily with the Franklin Beauty School in Texas, many of the same tropes existed nationwide.

57. "C. J. Walker College Graduates Large Class," *Negro World*, 21 February 1925.

58. See Myrtle Evangeline Pollard, "Harlem as It Is," vol. 1, "Sociological Notes on Harlem's Social Life" (master's thesis, College of the City of New York, 1935).

59. Hine argues that black professionals as early as the 1890s "embraced the ideology of self-determination" and began "the arduous task of creating a separate network of professional associations." Darlene Clark Hine, "The Intersection of Race, Class, and Gender in the Nursing Profession," in *Speak Truth to Power: Black Professional Class in the United States History*, by Darlene Clark Hine (Brooklyn, N.Y.: Carlson, 1996), 171.

60. Vernice Mark, *The National Beauty Culturists' League, Inc.*, 2nd ed. (Detroit: Harlo Press, 1994), 18.

61. Quoted in Bundles, *On Her Own Ground*, 212–213.

62. For more information on the founding of the National Negro Cosmetic Manufacturer's Association, see "Minutes," 5 September 1917, Box 1, Folder 9, MCJW, IHS; and "Press Release," n.d., Box 1, Folder 10, MCJW, IHS.

63. See Peiss, *Hope in a Jar*; and Willett, *Permanent Waves*.

64. Willett, in *Permanent Waves*, describes a dormant white hairdressing industry until at least the 1920s, asserting that prior to World War I, the services of a cosmetologist were limited to women of the middle class. She notes that unlike many black women, white women were not encouraged to enter into the industry (30–34).

65. Proceedings of the National Negro Business League's Thirteenth Annual Meeting.

66. Julie Willett considers those in the hair care industry as doing "women's service work" and links "hairdressing" to other "female dominated service occupations such as retail sales and waitressing in which women as workers faced the contradictory demands of managers and customers." *Permanent Waves*, 10. Both Willett and her reviewers place this work within labor history. While certainly most black beauty culturists did not achieve the wealth and status of Malone and Walker, the industry

was not looked at as a service industry until after the Great Depression, and even then the needs of shop and school owners dominated. The lure of the industry was its ability to make black women entrepreneurs and professionals.

67. Mark, *National Beauty Culturists' League*, 21, 31.

68. Willett, *Permanent Waves*, 30

69. Mark, *National Beauty Culturists' League*, 37.

70. Marjorie Stewart Joyner (hereafter cited as MSJ), interview with Michael Flug, Marjorie Stewart Joyner Papers (hereafter cited as MSJP), Vivian G. Harsh Collection, Carter G. Woodson Regional Library, Chicago Public Library (hereafter cited as VGHC).

71. Willett, *Permanent Waves*, 6.

72. For a larger discussion of the move toward professionalism in the medical industry and its impact on black women, especially in the fields of childbirth and midwifery, see Hine, *Black Women in White*; and Susan Smith, *Sick and Tired of Being Sick and Tired: Black Women's Health Activism in America, 1890–1950* (Philadelphia: University of Pennsylvania Press, 1995).

73. Jervis Anderson, *A. Philip Randolph: A Biographical Portrait* (New York: Ferrar, Straus, Giroux, 1972), 70.

74. Ibid., 72.

75. Ibid.

76. William Dufty quoted in Melinda Chateauvert, *Marching Together: Women of the Brotherhood of Sleeping Car Porters* (Urbana: University of Illinois Press, 1998), 8.

77. Ibid.

78. Anderson, *A. Philip Randolph*, 73.

79. Ibid., 70.

80. See Robinson. "Class, Race, and Gender," 395.

81. Beth Tompkins Bates argues that 1925 witnessed the burgeoning of a new moment in radical black politics, which she describes as "new-crowd protest politics." In particular, Bates credits the Brotherhood of Sleeping Car Porters and A. Phillip Randolph for advocating a politics that linked economic and political citizenship rights. This shift, as Bates notes, was initially met by opposition by many blacks in positions of leadership. Black beauty culturists would come to embrace a similar agenda in the 1940s. Perhaps this transition period was difficult for Lucille Randolph's clients and colleagues to support, thereby causing a decline in her business. For a larger discussion of the shift in black politics that occurs about 1925, see Beth Tompkins Bates, *Pullman Porters and the Rise of Protest Politics in Black America, 1925–1945* (Chapel Hill: University of North Carolina Press, 2001).

82. Richards, *Maida Springer Kemp*, 34–35.

83. Judith Stein, "Marcus Garvey," in *The Reader's Companion to American History*, ed. Eric Foner and John Garraty (New York: Houghton Mifflin, 1991), 440–441.

84. According to Barbara Bair, "It is very difficult to track employment of Garveyites, even through mention of them in the *Negro World*, because the focus there was on

UNIA activism and opinion, versus what a person 'was' or 'did' for a job or profession outside the movement (they 'were' the movement/activists/auxiliary members, and not elevator operators, nurses, beauticians, lawyers, etc., when they participated in the UNIA dialogue and activities)." Barbara Bair to the author, e-mail, 15 September 2002.

85. From Amy Jacques Garvey, *Garvey and Garveyism* (New York: Collier Books, 1970), 86, quoted in Walker, *History of Black Business in America*, 219.

86. Tony Martin, *Race First: The Ideological and Organizational Struggles of Marcus Garvey and the UNIA* (Boston: Majority Press, 1976), 33.

87. Emory Tolbert, *UNIA and Black Los Angeles: Ideology and Community in the American Garvey Movement* (Los Angeles: UCLA Press, 1980).

88. Walker, *History of Black Business in America*, 222.

89. For more analysis of the economic dimensions and ideologies of Marcus Garvey and the UNIA, see Milfred Fierce, "Economic Aspects of the Marcus Garvey Movement," *Black Scholar* 3 (March–April 1972): 50–61; "Garvey and Negro Business," *Negro World*, 7 April 1923; and Mrs. Johnie Terry, "Talk Alone Cannot Liberate a Race," *Negro World*, 10 July 1926.

90. For a larger discussion of the gendered nature of Garvey's racial pride, see Martin Summers, *Manliness and Its Discontents: The Black Middle Class and the Transformation of Masculinity, 1900–1930* (Chapel Hill: University of North Carolina Press, 2004); Mitchell, *Righteous Propagation*; Barbara Bair, "True Women, Real Men: Gender Ideology, and Social Roles in the Garvey Movement," in *Gendered Domains: Rethinking Public and Private in Women's History*, ed. Dorothy O. Helly and Susan Reverby (Ithaca, N.Y.: Cornell University Press, 1992): 154–166; Barbara Bair, "Re-negotiating Liberty: Garveyism, Women, and Grassroots Organizing in Virginia," in *Women of the American South*, ed. Christie Anne Farham (New York: New York University Press, 1997): 220–240; Beryl Satter, "Marcus Garvey, Father Divine, and the Gender Politics of Race Difference and Race Neutrality," *American Quarterly* 48 (March 1996): 43–76; Ula Taylor, *The Veiled Garvey: The Life and Times of Amy Jacques Garvey* (Chapel Hill: University of North Carolina Press, 2002); and Kate Dossett, *Bridging Race Divides: Black Nationalism, Feminism, and Integration in the United States, 1896–1935* (Gainesville: University of Florida, 2008), especially chapter 4; also see White's discussion in *Too Heavy a Load*, chap. 4.

91. Quoted in White, *Too Heavy a Load*, 121.

92. "Negro Women Leaving Domestic Service Alone," *Negro World*, 6 December 1924.

93. Ula Taylor, "Negro Women are Great Thinkers as well as Doers: Amy Jacques Garvey and Community Feminism, 1924–1927," *Journal of Women's History* 12 (Summer 2000): 112.

94. The full text of Marcus Garvey's poem, "The Black Woman," is quoted in Rupert Lewis and Patrick Bryan, eds., *Garvey: His Work and Impact* (Trenton, N.J.: Africa World Press, 1991), 75.

95. "For the Searcher of Beauty," *Negro World*, 17 January 1925; "True Beauty Not of Face but of Heart and Soul," *Negro World*, 8 November 1924.

96. Chandler Owen, "Good Looks Supremacy: A Perspicacious Perusal of the Potencies of Pulchritude by a Noted Authority," *Messenger*, March 1924.

97. The *Negro World* was certainly not the only black newspaper that relied heavily on advertising dollars from the black beauty industry. One need only to examine the pages of the *Messenger*, *Crisis*, *Pittsburgh Courier*, and *Chicago Defender* to see that the black beauty industry almost single handedly supported the black press. For further analysis, see Owen, "Good Looks Supremacy."

98. "Are We Proud of our Black Skins and Curly Hair?" *Negro World*, 1 August 1925.

99. "I Am a Negro—And Beautiful," *Negro World*, 10 July 1926.

100. *Negro World*, 1 August 1925.

101. Bair, "True Women, Real Men," 165.

102. Ibid., 165.

103. "Marcus Garvey's Contribution to His Race," *Negro World*, 28 August 1926.

104. See Advertisement on Woman's Page, *Negro World*, 20 November 1926.

105. *New York Amsterdam News*, 6 July 1940.

106. For more information on the ILDP see Judith Stein, *The World of Marcus Garvey: Race and Class in Modern Society* (Baton Rouge, La.: Louisiana University Press, 1991), 50–52.

107. Jacques Garvey, "Shopping at This Time of Year a Pleasure," *Negro World*, December 13, 1924.

108. *Negro World*, 24 August and 7 September 1929.

109. *Negro World*, 24 July 1926.

110. *Negro World*, 21 February 1925.

111. See *Negro World*, 8 August and 24 January 1925. It is important to point out that Burrows did not garner enough votes to win.

112. For the decline of the NACW, see White, *Too Heavy a Load*. Also, Tera Hunter in *To 'Joy My Freedom: Black Women's Lives and Labors After the Civil War* (Cambridge: Harvard University Press, 1998), describes how blues music and dance halls operated as an expression of working-class freedom in direct opposition to the aims of middle-class reformers and undermined their authority.

Chapter 3. Redefining Entrepreneurship and Activism in the 1930s and 1940s

The title of the chapter is from John F. Fenwick, "Reflections," in *National Beauty Creator*, July 1935, quoted in Pollard, "Harlem as It Is," 1:56–57.

1. Pollard, "Harlem as It Is," 1:43. LeRoy Jeffries noted 382 beauty shops in Harlem at the height of the Great Depression in "The Decay of the Beauty Parlor Industry in Harlem." *Opportunity: Journal of Negro Life* 15 (January 1938): 349–360.

2. For example, Walker, *History of Black Business in America*, 227, shows that only 83 out of 237 businesses in a mile-long strip on Chicago's South Side were black owned in 1938.

3. See Table 2.1 in Cheryl Lynn Greenberg, "Or Does It Explode?" *Black Harlem in Great Depression* (New York: Oxford University Press, 1991), 44, which shows that both black men and black women in Manhattan, Chicago, Detroit, and Birmingham were disproportionately represented among the unemployed.

4. For statistics on the financial decline of the beauty culture industry, see Walker, *Style and Status,* 23.

5. Annie Turnbo Malone to Poro Dealers, 1930, Box 1, Robert O. French Papers, VGHC.

6. See Ethel Erickson, *Employment Conditions in Beauty Shops: A Study of Four Cities,* U.S. Department of Labor, Bulletin of the Women's Bureau No.133 (Washington, D.C.: Government Printing Office, 1935); Works Progress Administration, "Harlem Beauty Shops," *American Life Histories: Manuscripts from the Federal Writers' Project, 1936–1940,* http://lcweb2.loc.gov/ammem/wpaintro/wpahome/ (accessed 16 February 2003); and Jeffries, "Decay of the Beauty Parlor Industry in Harlem," 349–360.

7. Erickson, Employment Conditions in Beauty Shops, 37.

8. Ibid., 39.

9. Jones, *Labor of Love, Labor of Sorrow,* 214–215.

10. Pollard, "Harlem as It Is," 1:56.

11. The notion of the black beauty industry as "depression proof" was touted by Fenwick, "Reflections," 56–57, and in the advertisements of Sara Spencer Washington's Apex Company.

12. This categorization is similar to a categorization of beauty shops by a white Cincinnati beauty shop owner, Murray Kane, who found "four classes" of beauty salons: salons in department stores, average beauty shops, large downtown shops, and shops operated in homes. See Willett, *Permanent Waves,* 66–67.

13. Works Progress Administration, "Harlem Beauty Shops."

14. See Mathilde Bunton, "Negro Business-Policy," Negroes in Illinois, Illinois Writers Project, Works Progress Administration, Box 35, Folder 11, VGHC.

15. See both volumes of Pollard's "Harlem as It Is."

16. Pollard, "Harlem as It Is," vol.2, "The Negro Business and Economic Community" (master's thesis, College of the City of New York, 1937), 243. For a larger discussion of beauty school education in general, see Blackwelder, *Stylin' Jim Crow.*

17. "Biographical Sketch of Miss Ruth Matilda Carter," Marie Steward Smith Collection, Afro-American Museum of Philadelphia (hereafter cited as AAMP).

18. "History of the Craig School of Beauty Culture," Alberta Colvard Collection, AAMP.

19. "Souvenir of Poro College," Box 2, Robert O. French Papers, VGHC; "Friends Gather at Poro College," *Chicago Defender,* 22 April 1933, 21; Thelma Wheaton is quoted in Bates, *Pullman Porters,* 220–221.

20. For more information on the Walker Building and Theater, see Gloria J. Gibson-Hudson, "'To all classes; to all races; this house is dedicated': The Walker Theater Revisited," Indiana Historical Society *Black History News and Notes* 35 (February 1989); and Mark David Higbee, "W. E. B. Du Bois, F. B. Ransom, the Madam Walker Company, and Black Business Leadership in the 1930s," *Indiana Magazine of History* 89 (June 1993): 101–124. Higbee notes that the Walker Building faced financial difficulty as a result of the Great Depression and that it was a "financial drain for the [Walker] Company" (111). The Walker Theatre became a separate legal entity and was leased to a white businessman.

21. Sobek, Matthew, "Detailed occupations—nonwhite females: 1860–1990 [Part 1]." Table Ba2845–3081 in *Historical Statistics of the United States, Earliest Times to the Present: Millennial Edition*, edited by Susan B. Carter, Scott Sigmund Gartner, Michael R. Haines, Alan L. Olmstead, Richard Sutch, and Gavin Wright (New York: Cambridge University Press, 2006). http://dx.doi.org.ezproxy.lib.utexas.edu/10.1017/ISBN-9780511132971.Ba1033–4213 (accessed May 26, 2009).

22. Robert L. Boyd, "Survivalist Entrepreneurship among Urban Blacks during the Great Depression: A Test of the Disadvantage Theory of Business Enterprise," *Social Science Quarterly* 81 (December 2000): 972.

23. For statistical evidence of the growth in the number of black female beauticians in northern cities with the highest unemployment rates, see Boyd's findings, "Survivalist Entrepreneurs," 978–980.

24. Mahalia Jackson, *Movin' On Up* (New York: Hawthorn Books, 1966), 49.

25. Ibid., 80.

26. Ibid.

27. For an insightful study of the connections between these two industries, see Baldwin, *Chicago's New Negroes*.

28. The historical record on Sara Spencer Washington's early life is sparse. I have seen three different years for her birth: 1881 (Robinson, "Class, Race, and Gender"), 1889 (Jim Waltzer, "Sara Spencer Washington," http://www.shorecast.com/html/Features/Legends/legendsswah.html/ [accessed 21 December 2001]), and 1894 (Marianna Davis, *Contributions of Black Women in America*, vol.1 [South Carolina: Kenday Press, 1982]).

29. For more information on Atlantic City's early black community, see Herbert James Foster, "Urban Experience of Blacks in Atlantic City, New Jersey, 1850–1915" (Ph.D. diss., Rutgers University, 1981).

30. Apex advertisement quoted in Peiss, *Hope in a Jar*, 237. Katina Manko also describes the Avon Company, known during the 1930s as the California Perfume Company, as having a "depression proof business strategy." The company had an average increase of sales of 10–15 percent every year from 1930 to 1939. Manko attributes Avon's ability to prosper to (1) its unique market niche in rural America, (2) its devotion to selling business opportunities to women, and (3) its strong commitment to maintaining door-to-door sales and services. In many ways, the success of

the Apex Company and other sectors of the black beauty industry (namely, beauty education) occurred for similar reasons—it had a unique mark, a devotion to business opportunity, and a strong personal commitment to its customers. See Katina Manko, "A Depression Proof Business Strategy: The California Perfume Company's Motivational Literature," in *Beauty and Business: Gender, Commerce, and Culture in Modern America*, ed. Philip Scranton (New York: Routledge Press, 2001), 142–168.

31. Frank Linn, "Ethiopian Invasion in America," *Apex News*, (November-December 1935).

32. Wesley Curtwright, "Negro Beauty Parlors in New York," WPA Writers Project, 1936.

33. "Sara Spencer Washington," in Marianna Davis, "Beauty Culture, Fashion, and Modeling," in *Contributions of Black Women in America,* vol. 1, by Marianna Davis (South Carolina: Kenday Press, 1982).

34. Jim Waltzer, "Sara Spencer Washington."

35. While domestic work was always a profession black women could fall back on, even that work was limited in the 1930s. Employers who could afford such luxuries during the Depression often hired whites and many black women in cities like New York who lined up on street corners in what was called "slave markets" waiting to be hired for low-paying day labor. See White, *Too Heavy a Load*. Not even the professionalization of domestic labor that Burroughs advocated could withstand these setbacks.

36. "Nannie Burrough's Address at Apex Commencement," *Apex News* (January/ February/March 1938). See Peiss's discussion of the shift in black beauty culture from race politics to a discourse on sexual attractiveness. *Hope in a Jar*, 237.

37. Of beauticians in this period, Victoria Wolcott argues that "although beauty culture had long been lauded as a model of female entrepreneurship, during the Great Depression, African American beauticians and entrepreneurs gained even more prominence for the race." *Remaking Respectability*, 173.

38. For a larger discussion of the attention the federal government was giving to the beauty industry, see Willett, *Permanent Waves*.

39. Vivian Morris, "Harlem Beauty Shops."

40. This law did, however, address some health concerns of beauticians who often complained of beautician's eczema, headaches, and sore throats from using certain chemical concoctions. According to Julie Willett, black women were particularly prone to such work-related illnesses. *Permanent Waves*, 73–74. For a larger discussion of the federal food, drug, and cosmetic laws, see Gwen Kay, *Dying to Be Beautiful: The Fight for Safe Cosmetics* (Columbus: Ohio State University Press, 2005).

41. For example, Julie Willett's discussion of the "hundreds of women working in the beauty industry [who] wrote to the federal government for answers, advice, and help" (87) does not recount any direct requests from black beauty culturists to the federal government. My own research has yielded little evidence of beauty operators asking for government intervention. Ethel Erickson's 1935 report states, "At the time

of this survey, because of the absence of an industry code and the fact that very few Negro shops had signed the President's Reemployment Agreement, wages had not been raised nor hours of work reduced in these shops." *Employment Conditions in Beauty Shops,* 42.

42. James Kefford quoted in Willett, *Permanent Waves,* 105.

43. Ethel Erickson's report to the Department of Labor Women's Bureau explained that more than two-fifths of black beauty operators worked more than fifty-four hours a week while 50 percent of white women worked less than a forty-eight-hour week on average. Erickson explains, "The schedules seem to reflect the long days of domestic workers, the group that furnished a large part of the customers of Negro shops." *Employment Conditions in Beauty Shops,* 42.

44. Edna Emme and Nathan Jacobs, *NHCA's Golden Years: From the Historical Records, Minutes, and Reports of the National Hairdressers and Cosmetologists Association and the Reminiscences of Edna L. Emme* (Racine, Wisc.: Western Publishing, 1970), 23.

45. Willett, *Permanent Waves,* 96.

46. Ibid., 90.

47. Erickson, *Employment Conditions in Beauty Shops,* 37.

48. Ibid., 43.

49. Jeffries, "Decay of the Beauty Parlor Industry in Harlem," 49.

50. Elizabeth Cardozo Barker, interview by Marcia McAdoo Greenlee, 8 December 1976, in *The Black Women Oral History History Project: The Arthur and Elizabeth Schlesinger Library on the History of Women in America,* ed. Ruth Edmonds Hill (Westport, Conn.: Meckler Press, 1991), 114.

51. Pollard, "Harlem as It Is," 2:248.

52. Willett argues that the NRA standards perhaps came the closest to a national code, but that the national discussion essentially came to a close once the NRA was declared unconstitutional. *Permanent Waves,* 119.

53. Mark, *National Beauty Culturists' League,* 181.

54. Ibid., 180.

55. Ibid., 19.

56. White, *Too Heavy a Load,* 155.

57. Michael Flug, "Marjorie Stewart Joyner: Entrepreneur, Educator, Philanthropist," in Jessie Carney Smith, ed., *Notable Black American Women,* bk. 2 (New York: Gale Research Group, 1996), 367.

58. Howell was indeed an anomaly. Ethel Erickson, for example, only found fifteen black women working in the 390 white salons she chronicled in her report, *Employment Conditions in Beauty Shops,* 3. None of the black women–owned salons were frequented by whites. "Beauty Salon for the Social Register," *Ebony,* May 1949, 31.

59. Christine Moore Howell, *Beauty Culture and Care of the Hair* (New Brunswick, N.J.: Hill Publishing, 1936).

60. Based on Cordelia Greene Johnson's success with the Modern Beauticians'

Association of New Jersey and her tireless campaign for Howell's representation on the New Jersey Beauty Board, Johnson was elected as president of the NBCL in 1939, a post she held until 1957. See Mark, *National Beauty Culturists' League*, 34–35.

61. All direct quotes from Rose Morgan, interview by James Briggs Murray, 21 April 1988. Schomburg Center for Research in Black Culture, New York, New York.

62. Pollard, "Harlem as It Is," 1:43.

63. Jeffries, "Decay of the Beauty Parlor Industry in Harlem," 50.

64. Erickson, *Employment Conditions in Beauty Shops,* 37.

65. "House of Beauty: Rose-Meta Salon Is Biggest Negro Beauty Parlor in World," *Ebony* (May 1946).

66. State of New York Department of Labor, *Beauty Service Minimum Wage Board, 1947* (Albany: New York State Printing Office, 1947).

67. Barker interview by Greenlee, 8 December 1976, 97.

68. Ibid.

69. Margaret Cardozo Holmes, interview by Marcia McAdoo Greenlee, 9 November 1977, in *The Black Women Oral History History Project: The Arthur and Elizabeth Schlesinger Library on the History of Women in America*, ed. Ruth Edmonds Hill (Westport, Conn.: Meckler Press, 1991), 57.

70. Barker interviewed by Greenlee, 8 December 1976, 115.

71. "Beauty Salon for the Social Register," 32.

72. J. H. Jemison to Faye Stewart, 8 January 1939, Box 30, Folder 1, Franklin Papers, Metropolitan Research Collection, Houston Public Library (hereafter cited as FP, HPL).

73. See Souvenir Program, Tenth Annual Convention, Texas State Association and Beauty Culturist League, October 4–7, 1953, Box 7, FP, HPL.

74. Transcript of the film The *Black Press: Soldiers Without Soldiers*, http://www.pbs.org/blackpress/film/index.html/ (accessed 5 June 2003). A photo of the Double V hairdo is also displayed in the documentary.

75. Brenda L. Moore, *To Serve My Country, To Serve My Race: The Story of the Only African Amercan WACs Stationed Overseas During World War II* (New York: New York University Press, 1996), 186.

76. Advertisement quoted in Rhonda Mawhood, "Tales to Curl Your Hair: African Americans Beauty Parlors in Jim Crow Durham" (unpublished seminar paper, Duke University, 1993, author's possession), 7.

77. Lawrence Samuel, *Pledging Allegiance: American Identity and the Bond Drive of World War II* (Washington, D.C.: Smithsonian Institution Press, 1997), xiv, xxi.

78. For more information about why the government chose not to record giving according to these demographic categories, see ibid.

79. "Maude I. Gaston," *Many Ways to Beautify*, June 1974, Alberta Colvard Collection, AAMP.

80. See Samuel, *Pledging Allegiance*, 196.

81. Pamphlet listing the places were war bonds could be purchased in Philadelphia;

sixteen beauty shops were listed out of the thirty-two locations. Marie Steward Smith Collection, AAMP.

82. See Samuel, *Pledging Allegiance*, 196.

83. Marva Louis to MSJ, 16 September 1942, Box 8, MSJP.

84. For more information on Mayor Edward Kelley and the work black women did in Chicago during the war, see Lionel Kimble, "'I Too Serve America': African American Women War Workers in Chicago, 1940–1945," *Journal of the Illinois State Historical Society* 93 (2000): 415–434. William Pickens to MSJ, 11 March 1948, Box 8, MSJP.

85. Bates, *Pullman Porters*, 7.

86. Ibid.

87. Randolph quoted in Bates, *Pullman Porters*, 155–156.

Chapter 4. The International Presence of African American Beauticians in the Postwar Era

The chapter title is from Bethune, quoted in *Ebony*, August 1942, 41.

1. Mary McLeod Bethune, "Writer Pays Tribute to Negro Beauticians as Ambassadors," *Chicago Defender*, 15 May 1954.

2. For more information on Robeson and Baker's clashes with the U.S. government, see Borstelmann, *The Cold War and the Color Line: American Race Relations in the Global Arena* (Cambridge: Harvard University Press, 2001), especially chapter 2.

3. The historiography on race and American foreign policy in the cold war era is rich and expanding. The most useful texts are Mary L. Dudziak, *Cold War Civil Rights: Race and the Image of American Democracy* (Princeton, N.J.: Princeton University Press, 2000); Borstelmann, *Cold War and the Color Line*; Brenda Gayle Plummer, ed., *Window on Freedom: Race, Civil Rights, and Foreign Affairs, 1945–1988* (Chapel Hill: University of North Carolina Press, 2003); and Brenda Gayle Plummer, *Rising Wind: Black Americans and United States' Foreign Policy, 1935–1960* (Chapel Hill: University of North Carolina Press, 1996); William Jelani Cobb, "Antidote to Revolution: Afro-American Anticommunism and the Quest for Civil Rights, 1931–1945" (Ph.D. diss., Rutgers University, 2003); Penny Von Eschen, "Challenging Cold War Habits: African Americans, Race, and Foreign Policy," *Diplomatic History* 20 (Fall 1996): 627–638; and Penny Von Eschen, *Satchmo Blows Up the World: Jazz Ambassadors Play the Cold War* (Cambridge: Harvard University Press, 2004). Shockley's discussion of the ideological negotiations made by black clubwomen in the Cold War is particularly insightful. "*We, Too, Are Americans*," chap. 3.

4. To better understand my preference of the term "professional class" as opposed to the more traditional "middle class," see Darlene Clark Hine, *Speak Truth to Power: Black Professional Class in United States History* (Brooklyn, N.Y.: Carlson, 1996). I also find Michele Mitchell's use of "aspiring class" useful in describing the complicated and tenuous class position of African American beauticians. Mitchell, *Righteous Propagation*.

5. MSJ interview by Michael Flug.

6. Ibid.

7. For more information on segregated beauty training, see Blackwelder, *Styling Jim Crow*; and Julie Willett, *Permanent Waves*.

8. Bettye Collier-Thomas, "The National Council of Negro Women," in Darlene Clark Hine, Rosalyn Terborg-Penn, and Elsa Barkley Brown, eds., *Black Women in America: An Historical Encyclopedia* (Brooklyn: Carlson, 1993), 856.

9. See White, *Too Heavy a Load*.

10. Wolcott, *Remaking Respectability*; and White, *Too Heavy a Load*, especially chapter 5.

11. MSJ interview by Michael Flug.

12. Bethune to MSJ, 19 April 1944, MSJP.

13. Ransom to Bethune, 10 February 1944, Series 18, Box 6, Folder 10, Records of the NCNW—National Association of Madam C. J. Walker Agents, Mary McLeod Bethune Council House, National Parks Service, Washington, D.C. (hereafter cited as MMBCH). However, Ransom later warned Joyner that soliciting funds directly from students in beauty college was not a good idea since "students feel that they are out of enough money to take care of their tuition, tools and other expenses." Ransom to MSJ, 23 February 1943, Series 18, Box 6, Folder 10, Records of the NCNW—National Association of Madam C. J. Walker Agents, MMBCH.

14. Violet Reynolds to MSJ, 23 April 1947, Box 8, MSJP.

15. See Flug, "Marjorie Stewart Joyner," 367. Bethune quoted in *Ebony*, August 1942, 41.

16. *Bulletin* 18 (November/December 1947–January 1948), Box 6, Folder 10, Records of the National Council of Negro Women—National Beauty Culturists League, MMBCH.

17. United Beauty School Owners and Teacher's Association, *Bulletin* No. 5, June 1946 Series 18, Box 6, Folder 10, Records of the National Council of Negro Women—National Beauty Culturists League, MMBCH.

18. Handwritten note, MSJ to unknown, n.d., Series 18, Box 8, Folder 12, Records of the National Council of Negro Women—United Beauty School Owners and Teacher's Association, MMBCH.

19. See Toni Costonie, "Renaissance Woman: Marjorie Stewart Joyner," *Renaissance*, November/December 1990, 6; Marjorie Stewart Joyner Hall was dedicated in Joyner's presence on October 28, 1982.

20. Press Release—UBSOTA and ACPO, 24 April 1952, Box 30, Folder 15, FP, HPL.

21. Ibid.

22. White served as executive secretary of the NAACP from 1931 until his death in 1955. For more on Walter White, see Walter White, *A Man Called White: The Autobiography of Walter White* (New York: Viking Oress, 1948); Kenneth Janken, *Walter White, Mr. NAACP* (Chapel Hill: University of North Carolina Press, 2006).

23. Walter White quoted in Millery Polyne, "Modernizing the Race: Political and

Cultural Engagements Between African Americans and Haitians, 1930–1964" (Ph.D. diss., University of Michigan, 2003), 75, 79.

24. Press release, UBSOTA and ACPO, 24 April 1952, Box 30, Folder 15, FB, HPL.

25. According to Harvey Levenstein, "Only one kind of visitor seemed immune from French disapproval and criticism [during the Cold War]: African Americans." *We'll Always Have Paris: American Tourists in France Since 1930* (Chicago: University of Chicago Press, 2004), 147.

26. Bethune, *Chicago Defender*, May 1954.

27. Unless otherwise noted, information on the European voyages has been derived from Katie Whickham, "Our Trip: Memoirs of Our European Tour, 1956," Marie Steward Smith Collection, AAMP; and "Beauty Pilgrimage: 195 Women Learn Latest Continent Hair Styles," *Ebony*, August 1954, 38–44.

28. MSJ to Amory Houghton, 22 January 1960, MSJP.

29. Dudziak, *Cold War Civil Rights*, 56.

30. Von Eschen, "Challenging Cold War Habits," 635.

31. Marjorie Stewart Joyner, "Our European Scrapbook: Some Clippings of a Memorable Trip," *Beauty Trade*, October 1954.

32. MSJ interview by Flug; emphasis added.

33. According to Andrew Wiese, African American incomes tripled during the 1940s and increased by another 50 percent during the 1950s. Andrew Wiese, *Places of Their Own: African American Suburbanization in the Twentieth Century* (Chicago: University of Chicago Press, 2004), 124.

34. For the changing consumption practices of African Americans in the postwar period see Robert Weems, *Desegregating the Dollar: African American Consumerism in the Twentieth Century* (New York: New York University Press, 1998), chapter 2 and Jason Chambers, *Madison Avenue and the Color Line: African Americans in the Advertising Industry* (Philadelphia: University of Pennsylvania Press, 2007), chapter 2.

35. Mrs. Joseph N. Grant to MSJ and Willa Lee Calvin, 1 October 1962, MSJP (unprocessed).

36. "European Travellers," *Beauty Trade*, September, 1958, 39.

37. "Back to Vacation Coifs," *Beauty Trade*, September 1957, cover.

38. "Beauty Pilgrimage," *Ebony*, 44.

39. For more on the politics of respectability, see Higginbotham, *Righteous Discontent*, chapter 7.

40. For a firsthand account of the trips from a beautician's point of view, see Whickham, "Our Trip."

41. Whickham, "Our Trip," p. 2.

42. "Travel by Freddye," *Pittsburgh Courier*, February 17, 1962.

43. E. Franklin Frazier, *Black Bourgeoisie* (1962; reprint, New York: Free Press, 1997), 192, 194.

44. "Beauty Pilgrimage," *Ebony*, 46.

45. Bethune, *Chicago Defender*, August 1954.

46. Borstelmann, *Cold War and the Color Line*.

47. See Levenstein, *We'll Always Have Paris*, 148–149.

48. Whickham, "Our Trip," 23.

49. Ibid., 20.

50. Ibid., 22.

51. "Eastern News," *Beauty Trade,* April 1958.

52. "School News," *Beauty Trade*, May 1958, 33.

53. "Daughter of Ghana Ambassador Studying at Mme. Walker College in Washington," *Beauty Trade*, April 1960, 34.

54. "Haiti Gets First Negro Beauty School," *Beauty Trade*, November 1960, 57.

55. "Bermuda's Only Beauty School Graduates 12 in First Year," *Beauty Trade*, February 1961, 37.

56. "Beauty Trade Introduces Pressing for First Time at Puerto Rico Show," *Beauty Trade*, 30–31.

57. Ibid.

58. "Around the World," *Beauty Trade*, November 1961.

59. Grant to MSJ and Calvin, 1 October 1962.

Chapter 5. Southern Beauty Activists and the Modern Black Freedom Struggle

1. Anne Moody, *Coming of Age in Mississippi* (1968; reprint, New York: Delta Trade Paperbacks, 2004), 293.

2. Christina Royster-Hemby, "Reflected in the Lens," *Baltimore City Paper*, 30 March 2005, http://www.citypaper.com/arts/prinready.asp?id=9785/ (accessed December 15, 2005).

3. National Beauty Culturists League, *Daily Bulletin*, 11 August 1948, Series 18, Box 7 Folder 3, Records of the National Council of Negro Women, National Beauty Culturists League, MMBCH.

4. For a larger discussion of the nature and scope of postwar black women's activism, see Martha Biondi, *To Stand and Fight: The Struggle for Civil Rights in Postwar New York City* (Cambridge: Harvard University Press, 2003); Shockley, "We, Too, Are Americans"; Gretchen Lemke-Santangelo, *Abiding Women: African American Migrant Women and the East Bay Community* (Chapel Hill: University of North Carolina Press, 1996); Shockley, "We, Too, Are Americans"; Christina Greene, *Our Separate Ways: Women and the Black Freedom Movement in Durham, North Carolina* (Chapel Hill: University of North Carolina Press, 2005); and Laurie Green, *Battling the Plantation Mentality: Memphis and the Black Freedom Struggle* (Chapel Hill: University of North Carolina Press, 2007).

5. Convention information is derived from Mark, *National Beauty Culturists' League,* 36.

6. Martin Luther King to Katie Whickham, 7 July 1958, in Martin Luther King Jr., Peter Halloran, and Clayborne Carson, eds., *The Papers of Martin Luther King, Jr.*, vol. 4, *Symbol of the Movement* (Berkeley and Los Angeles: University of California Press, 1992).

7. Quoted in Belinda Robnett, *How Long? How Long? African American Women and the Struggle for Civil Rights* (New York: Oxford University Press, 1997), 93.

8. See Robnett's discussion of the gender politics of the SCLC in ibid., 93.

9. Mark, *National Beauty Culturists' League*, 288–289.

10. Louis Martin, interviewed by Michael L. Gillette, 12 June 1986, Internet copy, Lyndon Baines Johnson Library, University of Texas, Austin. For more information on Louis Martin see, Alex Poinsett, *Walking with the Presidents: Louis Martin and the Rising of Black Political Power* (New York: Rowan and Littlefield, 2000).

11. Martin interviewed by Gillette.

12. "So This Is Washington," *Chicago Defender*, 24 May 1958.

13. Ethel L. Payne to MSJ, 11 January 1958, MSJP.

14. South Carolina Beauticians Club (1936), North Carolina State Beauticians and Cosmetologists Association (1939), the Orange Blossom Cosmetologist Association of Florida (1939), Arkansas Beauticians Association (1940), Mississippi Independent Beautician Association (1941), Tennessee State Beauticians Association (1956), Texas State Association and Beauty Culturists League (1942), Virginia State Beauticians Association (1943), Alabama Modern Beauticians (1944), Georgia State Beauty Culturists' League (1946), Louisiana State Beauticians Association (1946). See Mark, *National Beauty Culturists' League*.

15. Mark, *National Beauty Culturist's League*, 158–163.

16. Quoted in Davidson M. Douglas, *Reading, Writing, and Race: The Desegregation of Charlotte Public Schools* (Chapel Hill: University of North Carolina Press, 1995), 26.

17. "State Beauticians Praise Supreme Court Decision; Group Urged to Resist Any Form of Continued Segregation," *Jackson Advocate*, 24 July 1954, 1.

18. See Charles Payne, *I've Got the Light of Freedom: The Organizing Tradition in the Mississippi Civil Rights Movement*, 2nd ed. (Berkeley and Los Angeles: University of California Press, 2007).

19. See *Carolina Times*, 22 August 1950, 22.

20. See undated letter, Box 4, Ruby Parks Blackburn Papers, Auburn Avenue Research Library on African American Culture and History, Atlanta (hereafter cited as RPBP).

21. See appointment books and receipts from Blackburn's beauty salon, RPBP.

22. Kathryn Nasstrom, "Women, the Civil Rights Movement, and the Politics of Historical Memory, 1946–1973" (Ph.D. diss., University of North Carolina- Chapel Hill, 1993), 71.

23. For more on the segregated housing and public transportation system in Atlanta during the early years of Jim Crow, see Hunter, *To 'Joy My Freedom;* for the postwar

period, see Gary Pomerantz, *Where Peachtree Meets Sweet Auburn: A Saga of Race and Family* (New York: Penguin Books, 1997); Herman "Skip" Mason, *Politics, Civil Rights and Law in Black Atlanta, 1870–1970* (Charleston: Arcadia Publishing, 2000).

24. See Georgia Public Service Commission vs. Dixie Hills Bus Lines, 6 October 1953; and J. C. Steinmetz to Ruby Blackburn, 14 October 1953, both in RPBP; Mason, *Politics, Civil Right and Law*, 49–54.

25. bell hooks, *Bone Black: Memories of Girlhood* (New York: Henry Holt, 1996), 112.

26. Coazell Frazier, interviewed by Tunga White, St. Helena, S.C., 7 August 1994, BTV.

27. Bernice Toy Caldwell, interviewed by Leslie Brown, Charlotte, N.C., 7 June 1993, BTV.

28. Weems, *Desegregating the Dollar*, 34.

29. "Integration Comes to the Beauty Business," *Ebony*, August 1966.

30. Craig, *Ain't I a Beauty Queen*, 35.

31. For collections of photographs of the civil rights movement, see Bruce Davidson, *Time of Change: Civil Rights Photographers, 1961–1965* (Los Angeles: St. Ann's Press, 2002); Herbert Randall, *Faces of Freedom Summer* (Tuscaloosa: University of Alabama Press, 2001); Manning Marable and Leith Mullings, *Freedom: A Photographic History of the African American Struggle* (London: Phaidon, 2002); Steven Kasher, *The Civil Rights Movement: A Photographic History, 1954–1968* (New York: Abbeyville Press, 1996); Cecil Williams, *Freedom and Justice: Four Decades of the Civil Rights Struggle as Seen By a Black Photographer of the Deep South* (Macon, Ga.: Mercer University Press, 1995).

32. Marisa Chappell, Jenny Hutchinson, and Brian Ward, "'Dress modestly, neatly . . . as if you were going to church': Respectability, Class and Gender in the Montgomery Bus Boycott and the Early Civil Rights Movement," in *Gender and the Civil Rights Movement*, ed. Peter Ling and Sharon Monteith (New Brunswick, N.J.: Rutgers University Press, 2004), 96n1.

33. See Madam C. J. Walker Company Advertisements in the 1960s in black publications like *Ebony* as well as in the Madam C. J. Walker Papers at the Indiana Historical Society, Indianapolis.

34. Pitts quoted in Mawhood, "Tales to Curl Your Hair," 17.

35. Margaret Williams Neal, interviewed by Rhonda Mawhood, Charlotte, N.C., 19 July 1993, BTV.

36. Ibid.

37. Greene, *Our Separate Ways*, 32.

38. Martin interviewed by Gillette.

39. Julie Willett, *Permanent Waves*, 150.

40. Harriet Vail Wade interviewed by Rhonda Mawhood, Wilmington, N.C., 1 August 1993, BTV.

41. Neal interviewed by Mawhood.

42. John M. Glen, *Highlander: No Ordinary School*, 2nd ed. (Knoxville: University of Tennessee Press, 1996), 154.

43. John M. Glen, introduction to Glen, *Highlander*.

44. All direct quotes from Bernice Robinson's life have been taken from typed, unedited interview: Bernice Robinson, interviewed by Sue Thrasher and Elliot Wiggington, Charleston, S.C., 9 November 1980, Box 1, Folder 5, Avery Research Center, College of Charleston, Charleston, S.C.

45. Ibid.

46. Ibid.

47. For a larger discussion of black women's precarious situation with factory work, see Jones, *Labor of Love, Labor of Sorrow*.

48. On the resiliency of the black beauty market, see Bundles, *On Her Own Ground*; and Walker, *History of Black Business in America*.

49. Robinson interview by Thrasher and Wiggington.

50. Elliot Wigginton, ed., *Refuse to Stand Silently By: An Oral History of Grassroots Social Activism in America, 1921–1964* (New York: Doubleday Books, 1991).

51. Robinson quoted in LaVerne Grant, "Contributions of African-American Women to Nonformal Education During the Civil Rights Movement, 1955–1965" (Ed.D. diss., Pennsylvania State University, 1990), 46.

52. For more information on the life of Septima Clark, see Septima Clark, *Echo in My Soul* (New York: E. P. Dutton, 1962); Cynthia Stokes Brown, *Refuse to Stand Silently By: Septima Clark and the Civil Rights Movement* (Navarro, Calif.: Wild Trees Press, 1986); and Katherine Mellen Charron, "Teaching Citizenship: Septima Poinsette Clark and the Transformation of the African American Freedom Struggle" (Ph.D. diss., Yale University, 2005).

53. R. Scott Baker, "Ambiguous Legacies: The NAACP's Legal Campaign Against Segregation in Charleston, SC, 1935–1975" (Ph.D. diss., Columbia University, 1993), 180.

54. Bernice Robinson to Lucille Black, 28 January 1956, in *Papers of the NAACP, Selected Branch Files, 1956–1965* (Bethesda, Md.: University Publications of America, 1991).

55. Robinson interview by Thrasher and Wiggington.

56. Sandra Brenneman Oldendorf, "Highlander Folk School and the South Carolina Sea Island Citizenship Schools: Implications for the Social Studies" (Ph.D. diss., University of Kentucky, 1987).

57. For a larger analysis of the hesitancy of African American schoolteachers to get involved in civil rights activities, see Charron, "Teaching Citizenship," 345–348. For an analysis of Clark's reasons not to use teachers, see 479.

58. Clark, *Ready from Within*, 51; Horton, *Long Haul*, 105.

59. See Mellon, "Teaching Citizenship," 480–484.

60. Glen, *Highlander*, 197; Mellen, "Teaching Citizenship," 487.

61. See "Announcing a workshop on New Leadership Responsibilities" and Septima

Clark to beauticians in Tennessee, Alabama, and Georgia, 12 December 1960, Box 80, Folder 10, Highlander Folk School Papers, Social Action Collection, Wisconsin Historical Society, Madison (hereafter cited as HFSP); emphasis added.

62. Horton quoted in Aldon Morris, *The Origins of the Civil Rights Movement*: Black Communities Organizing for Change (New York: Free Press, 1984), 145.

63. A press release dated 17 January 1961 claims the attendance of "fifty-two women beauticians from Tennessee and Alabama," but the sign in sheets reflect thirty-four women and one male beautician. I find it interesting that the press release ignored the presence of the man. See MSS 265, Box 80, Folder 10, HFSP.

64. Charron, "Teaching Citizenship," 514–515.

65. See untitled press release, 17 January 17 1961, and Notes from the Board of Directors meeting, 16 January 1961, MSS 265, Box 80, Folder 10, HFSP.

66. Septima Clark to Eva Bowman, n.d., Box 38, Folder 6; Bowman to Co-workers, 19 April 1961, Box 38, Folder 6 (HFSP); quotation from handwritten note Clark to Bowman, n.d., Box 38, Folder 6 (HFSP).

67. Charron, "Teaching Citizenship," 518.

68. Announcement of Workshop for Beauticians on "New Leadership Responsibilities," 28–29 October 1962, Box 80, Folder 10, HFSP.

69. Oldendorf, "Highlander Folk School," 67.

70. For more information about the raid on Highlander and its legal battles, see Glen, *Highlander*; Horton, *Long Haul*; Aimee Isgrig Horton, *The Highlander Folk School: A History of its Major Programs, 1939–1961* (Brooklyn, N.Y.: Carlson Publishing, 1989). See "Highlander School's Septima Clark Among Seven Taking Peace Corps Test," *Chattanooga Free Press*, 29 May 1961, clipping in Clark/Robinson Papers, Folder 5, Avery Research Center, College of Charleston, Charleston, S.C.

71. For a larger discussion of the SCLC, namely, its gender politics, see Robnett, *How Long? How Long?*

72. Young quoted in Mellon, "Teaching Citizenship," 536.

73. For a larger discussion of the situation in Clarksdale with regard to resistance and repression, see Annelieke Dirks, "Between Threat and Reality: The National Association for the Advancement of Colored People and the Emergence of Armed Self-Defense in Clarksdale and Natchez, Mississippi, 1960–1965," *Journal for the Study of Radicalism* 1, no. 1 (2007): 71–98.

74. For more on Pigee, see Françoise Nicole Hamlin, "Vera Mae Pigee (1925–): Mothering the Movement," in *Mississippi Women: Their Histories, Their Lives*, ed. Martha Swain, Elizabeth Anne Payne, Marjorie Spruill, and Susan Ditto (Athens: University of Georgia Press, 2003), 281–93; Charron, "Teaching Citizenship," 557–5588; and Vera Pigee, *The Struggle of Struggles* (Detroit: Harlo Press, 1975).

75. Pigee, *Struggle of Struggles,* 99–100.

76. Morris's interview with Myles Horton in *Origins of the Civil Rights Movement*, 145.

77. Clark, *Echo in My Soul*, 161.

Chapter 6. Beauticians, Health Activism, and the Politics of Dignity in the Post–Civil Rights Era

1. Alice Walker, "Oppressed Hair Puts a Ceiling on the Brain," in *Living by the Word*, by Alice Walker (New York: Harcourt Brace and Javanovich, 1988), 72–73.

2. See Walker, *Style and Status;* Craig, *Ain't I a Beauty Queen.*

3. For a discussion of the declension model of post–civil rights history, see Jaquelyn Dowd Hall, "The Long Civil Rights Movement and the Political Uses of the Past," *Journal of American History* 91 (March 2005): 1233–1263.

4. Gloria Wade-Gayles, "The Making of a Permanent Afro," *Pushed Back to Strength: A Black Woman's Journey Home* (Boston: Beacon Press, 1993), 157.

5. For a larger discussion of the Afro, particularly the black beauty culture industry's response, see Walker, "Black Is Profitable," 254–277. On a discussion of the political and nonpolitical elements of "soul culture," see Craig, *Ain't I a Beauty Queen;* Angela Davis, "Afro Images: Politics, Fashion, and Nostalgia," in *Soul: Black Power, Politics, and Pleasure*, ed. Monique Guillory and Richard Green (New York: New York University Press, 1998):23–31; and William Van DeBurg, *New Day in Babylon: The Black Power Movement and American Culture* (Chicago: University of Chicago Press, 1992).

6. Willi Coleman, "Among the Things That Used to Be," in *Home Girls: A Black Feminist Anthology*, ed. Barbara Smith (New Brunswick, N.J.: Rutgers University Press, 2000), 213–215. I am so grateful to have had the chance to become Coleman's colleague at the University of Vermont (2002–3) and to speak with her about the sentiment expressed in her poem.

7. "The Natural Look—Is It Here to Stay?" *Ebony*, June 1969.

8. Ibid.

9. For a larger discussion of the commercialization of the Afro, see Walker, "Black Is Profitable," 254–277, and Walker, *Style and Status*, chap. 6.

10. Juliet Walker notes that as early as the mid-1940s, the Walker Company only had a 1.1 percent share of the overall black hair product manufacturing industry and that the company's annual earnings dropped from $595,000 in 1920 to $48,000 in 1933. The company never fully rebounded. *History of Black Business in America*, 305.

11. Ibid., 306.

12. Penelope Wang and Maggie Malone, "Targeting Black Dollars," *Newsweek*, 13 October 1986, 54.

13. Operation PUSH under the leadership of Rev. Jesse Jackson called for a "bury Revlon" national boycott and insisted that Revlon sell their manufacturing plant in South Africa and sever economic ties with the apartheid nation. *Essence* magazine banned advertising from Revlon, which was valued at more than four hundred thousand dollars a year. See Penelope Wang and Maggie Malone, "Can Revlon Repair Its Image?" *Newsweek*, 23 February 1987, 53.

14. See "Ethnic Hair Care Is $1.2 Billion a Year Sector," *Forbes*, 27 November 2000; and Mintel Report, "Manufacturer Sales of Black Haircare Products in the U.S., 2004 and 2006," http://academic.mintel.com.ezproxy.lib.utexas.edu/sinatra/oxygen_academic/search_results/show&/display/id=226583/displaytables/id=226583/ (accessed March 12, 2008).

15. According to Julie Willett, by 1995 at least half of the 343,294 nail technicians were Vietnamese. For more information on the decline of the Asian American manicurist and the rise of the Asian American nail technicians, see Julie Willett, "'Hands Across the Table': A Short History of the Manicurist in the Twentieth Century," *Journal of Women's History* 17, no. 3 (Fall 2005): 59–80.

16. For a larger discussion of Korean domination in beauty product distribution, see the documentary *Black Hair: The Korean Takeover of the Black Haircare Industry*, directed by Aron Ranen, 2006.

17. For more information on the growth of community colleges in the 1960s, see *Community Colleges: A Century of Innovation* (Annapolis, Md.: Community College Press, 2001).

18. Joyner, *Beauty Trade,* 1973.

19. Gregory Lewis and Alva James Johnson, "Black Hair Grows into Lucrative Industry," *Sun-Sentinel,* 27 February 2005, 2H.

20. Wade interviewed by Mawhood.

21. Katie Catalon, "News from the NBCL National Office," NBCL, http://www.nbcl.org/news.php/ (accessed March 3, 2008).

22. Tommie Flanagan, interviewed by Tiffany Gill, San Diego, 8 December 2005.

23. See brochure for Bronner Bros. International Hair Show, 9–12 February 2008, http://www.bronnerbros.com/show/pdf/brochure.pdf/ (accessed March 3, 2008).

24. Sarah Klien, "Tressed to Kill: Through Tease and Spray Detroit's *Hair Wars* Plumbs Issues of Race, Gender, and Multiculturalism," 7 April 2004, www.metrotimes.com/editorial/printstory.asp?id=6098/ (accessed January 30, 2008).

25. For a larger discussion of hair shows, see David Yellen and Johanna Lenander, *Hair Wars* (Brooklyn, N.Y.: Powerhouse Press, 2007).

26. For a larger discussion of the rise of the black women's health movement, see Byllye Avery, "Breathing Life into Ourselves: The Evolution of the National Black Women's Health Project," in *Feminism and Community,* ed. Penny A. Weiss and Marilyn Friedman (Philadelphia: Temple University Press, 1995), 147–153; "Our Story: Black Women's Health Imperative," http://www.blackwomenshealth.org/site/c.eeJIIWOCIrH/b.3561065/ (accessed January 18, 2008); Evelyn White, ed., *The Black Women's Health Book: Speaking for Ourselves* (New York: Seal Publishing, 1994) and Deborah Grayson, "'Necessity Was the Midwife of Our Politics': Black Women's Health Activism in the 'Post'–Civil Rights Era, 1980–1996," in *Still Lifting, Still Climbing: Contemporary African American Women's Activism,* ed. Kimberly Springer (New York: New York University Press, 1999), 131–148.

27. In fact, Grayson argues that health activism is indeed a form of political activ-

ism: "Recognizing that achieving good health is still a central component within the struggle for civil rights, Black women activists work to make the health needs of Black people a central political concern in the national arena." "Necessity was the Midwife," 134–135.

28. For a list of the twenty-two targeted sites, see Selina A. Smith, Sandra Hamilton, Joyce Q. Sheats, Ernest Mensch, Funmi Apantaku, and Louis Sullivan, "Stay Beautiful/Stay Alive: A Successful Approach to Community-Based Participatory Research," *American Journal of Health Studies* 18, no.4 (2003): 220.

29. Christmas quoted in Betty Norwood Chaney, "Black Women's Health Conference," *Southern Changes: The Journal of the Southern Regional Council, 1978–2003* 5 (1983): 18.

30. For more information on beauty salons and breast cancer prevention, see Julie Halenar, "Beauty Shops Helping Women Prevent Breast Cancer," Stop Getting Sick, http://www.stopgettingsick.com/templates/news_template.cfm/6217. Jenny M. Baum, "Turning a Salon into 'A Salon': Talking Health at the Hairdresser's," Media Rights, http://www.mediarights.org/news/article/php?art_id=00053/; "Stay Beautiful, Stay Alive," NBLIC, http://www.nblic.org/beautiful.htm/; Olivia Reyes Garcia, "Getting the Word Out," Ecoalition, http://www.ecoalition.org/articals/04–24–01%20Getting%20 the%20word%20out,htm/ (all accessed February 10, 2008); *Community Health News and Views: A Publication of Community Health Nursing Program, Genessee County (MI) Health Department* 4, no.3 (Fall 2001).

31. Georgia Robin Sadler quoted in Malcolm Gladwell, *The Tipping Point: How Little Things Can Make a Big Difference* (New York: Back Bay Books, 2000), 254.

32. Georgia Robins Sadler, Margaret W. Meyer, Celine Marie Ko, Crystal Butcher, Shianti Lee, Tiffany Neal, Lynn Reed, Aaron E. Veals, and Elizabeth A. Gilpin, "Black Cosmetologists Promote Diabetes Awareness and Screening Among African American Women," *Diabetes Educator* 30 (July/August 2004): 677.

33. Sylvia Bennett [name changed], interview by Tiffany Gill, San Diego, 10 December 2005.

34. Sadler et al., "Black Cosmetologists Promote Diabetes," 678; and Georgia Robins Sadler, Melanie Peterson, Linda Wasserman, Paul Mills, Vanessa Malcame, Cheryl Rock, Sonia Ancoli-Israel, Amanda Moore, Rai-Nesha Welson, Tenisha Garcia, and Richard Kolodner, "Recruiting Research Participants at Community Education Sites," *Journal of Cancer Education* 20 (2005): 235–239.

35. Smith et al., "Stay Beautiful/Stay Alive," 220.

36. For more on the role of beauty salons in HIV/AIDS prevention in the South and beyond, see *DiAna's Hair Ego: AIDS Info Upfront*, directed by Ellen Spiro, Women Make Movies, Inc., New York, 1990; Mike Billington, "Man Crusades to Help Prevent Spread of AIDS," Delaware Online, http://www.delawareonline.com/newsjournal/ local/2001/08/13mancrusade.html/; Wevonneda Minis, "South Carolina: Salons, Churches Reach out to Educate," The Body, http://www.thebody.com/cdc/news_ updates_archive/2003/jun27_03/south_carolina_prevent.html/; "Significant Increase

in HIV counseling and Testing Reported at State Funded Test Sites: California AIDS Prevention," Aegis, http://www.aegis.com/news/bw/1997/bw970624.html/. All accessed June 12, 2004.

37. Brad Bonhall, "Sex, Seriously Education: Orange-based Hannah's Children Homes Is Trying to Reach African Americans with a Message about HIV Infection," *Los Angeles Times*, 29 January 1997, Life and Style page.

38. P. Tjaden and N. Thoennes, "Full Report of the Prevalence, Incidence, and Consequences of Violence Against Women," Report NCJ 183781, National Institute of Justice, Washington, D.C., 2000.

39. G. E. Wyatt, "The Sociocultural Context of African American and White American Women's Rape," *Journal of Social Issues* 48 (2002): 77–91.

40. John Spragens, "Relief in Black and White," *Nashville Scene*, 15 September 2005, http://www.nashvillescene.com/stories/news/2005/09/15/Relief_in_black_and_white/ (accessed May 26, 2009).

41. "Dr. Willie Morrow Helps Black Hair Care Professionals Hit by Hurricane," Unity First, www.unityfirst.com/ufthisweek.htm/ (accessed October 2006).

42. Audie Cornish, "Hopefuls Court South Carolina's Black Voters," 15 October 2007, Transcript, Morning Edition, National Public Radio, http://www.npr.org/templates/story/story.php?storyId=15276494/ (accessed May 26, 2009). Also see Melissa Victoria Harris-Lacewell, *Barbershops, Bibles, and BET: Everyday Talk and Black Political Thought* (Princeton, N.J.: Princeton University Press, 2004).

43. Vcubed, comment on "Beauty Shops/ Barber Shops Politics—A Gold Mine for Obama," Obama '08 Community Blogs, http://my.barackobama.com/page/community/post/vcubed/ChQP comment posted 14 October 2007 (accessed May 26, 2009).

44. For coverage of the South Carolina primary and the beauty shop vote, see Krissah Williams, "In S.C., Beauty Salons Are Also Political Soapboxes," *Washington Post*, 14 October 2007, A01; Katharine Q. Seelye, "Clinton-Obama Quandary for Many Black Women," *New York Times*, 14 October 2007, http://www.nytimes.com/2007/10/14/us/politics/14carolina.html/ (accessed May 26, 2009); Cornish, "Hopefuls Court South Carolina's Black Voters."

Bibliography

Primary Sources

MANUSCRIPT COLLECTIONS

Afro-American Museum of Philadelphia. Philadelphia.
Lillian Barkley Papers
Alberta Colvard Papers
Grace Lindsey Collection
Lucille McKnight Collection
Marie Steward Smith Collection

Auburn Avenue Research Library on African American Culture and History. Atlanta.
Ruby Parks Blackburn Papers

Avery Research Center. College of Charleston, Charleston, S.C.
Septima Poinsette Clark Papers
Bernice Robinson Papers

Indiana Historical Society. Indianapolis.
Madam C. J. Walker Papers

Mary McLeod Bethune Council House. National Parks Service, Washington, D.C.
Susie Greene Papers
National Association of Negro Business and Professional Women's Clubs Papers
National Association of Walker Agents Papers
National Beauty Culturists' League Papers

Metropolitan Research Center. Houston Public Library, Houston.
Franklin Beauty School Papers

Social Action Collection. Wisconsin Historical Society. Madison.

Highlander Research and Education Center Papers

Myles Horton Papers

Pressley Beauty School

Vivian G. Harsh Collection. Carter G. Woodson Regional Library.
Chicago Public Library, Chicago.

Robert O. French Papers

Negroes in Illinois. Illinois Writers Project, Works Progress Administration.

Marjorie Stewart Joyner Papers

United Beauty School Owners and Teachers Association Papers

MANUSCRIPTS ON MICROFILM

Claude A. Barnett Papers

Mary McLeod Bethune Papers. Frederick, Md.: University Publications of America.

Records of the National Association of Colored Women's Clubs, 1895–1992. Bethesda, Md.: University Publications of America, 1993– .

Records of the National Negro Business League. Frederick, Md.: University Publications of America.

INTERVIEWS

Behind the Veil Collection. John Hope Franklin Research Center for African and African American Documentation. Duke University, Durham, N.C.

Alexander, Almetto. Interview by Karen Ferguson. 11 June 1993.

Caldwell, Bernice Toy. Interview by Leslie Brown. 7 June 1993.

Conway, Alice Lois. Interview by Tunga White. 28 June 1994.

Frazier, Coazell. Interview by Tunga White. 7 August 1994.

Grantham, Rosa Hopkins. Interview by Sonya Ramsey. 5 August 1993.

Griffin, Lovie Mae. Interview by Laurie Green. 15 August 1999.

Little, JoAnna. Interview by Tywanna Whorley. 21 June 1994

McWilliam, Ada Whitaker. Interview by Rhonda Mawhood. 29 June 1993.

Mungo, Alma, and Lucille Lynch. Interview by Sonya Ramsey. 13 June 1993.

Neal, Margaret Williams. Interview by Rhonda Mawhood. 19 July 1993.

Roberts, Mary Elizabeth. Interview by Rhonda Mawhood. 12 August 1993.

Spears, Alphatene Keith. Interview by Kara Miles. 10 June 1993.

Trailor, Christine. Interview by Doris Dixon. 15 July 1995.

Wade, Harriet Vail. Interview by Rhonda Mawhood. 1 August 1993.

Ware, Elizabeth. Interview by Doris Dixon. 2 July 1995.

Wilson, Rosetta. Interview by Mausiki Scales. 11 July 1995.

Hill, Ruth Edmonds, ed. *The Black Women Oral History Project: The Arthur and Elizabeth Schlesinger Library on the History of Women in America.* Westport, Conn.: Meckler Press, 1991.

Barker, Elizabeth Cardozo. Interview by Marcia McAdoo Greenlee. 8 December 1976; 29 January, 10 November 1977.

Holmes, Margaret Cardozo. Interview by Marcia McAdoo Greenlee. 9 November 1977.

Kemp, Maida Springer. Interview by Elizabeth Balanoff. 4, 5 January, 11 May, 7 June 1977.

Lewis, Catherine Cardozo. Interview by Marcia McAdoo Greenlee. 12 September 1980.

Joyner, Marjorie Stewart. Interview by Michael Flug. Vivian G. Harsh Collection. Carter G. Woodson Regional Library. Chicago Public Library, Chicago.

Morgan, Rose. Interviewed by James Briggs Murray. 21 April 1988. Schomburg Center for Research in Black Culture. New York.

Bennett, Sylvia (name changed). Interview by Tiffany Gill. San Diego, 10 December 2005. In author's possession.

Flanagan, Tommie. Interview by Tiffany Gill. San Diego. 8 December 2005. In author's possession.

Sadler, Georgia Robins. Interview by Tiffany Gill. San Diego, 8 December 2005. In author's possession.

Newspapers and Serials

Advocate (Jackson, Miss.)
Apex News (Atlantic City, N.J.)
Atlanta Daily World
Beauty Trade (New York)
Carolina Times (Durham, N.C.)
Chicago Defender
Colored American Magazine (Tuskegee, Ala.)
Crisis (New York)
Ebony (Chicago)
Essence (New York)
Interstate Tattler (New York)
Messenger (New York)
Negro World (New York)
Newsweek (New York)
New York Age
New York Amsterdam News
New York Times
Opportunity (New York)
Pittsburgh Courier
Responsibility (Washington, D.C.)

Government Documents

Erickson, Ethel. *Employment Conditions in Beauty Shops: A Study of Four Cities.* U.S. Department of Labor. Bulletin of the Women's Bureau No. 133. Washington, D.C.: Government Printing Office, 1926.

Gordon, Edith. *Establishing and Operating a Beauty Shop.* Washington, D.C.: Government Printing Office, 1946.

State of New York. Department of Labor. *Beauty Service Minimum Wage Board.* Albany: New York State Printing Office, 1947.

Works Progress Administration. "Harlem Beauty Shops." *American Life Histories: Manuscripts from the Federal Writers' Project, 1936–1940.* http://lcweb2.loc.gov/ ammem/wpaintro/wpahome/(accessed October 12, 2002).

Secondary Sources

BOOKS AND ARTICLES

Alexis, Marcus. "Pathways to the Negro Market." *Journal of Negro Education* 28 (Spring 1959): 114–27.

Amott, Theresa, and Julie Matthaei. *Race, Gender, and Work: A Multicultural Economic History of Women in the United States.* Boston: South End Press, 1991.

Anderson, Jervis. *A. Philip Randolph: A Biographical Portrait.* Berkeley and Los Angeles: University of California Press, 1972.

———. *This Was Harlem, 1900–1950.* New York: Ferrar, Strauss, and Giroux, 1981.

Avery, Byllye. "Breathing Life into Ourselves: The Evolution of the National Black Women's Health Project." In *Feminism and Community,* edited by Penny A. Weiss and Marilyn Friedman, 147–153. Philadelphia: Temple University Press, 1995.

Bailey, Ronald, ed. *Black Business Enterprises: Historical and Contemporary Perspectives.* New York: Basic Books, 1971.

Bair, Barbara. "Renegotiating Liberty: Garveyism, Women, and Grassroots Organizing in Virginia." In *Women of the American South,* edited by Christie Anne Farham. New York: New York University Press, 1997: 220–240.

———. "True Women, Real Men: Gender, Ideology, and Social Roles in the Garvey Movement." In *Gendered Domains: Rethinking Public and Private in Women's History,* edited by Dorothy O. Helly and Susan Reverby. Ithaca, N.Y.: Cornell University Press, 1992: 154–166.

Baker, Paula. "The Domestication of Politics: Women and American Political Society, 1780–1920." *American Historical Review* 89 (1984): 620–647.

Baldwin, Davarian. *Chicago's New Negroes: Modernity, the Great Migration, and Black Urban Life.* Chapel Hill: University of North Carolina, 2007.

Barnes, Annie. "The Black Beauty Parlor Complex in a Southern City." *Phylon* 36 (1975): 149–154.

Barnett, Bernice McNair. "Invisible Southern Black Women Leaders in the Civil Rights Movement: The Triple Constraints of Gender, Race, and Class." *Gender and History* 7 (June 1993): 162–182.

Bates, Beth Tompkins. *Pullman Porters and the Rise of Protest Politics in Black America, 1925–1945*. Chapel Hill: University of North Carolina Press, 2001.

Baylor, Ronald. "Roads to Racial Segregation: Atlanta in the Twentieth Century." *Journal of Urban History* 15 (November 1988): 3–21.

Bederman, Gail. *Manliness and Civilization: A Cultural History of Gender and Race in the United States, 1880–1917.* Chicago: University of Chicago Press, 1995.

Billingsley, Andrew. *Mighty Like a River: The Black Church and Social Reform*. New York: Oxford University Press, 1999.

Biondi, Martha. *To Stand and Fight: The Struggle for Civil Rights in Postwar New York City*. Cambridge: Harvard University Press, 2003.

Blackwelder, Julia Kirk. "Quiet Suffering: Atlanta Women in the 1930s." *Georgia Historical Quarterly* 61 (1977): 112–124.

———. *Stylin' Jim Crow: African American Beauty Training During Segregation*. College Station: Texas A&M Press, 2003.

Borchert, James. *Alley Life in Washington: Family, Community, Religion, and Folklife in the City, 1850–1970*. Urbana: University of Illinois Press, 1982.

Borstelmann, Thomas. *The Cold War and the Color Line: American Race Relations in the Global Arena*. Cambridge: Harvard University Press, 2001.

Boyd, Robert. "Survivalist Entrepreneurship among Urban Blacks During the Great Depression: A Test of the Disadvantage Theory of Business Enterprise." *Social Science Quarterly* 81 (December 2000): 972–984.

Branch, Taylor. *Pillar of Fire: America in the King Years, 1953–1965*. New York: Simon and Schuster Press, 1998.

Brand, Peg Zeglin, ed. *Beauty Matters*. Bloomington: Indiana University Press, 2000.

Bristol, Douglas. "The Victory of Black Barbers Over Reform in Ohio, 1902–1913." *Essays in Economic and Business History* 16 (1998): 251–260.

Brown, Cynthia Stokes. *Ready from Within: Septima Clark and the Civil Rights Movement*. California: Wild Tree Press, 1986.

Brown, Elsa Barkley. "Negotiating and Transforming the Public Sphere: African American Political Life in the Transition from Slavery to Freedom." *Public Culture* 7 (1994): 107–146.

———. "Womanist Consciousness: Maggie Lena Walker and the Independent Order of St. Luke." *Signs* 14 (Spring 1989): 610–633.

Bunch-Lyons, Beverly. *Contested Terrain: African American Women Migrate from the South to Cincinnati, Ohio, 1900–1950*. New York: Routledge Press, 2002.

Burroughs, Nannie Helen. "Not Color, But Character." *Voice of the Negro*, July 1904.

Burrows, John. *The Necessity of Myth: A History of the National Negro Business League, 1900–1945*. Auburn, Ga.: Hickory Hill Press, 1998.

Bundles, A'Lelia. *Madam C. J. Walker*. New York: Chelsea Publishing, 1994.

———. *On Her Own Ground: The Life and Times of Madam C. J. Walker*. New York: Scribner Books, 2001.

Butler, John. *Entrepreneurship and Self-Help Among Black Americans*. Albany, N.Y.: State University of New York Press, 1991.

Byrd, Ayanna, and Lori Tharps. *Hair Story: Untangling the Roots of Black Hair in America*. New York: St. Martin's Press, 2001.

Candelario, Ginetta. "Hair Race-ing: Dominican Beauty Culture and Identity Production." *Meridians: Race, Feminism, Transnationalism*. 1(Autumn 2000): 128–156.

Carby, Hazel. "Policing the Black Woman in an Urban Context." *Critical Inquiry* 18 (Summer 1992): 738–755.

Carson, Clayborne. *In Struggle: SNCC and the Black Awakening of the 1960s*. Cambridge: Harvard University Press, 1981.

Chambers, Jason. *Madison Avenue and the Color Line: African Americans in the Advertising Industry*. Philadelphia: University of Pennsylvania Press, 2007.

Chappell, Marisa, Jenny Hutchinson, and Brian Ward. "'Dress modestly, neatly . . . as if you were going to church': Respectability, Class and Gender in the Montgomery Bus Boycott and the Early Civil Rights Movement." In *Gender and the Civil Rights Movement*, edited by Peter Ling and Sharon Monteith. New Brunswick, N.J.: Rutgers University Press, 2004:69–99.

Chateauvert, Melinda. *Marching Together: Women of the Brotherhood of Sleeping Car Porters*. Chicago: University of Chicago Press, 1998.

Clark, Septima. *Echo in My Soul*. New York: E. P. Dutton, 1962.

Clark-Lewis, Elizabeth. *Living In, Living Out: African American Domestics in Washington, D.C., 1910–1940*. Washington, D.C.: Smithsonian Institution Press, 1994.

———. "'This Work Had an End': African American Domestic Workers in Washington, D.C., 1910–1940." In *To Toil the Livelong Day: America's Women at Work, 1780–1980*, edited by Carol Groneman and Mary Beth Norton. Ithaca, N.Y.: Cornell University Press, 1987:196–212.

Clarke, Alison. *Tupperware: The Promise of Plastic in 1950s America*. Washington, D.C.: Smithsonian Institution Press, 1999.

Cobble, Dorothy Sue. *Dishing It Out: Waitresses and Their Unions in the Twentieth Century*. Urbana: University of Illinois Press, 1991.

Cohen, Lizabeth. *A Consumers' Republic: The Politics of Mass Consumption in Postwar America*. New York: Vintage Books, 2003.

Coleman, Willi. "Among the Things That Used to Be." In *Home Girls: A Black Feminist Anthology*, edited by Barbara Smith. New Brunswick, N.J.: Rutgers University Press, 2000: 213–215.

Collier-Thomas, Bettye, and V. P. Franklin, eds. *Sisters in the Struggle: African American Women in the Civil Rights and Black Power Movements*. New York: New York University Press, 2001.

Craig, Maxine Leeds. *Ain't I a Beauty Queen: Black Women, Beauty, and the Politics of Race*. New York: Oxford University Press, 2002.

Crawford, Vicki Lynn, Jacqueline Anne Rouse, and Barbara Woods, eds. *Women in the Civil Rights Movement: Trailblazers and Torchbearers*. Brooklyn, N.Y.: Carlson, 1998.

Cruse, Harold. *The Crisis of the Negro Intellectual: A Historical Analysis of the Failure of Black Leadership.* New York: Quill Press, 1984.

Davis, Angela. "Afro Images: Politics, Fashion, and Nostalgia." In *Soul: Black Power, Politics, and Pleasure,* edited by Monique Guillory and Richard Green. New York: New York University Press, 1998:23–31.

Davis, Elizabeth Lindsay. *Lifting as They Climb.* Washington, D.C.: National Association of Colored Women, 1933.

Davis, Leroy. "Madam C. J. Walker: A Woman of Her Time." In *The African Experience in Community Development: The Continuing Struggle in Africa and the Americas,* vol. 2, edited by Edward W. Crosby, Leroy Davis, and Anne Adams Graves, 37–60. Needham Heights, Mass.: Advocate Publishing Group, 1980: 37–60.

Davis, Marianna. *Contributions of Black Women to America,* vol. 1. Columbia, S.C.: Kenday Press, 1982.

De Grazia, Victoria, ed. *The Sex of Things: Gender and Consumption in Historical Perspective.* Berkeley and Los Angeles: University of California Press, 1996.

Dirks, Annelieke. "Between Threat and Reality: The National Association for the Advancement of Colored People and the Emergence of Armed Self-Defense in Clarksdale and Natchez, Mississippi, 1960–1965." *Journal for the Study of Radicalism* 1, no. 1 (2007): 71–98.

Dittmer, John. *Local People: The Struggle for Civil Rights in Mississippi.* Urbana: University of Illinois Press, 1994.

Dossett, Kate. *Bridging Race Divides: Black Nationalism, Feminism, and Integration in the United States, 1896–1935.* Gainesville: University Press of Florida, 2008.

Douglas, Davidson. *Reading, Writing, and Race: The Desegregation of Charlotte Public Schools.* Chapel Hill: University of North Carolina Press, 1995.

Drake, St. Clair, and Horace Cayton. *Black Metropolis: A Study of Negro Life in a Northern City.* 1962. Reprint, New York: Harper and Row, 1945.

Du Bois, W. E. B. *Black Reconstruction in America, 1860–1880.* New York: Antheneum, 1935.

———, ed. *The Negro in Business.* Atlanta University Publication no. 4. Atlanta: Atlanta University Press, 1899.

Dudziak, Mary. *Cold War Civil Rights: Race and the Image of American Democracy.* Princeton, N.J.: Princeton University Press. 2000.

Ebong, Ima, ed. *Black Hair: Art, Style, and Culture.* New York: Universe Publishing, 2001.

Egerton, John. *Speak Now Against the Day: The Generation Before the Civil Rights Movement in the South.* Chapel Hill: University of North Carolina Press, 1994.

Emme, Edna, and Nathan Jacobs. *NHCA's Golden Years: From the Historical Records, Minutes, and Reports of the National Hairdressers and Cosmetologists Association and the Reminiscences of Edna L. Emme.* Racine, Wisc.: Western Publishing, 1970.

Evans, Sara, and Harry Boyte. *Free Spaces: The Sources of Democratic Changes in America.* New York: Harper and Row, 1986.

Ewen, Phyllis. "Beauty Parlor—A Woman's Space." *Radical America* 11 (May–June 1977): 47–58.

Fairclough, Adam. *To Redeem the Soul of America: The Southern Christian Leadership Conference and Martin Luther King.* Athens: University of Georgia, 1987.

Fields, Mamie Garvin, with Karen Fields. *Lemon Swamp and Other Places: A Carolina Memoir.* New York: Free Press, 1983.

Foner, Eric. *Reconstruction: America's Unfinished Revolution.* New York: Harper and Row, 1998.

Fox, Richard Wightman, and T. Jackson Lears, eds. *The Culture of Consumption: Critical Essays in American History, 1880–1980.* New York: Pantheon Books, 1983.

Frazier, E. Franklin. *Black Bourgeoisie.* 1962. Reprint, New York: Free Press, 1997.

Gaines, Kevin. *Uplifting the Race: Black Leadership, Politics, and Culture in the Twentieth Century.* Chapel Hill: University of North Carolina Press, 1996.

Gambler, Wendy. "A Gendered Enterprise: Placing Nineteenth Century Businesswomen in History." *Business History Review* 72 (Summer 1998): 188–218.

Garrow, David. *Bearing the Cross: Martin Luther King and the Southern Christian Leadership Conference.* New York: Quill Books, 1999.

Gaspar, David Barry, and Darlene Clark Hine, eds. *More than Chattel: Black Women and Slavery in the Americas.* Bloomington: Indiana University Press, 1996.

Gayles, Gloria Wade. "The Making of a Permanent Afro." *Catalyst: A Magazine of Heart and Mind.* Summer 1988, 20–26.

Giddings, Paula. *When and Where I Enter: The Impact of Black Women on Race and Sex in America.* New York: Bantam, 1984.

Gill, Tiffany M. "'I Had My Own Business So I Didn't Have to Worry': Beauty Salons, Beauty Culturists, and the Politics of African American Female Entrepreneurship." In *Beauty and Business: Commerce, Gender, and Culture in Modern America*, edited by Philip Scranton. New York: Routledge Press, 2001: 169–194.

———. "'The First Thing Every Negro Girl Does': Black Beauty Culture, Racial Politics, and the Construction of Modern Black Womanhood, 1900–1925." In *Cultures of Commerce: Representation and American Business Culture, 1877–1960.* New York: Palgrave Macmillan, 2006.

Gilmore, Glenda. *Gender and Jim Crow: Women and the Politics of White Supremacy in North Carolina, 1890–1920.* Chapel Hill: University of North Carolina Press, 1996.

Glen, John. *Highlander: No Ordinary School.* 2nd ed. Knoxville: University of Tennessee Press, 1996.

Goings, Kenneth, and Raymond Mohl, eds. *The New African American Urban History.* California: Sage, 1996.

Gordon, Linda. *Pitied But Not Entitled: Single Mothers and the History of Welfare.* Cambridge: Harvard University Press, 1994.

Grayson, Deborah. "'Necessity Was the Midwife of Our Politics': Black Women's Health Activism in the 'Post'–Civil Rights Era, 1980–1996." In *Still Lifting, Still*

Climbing: Contemporary African American Women's Activism, edited by Kimberly Springer, 131–148. New York: New York University Press, 1998.

Green, Laurie. *Battling the Plantation Mentality: Memphis and the Black Freedom Struggle*. Chapel Hill: University of North Carolina Press, 2007.

Greenberg, Cheryl Lynn. *Or Does It Explode? Black Harlem in the Great Depression*. New York: Oxford University Press, 1991.

Greene, Christina. *Our Separate Ways: Women and the Black Freedom Movement in Durham, North Carolina*. Chapel Hill: University of North Carolina Press, 2005.

Grossman, James. *Land of Hope: Chicago, Black Southerners, and the Great Migration*. Chicago: University of Chicago Press, 1989.

Hackley, Azalia. *The Colored Girl Beautiful*. Kansas City, Mo.: Burton Publishing Co., 1916.

Hall, Jacquelyn Dowd. "The Long Civil Rights Movement and the Political Uses of the Past." *Journal of American History* 91 (March 2005): 1233–1263.

Hamlin, Francoise Nicole. "Vera Mae Pigee (1925–): Mothering the Movement." In *Mississippi Women: Their Histories, Their Lives*, edited by Martha Swain, Elizabeth Anne Payne, Marjorie Spruill, and Susan Ditto, 281–293. Athens: University of Georgia Press, 2003.

Hammond, Theresa. *A White Collar Profession: African American Certified Public Accountants Since 1921*. Chapel Hill: University of North Carolina Press, 2002.

Hanson, Joyce. *Mary McLeod Bethune and Black Women's Political Activism*. Columbia: University of Missouri Press, 2003.

Harlan, Louis. *Booker T. Washington: The Making of a Leader*. New York: Oxford University Press, 1972.

———. *The Booker T. Washington Papers*. Urbana: University of Illinois Press, 1972.

Harley, Sharon. "When Your Work Is Not Who You Are: The Development of a Working Class Consciousness Among Afro-American Women." In *We Specialize in the Wholly Impossible: A Reader in Black Women's History*, edited by Darlene Clark Hine, Wilma King, Linda Reed. Brooklyn, N.Y.: Carlson, 1995.

Harley, Sharon, and Rosalyn Terborg-Penn, eds. *The Afro-American Woman: Struggles and Images*. Baltimore: Black Classic Press, 1978.

Harris, Juliette, and Pamela Johnson, eds. *Tenderheaded: A Comb-Bending Collection of Hair Stories*. New York: Pocket Books, 2001.

Harris, Michael. *The Rise of Gospel Blues: The Music of Thomas Andrew Dorsey in the Urban Church*. New York: Oxford University Press, 1992.

Hewitt, Nancy. *Southern Discomfort: Women's Activism in Tampa, Florida, 1880–1920s*. Urbana: University of Illinois Press, 2001.

Higbee, Mark David. "W. E. B. Du Bois, F. B. Ransom, the Madam Walker Company, and Black Business Leadership in the 1930s." *Indiana Magazine of History* 89 (June 1993): 101–124.

Higginbotham, Evelyn Brooks. *Righteous Discontent: The National Black Baptist Women's Convention*. Cambridge: Harvard University Press, 1994.

Hine, Darlene Clark. *Black Women in White: Racial Conflict and Cooperation in the Nursing Profession, 1890–1920.* Bloomington: Indiana University Press, 1989.

———. "The Housewives League of Detroit: Black Women and Economic Nationalism." In *Visible Women: New Essays on American Activism,* edited by Nancy Hewitt and Suzanne Lebsock. Urbana: University of Illinois Press, 1993: 223–242.

———. *Speak Truth to Power: Black Professional Class in United States History.* Brooklyn, N.Y.: Carlson, 1996.

———. "We Specialize in the Wholly Impossible." In *Lady Bountiful Revisited: Women, Philanthropy, and Power,* edited by Kathleen McCarthy. New Brunswick, N.J.: Rutgers University Press, 1991: 70–93.

hooks, bell. *Bone Black: Memories of Girlhood.* New York: Henry Holt, 1996.

Horowitz, Roger, and Arwen Mohun, eds. *His and Hers: Gender, Consumption, and Technology.* Charlottesville, Va.: University Press of Virginia, 1998.

Horton, Aimee Isgrig. *The Highlander Folk School: A History of Its Major Programs, 1939–1961.* Brooklyn, N.Y.: Carlson, 1989.

Horton, Myles. *The Long Haul: An Autobiography.* New York: Doubleday Books, 1990.

Howell, Christina Moore. *Beauty Culture and Care of the Hair.* New Brunswick, N.J.: Hill Publishing, 1936.

Hudson, Lynn. *The Making of "Mammy Pleasant": A Black Entrepreneur in Nineteenth-Century San Francisco.* Urbana: University of Illinois Press, 2003.

Hull, Gloria, ed. *Give Us Each Day: The Diary of Alice Dunbar-Nelson.* New York: Oxford University Press. 1984.

———. *The Works of Alice Dunbar-Nelson.* Vol. 2. New York: Oxford University Press, 1984.

Hunter, Tera. *To 'Joy My Freedom: Southern Black Women's Lives and Labors After the Civil War.* Cambridge: Harvard University Press, 1997.

Jackson, Mahalia. *Movin On Up.* New York: Hawthorn Books, 1966.

Janken, Kenneth. *Walter White, Mr. NAACP.* Chapel Hill: University of North Carolina Press, 2006.

Jeffries, LeRoy. "The Decay of the Beauty Parlor Industry in Harlem." *Opportunity: Journal of Negro Life* 15 (January 1938): 349–360.

Johnson, Kathryn. *What a Spelman Graduate Accomplished: Ezella Mathis Carter—A Biography and An Appeal.* Chicago: Pyramid Publishing, 1935.

Jones, Arthur. *Pierre Toussaint.* New York: Doubleday Books, 2003.

Jones, Jacqueline. *Labor of Love, Labor of Sorrow: Black Women, Work, and the Family From Slavery to the Present.* New York: Vintage Books, 1985.

Kay, Gwen. *Dying to Be Beautiful: The Fight for Safe Cosmetics.* Columbus: Ohio State University Press, 2005.

Kelley, Robin D. G. *Hammer and Hoe: Alabama Communists During the Great Depression.* Chapel Hill: University of North Carolina Press, 1990.

———. *Race Rebels: Culture, Politics, and the Black Working Class*. New York: Free Press, 1994.

Kessler- Harris, Alice. *In Pursuit of Equality: Women, Men and the Quest for Economic Citizenship in 20th Century America*. New York: Oxford University Press, 2003.

Kimble, Lionel. "'I Too Serve America': African American Women War Workers in Chicago, 1940–1945." *Journal of the Illinois State Historical Society* 93 (2000): 415–434.

King, Martin Luther, Peter Halloran, and Clayborne Carson. *The Papers of Martin Luther King, Jr. Vol. 4, Symbol of the Movement*. Berkeley and Los Angeles: University of California Press, 1992.

King, Wilma. *The Essence of Liberty: Free Black Women During the Slave Era*. Colombia: University of Missouri Press, 2006.

Knupfer, Anne Meis. *Toward a Tenderer Humanity and a Nobler Womanhood: African American Women's Clubs in the Turn-of-the-Century Chicago*. New York: Oxford University Press, 1984.

Kornweibel, Theodore. *No Crystal Stair: Black Life and the Messenger, 1917–1928*. Westport, Conn.: Greenwood Press, 1975.

Krenn, Michael. *Black Diplomacy: African Americans and the State Department, 1945–1969*. New York: M. E. Sharpe, 1999.

Kuhn, Clifford, Harlon Joye, and E. Bernard West, eds. *Living Atlanta: An Oral History of the City, 1914–1948*. Athens: University of Georgia, 1990.

Kwolek-Folland, Angel. *Engendering Business: Men and Women in the Corporate Office, 1870–1930*. Baltimore: Johns Hopkins Press, 1994.

———. *Incorporating Women: A History of Women and Business in the United States*. New York: Twayne, 1998.

Lacewell, Melissa Harris. *Barbershops, Bibles, and BET: Everyday Talk and Black Political Thought*. Princeton, N.J.: Princeton University Press, 2004.

Laird, Pamela. *Pull: Networking and Success Since Benjamin Franklin*. Cambridge: Harvard University Press, 2005.

Lears, T. Jackson. *Fables of Abundance: A Cultural History of Advertising in America*. New York: Basic Books, 1994.

Lee, Chana Kai. *For Freedom's Sake: The Life of Fannie Lou Hamer*. Urbana: University of Illinois Press, 1999.

Levenstein, Harvey. *We'll Always Have Paris: American Tourists in France Since 1930*. Chicago: University of Chicago Press, 2004.

Lewis, David Levering. *W. E. B. Du Bois: Biography of a Race, 1868–1919*. New York: Henry Holt Books, 1993.

———. *When Harlem Was in Vogue*. New York: Oxford University Press, 1979.

Ling, Peter. "Local Leadership in the Early Civil Rights Movement: The South Carolina Citizenship Education Program of the Highlander Folk School." *Journal of American Studies* 29 (1995): 399–422.

Livingston, James. *Pragmatism and the Political Economy of Cultural Revolution.* Chapel Hill: University North Carolina Press, 1994.

Lynk, B. S. *A Complete Course in Hair Straightening and Beauty Culture.* Memphis: 20th Century Art, 1919.

Marable, Manning, and Leith Mullings, Sophie Spencer Woods, eds. *Freedom: A Photographic History of the African American Struggle.* London: Phaidon Books, 2002.

Mark, Vernice. *The National Beauty Culturists' League History, 1919–1994.* Detroit: Harlo Press, 1994.

Martin, Tony. *Race First: The Ideological and Organizational Struggles of Marcus Garvey and the Universal Negro Improvement Association.* Boston: Majority Press, 1976.

Marwick, Arthur. *Beauty in History: Society, Politics, and Personal Appearance, 1500– the Present.* London: Thames and Hudson, 1988.

Mason, Herman. *Politics, Civil Rights and Law in Black Atlanta, 1870–1970.* Charleston, S.C.: Arcadia Publishing, 2000.

McArthur, Judith. *Creating the New Woman: The Rise of Southern Women's Progressive Culture in Texas, 1893–1918.* Urbana: University of Illinois Press, 1998.

McGerr, Michael. "Political Style and Women's Power, 1830–1930." *Journal of American History* (December 1998): 864–885.

Meyerowitz, Joanne. *Women Adrift: Independent Wage Earners in Chicago, 1880–1930.* Chicago: University of Chicago Press, 1988.

Michals, Debra. "Toward a New History of the Postwar Economy: Prosperity, Preparedness, and Women's Small Business Ownership." *Business and Economic History* 26 (Fall 1997): 45–56.

Miller, John. "Miss Americanizer: Frances Kellor." *Policy Review: The Journal of American Citizenship* 83 (May–June 1997): 64–65.

Mitchell, Jacquelyn. "Three Women: Cultural Rates and Leadership Roles in the Black Community." *Sage* 5 (Fall 1988): 9–19.

Mitchell, Michele. *Righteous Discontent: African Americans and the Politics of Racial Destiny after Reconstruction.* Chapel Hill: University of North Carolina Press, 2004.

Moody, Anne. *Coming of Age in Mississippi.* 1968. Reprint, New York: Delta Trade Paperbacks, 2004.

Moore, Brenda. *To Serve My Country, to Serve My Race: The Story of the Only African American WACs Stationed Overseas During World War II.* New York: New York University Press, 1996.

Morgan, Jennifer Lyle. "'Some Could Suckle Over Their Shoulder': Male Travelers, Female Bodies and the Gendering of Racial Ideology, 1500–1770." *William and Mary Quarterly* 54 (January 1997): 167–192.

Morris, Aldon. *The Origins of the Civil Rights Movements: Black Communities Organizing for Change.* New York: Free Press, 1984.

Newman, Kathy M. "The Forgotten Fifteen Million: Black Radio, the 'Negro Market' and the Civil Rights Movement." *Radical History Review* 76 (Spring 2000): 115–135.

Payne, Charles. *I've Got the Light of Freedom: The Organizing Tradition and the Mississippi Freedom Struggle.* Berkeley and Los Angeles: University of California Press, 1995.

Peiss, Kathy. "American Women and the Making of Modern Consumer Culture." *Journal of Multimedia History* 1 (Fall 1998). http://www.albany.edu/jmmh/vol1no1/peiss.html/. Accessed 1 May 2009.

———. *Cheap Amusements: Working Women and Leisure in Turn-of-the-Century New York.* Philadelphia: Temple University Press, 1986.

———. *Hope in a Jar: The Making of America's Beauty Culture.* New York: Metropolitan Books, 1998.

———. "Vital Industry and Women's Ventures: Conceptualizing Gender in Twentieth Century Business History." *Business History Review* 72 (Summer 1998): 219–241.

Pigee, Vera. *The Struggle of Struggles.* Detroit: Harlo Press, 1975.

Plummer, Brenda Gayle, ed. *Window on Freedom: Race, Civil Rights, and Foreign Affairs, 1945–1988.* Chapel Hill: University of North Carolina Press, 2003.

———. *Rising Wind: Black Americans and United States' Foreign Policy, 1935–1960.* Chapel Hill: University of North Carolina Press, 1996.

Poinsett, Alex. *Walking with the Presidents: Louis Martin and the Rising of Black Political Power.* New York: Rowan and Littlefield, 2000.

Pomerantz, Gary. *Where Peachtree Meets Sweet Auburn: A Saga of Race and Family.* New York: Penguin Books, 1997.

Potter, Eliza. *A Hairdresser's Experience in the High Life.* 1859. Reprint, New York: Oxford University Press, 1988.

Raines, Howell. *My Soul Is Rested: The Story of the Civil Rights Movement in the Deep South.* New York: Penguin Books, 1977.

Ransby, Barbara. *Ella Baker and the Black Freedom Movement: A Radical Democratic Vision.* Chapel Hill: University of North Carolina Press, 2003.

Richards, Yevette. *Maida Springer: Pan Africanist and International Labor Leader.* Pittsburgh: University of Pittsburgh Press, 2000.

Robnett, Belinda. *How Long? How Long? African American Women in the Struggle for Civil Rights.* New York: Oxford University Press, 1997.

Rooks, Noliwe. *Hair Raising: Beauty Culture and African American Women.* New Brunswick, N.J.: Rutgers University Press, 1996.

Sadler, Georgia Robins, Margaret W. Meyer, Celine Marie Ko, Crystal Butcher, Shianti Lee, Tiffany Neal, Lynn Reed, Aaron E. Veals, and Elizabeth A. Gilpin, "Black Cosmetologists Promote Diabetes Awareness and Screening Among African American Women." *Diabetes Educator* 30 (July/August 2004): 676–685.

———, Melanie Peterson, Linda Wasserman, Paul Mills, Vanessa Malcame, Cheryl Rock, Sonia Ancoli-Israel, Amanda Moore, Rai-Nesha Welson, Tenisha Garcia, and Richard Kolodner, "Recruiting Research Participants at Community Education Sites," *Journal of Cancer Education* 20 (2005): 235–239.

Samuel, Lawrence. *Pledging Allegiance: American Identity and the Bond Drive of World War II*. Washington, D.C.: Smithsonian Institution Press, 1997.

Santamarina, Xiomara. "Black Hairdresser and Social Critic: Eliza Potter and the Labors of Femininity." *American Literature* 77 (March 2005): 151–177.

Satter, Beryl. "Marcus Garvey, Father Divine, and the Gender Politics of Race Difference and Race Neutrality." *American Quarterly* 48 (March 1996): 43–76.

Saville, Julie. *The Work of Reconstruction: From Slave to Wage Laborer in South Carolina, 1860–1870*. Cambridge: Cambridge University Press, 1994.

Schuyler, George. *Black No More*. 1931. Reprint, Chicago: Northeastern University Press, 1989.

Scott, Joan. "Gender: A Useful Category of Historical Analysis." *American Historical Review* 91, no. 5 (December 1986): 1053–1075.

Sernett, Milton. *Bound for the Promised Land: African American Religion and the Great Migration*. Durham, N.C.: Duke University Press, 1997.

Shaw, Stephanie. *What A Woman Ought to Be and to Do: Black Professional Women During the Jim Crow Era*. Chicago: University of Chicago Press, 1995.

Shockley, Megan Taylor. *"We, Too, Are Americans": African American Women in Detroit and Richmond, 1945–1954*. Urbana: University of Illinois Press, 2004.

Smith, Selina, Sandra Hamilton, Joyce Q. Sheats, Ernest Mensch, Funmi Apantaku, and Louis Sullivan. "Stay Beautiful/Stay Alive: A Successful Approach to Community-Based Participatory Research." *American Journal of Health Studies* 18, no. 4 (2003).

Sparks, Edith. "Married Women and Economic Choice: Explaining Why Women Started Business in San Francisco Between 1890–1930." *Business and Economic History* 28 (Winter 1999): 287–300.

Stein, Judith. *The World of Marcus Garvey: Race and Class in Modern Society*. Baton Rouge, La.: Louisiana University Press, 1991.

Strasser, Susan. *Satisfaction Guaranteed: The Making of the American Mass Market*. New York: Pantheon Books, 1989.

Strasser, Susan, Charles McGovern, and Matthias Judt, eds. *Getting and Spending: European and American Consumer Societies in the Twentieth Century*. Cambridge: Cambridge University Press, 1998.

Sullivan, Patricia. *Days of Hope: Race and Democracy in the New Deal Era*. Chapel Hill: University of North Carolina Press, 1996.

Summers, Martin. *Manliness and Its Discontents: The Black Middle Class and the Transformation of Masculinity, 1900–1930*. Chapel Hill: University of North Carolina Press, 2004.

Taylor, Ula. *The Veiled Garvey: The Life and Times of Amy Jacques Garvey*. Chapel Hill: University of North Carolina Press, 2002.

Tolbert, Emory. *The UNIA and Black Los Angeles: Ideology and Community in the American Garvey Movement*. Los Angeles: UCLA Press, 1980.

Trotter, Joe William, ed. *The Great Migration in Historical Perspective: New Dimensions of Race, Class, and Gender.* Bloomington: Indiana University Press, 1991.

Turner, Joyce Moore. *Caribbean Crusaders and the Harlem Renaissance.* Urbana: University of Illinois Press, 2005.

Von Eschen, Penny. "Challenging Cold War Habits: African Americans, Race, and Foreign Policy." *Diplomatic History* 20 (Fall 1996): 627–638.

———. *Satchmo Blows Up the World: Jazz Ambassadors Play the Cold War.* Cambridge: Harvard University Press, 2004.

Wade-Gayles, Gloria. *Pushed Back to Strength: A Black Woman's Journey Home.* Boston: Beacon Press, 1993.

Walker, Alice. "Oppressed Hair Puts a Ceiling on the Brain." In *Living by the Word,* by Alice Walker. New York: Harcourt Brace and Jovanovich, 1988: 69–74.

Walker, Juliet E. K. *Encyclopedia of African American Business History.* Westport, Conn.: Greenwood Press, 1999.

———. *The History of Black Business in America: Capitalism, Race, and Entrepreneurship.* New York: Macmillian Reference Library, 1998.

Walker, Susannah. *Style and Status: Selling Beauty to African American Women, 1920–1975.* Lexington: University of Kentucky Press, 2007.

Ward, Martha. *Voodoo Queen: The Spirited Lives of Marie Laveau.* Jackson: University of Mississippi Press, 2004.

Washington, Booker T. *The Negro in Business.* New York: Devore & Sons, 1907.

———. *Tuskegee and Its People: Their Ideals and Achievements.* New York: D. Appleton, 1905.

Watkins-Owens, Irma. *Blood Relations: Caribbean Immigrants and the Harlem Community, 1900–1930.* Bloomington: Indiana University Press, 1996.

Weems, Robert. *Black Business in the Black Metropolis: The Chicago Metropolitan Assurance Company, 1925–1985.* Bloomington: Indiana University Press, 1996.

———. *Desegregating the Dollar: African American Consumerism in the Twentieth Century.* New York: New York University Press, 1998.

Wiese, Andrew. *Places of Their Own: African American Suburbanization in the Twentieth Century.* Chicago: University of Chicago Press, 2004.

Wigginton, Elliot, ed. *Refuse to Stand Silently By: An Oral History of Grassroots Social Activism in America, 1921–1964.* New York: Doubleday Books, 1991.

White, Deborah Gray. *Too Heavy a Load: Black Women in Defense of Themselves.* New York: W. W. Norton, 1998.

White, Shane, and Graham White. "Slave Hair and African American Culture in the Eighteenth and Nineteenth Centuries." *Journal of Southern History* 61 (February 1995): 45–76.

———. *Stylin': African American Expressive Culture from Its Beginning to the Zoot Suit.* Ithaca, N.Y.: Cornell University Press, 1998.

Willett, Julie Ann. "'Hands Across the Table': A Short History of the Manicurist in the Twentieth Century." *Journal of Women's History* 17, no. 3 (Fall 2005): 59–80.

———. *Permanent Waves: The Making of the American Beauty Shop*. New York: New York University Press, 2000.

Wolcott, Victoria. "'Bible, Bath, and Broom': Nannie Helen Burroughs, the National Training School and the Uplift of the Race." *Journal of Women's History* (Spring 1997): 88–110.

———. *Remaking Respectability: African American Women in Interwar Detroit*. Chapel Hill: University of North Carolina Press, 2001.

Yellen, David, and Johanna Lenander. *Hair Wars*. Brooklyn, N.Y.: Powerhouse Press, 2007.

Zunz, Oliver. *Making America Corporate, 1870–1970*. Chicago: University of Chicago Press, 1992.

DISSERTATIONS, THESES, AND UNPUBLISHED PAPERS

Baker, R. Scott. "Ambiguous Legacies: The NAACP Legal Campaign Against Segregation in Charleston, SC, 1935–1975." Ph.D. diss., Columbia University, 1993.

Bristol, Douglas. "From Outposts to Enclaves: A Social History of Black Barbers, 1750–1915." Ph.D. diss., University of Maryland, 2002.

Brown, Leslie. "Common Spaces, Separate Lives: Gender and Racial Conflict in the Capitol of the Black Middle Class." Ph.D. diss., Duke University 1997.

Charron, Katherine Mellen. "Teaching Citizenship: Septima Poinsette Clark and the Transformation of the African American Freedom Struggle." Ph.D. diss., Yale University, 2005.

Christenen, Lawrence Oland. "Black St. Louis: A Study in Race Relations, 1865–1916." Ph.D. diss., University of Missouri, 1972.

Cobb, William Jelani. "Antidote to Revolution: Afro-American Anticommunism and the Quest for Civil Rights, 1931–1945." Ph.D. diss., Rutgers University, 2003.

Foster, James Herbert. "Urban Experience of Blacks in Atlantic City, New Jersey, 1850–1915." Ph.D. diss., Rutgers University, 1981.

Franson, Jerome Donald. "Citizenship Education in the South Carolina Sea Islands, 1954–1966." Ph.D. diss., Georgia Peabody College for Teachers, 1977.

Grant, LaVerne. "Contributions of African American Women to Nonformal Education During the Civil Rights Movement, 1955–1965." Ed.D. diss., Pennsylvania State University, 1990.

Kanes, Candace. "American Business Women, 1890–1930: Creating an Identity." Ph.D. diss., University of New Hampshire, 1997.

Mawhood, Rhonda. "Tales to Curl Your Hair: African American Beauty Parlors in Jim Crow Durham." Unpublished seminar paper, Duke University, 1993.

Mills, Quincy T. "Color-Line Barbers and the Emergence of a Black Public Space: A Social and Political History of Black Barbers and Barber Shops, 1830–1970." Ph.D. diss., University of Chicago, 2006.

Millward, Jessica. "'A Choice Parcel of Country Born': African-Americans and the

Transition to Freedom in Maryland, 1770–1840." Ph.D. diss., University of California, Los Angeles, 2003.

Myers, Amrita Chakrabarti. "Negotiating Women: Black Women and the Politics of Freedom in Charleston, South Carolina, 1790–1860." Ph.D. diss., Rutgers University, 2004.

Nasstrom, Kathryn. "Women, the Civil Rights Movement, and the Politics of Historical Memory, 1946–1973." Ph.D. diss., University of North Carolina, 1993.

Oldendorf, Sandra Brenneman. "Highlander Folk School and the South Carolina Sea Island Citizenship Schools: Implications for the Social Studies." Ph.D. diss., University of Kentucky, 1987.

Polyne, Millery. "Modernizing the Race: Political and Cultural Engagements Between African Americans and Haitians, 1930–1964." Ph.D. diss., University of Michigan, 2003.

Robinson, Gwendolyn Keita. "Class, Race, and Gender: A Transcultural Theoretical and Sociohistorical Analysis of Cosmetic Institutions and Practices to 1920." Ph.D. diss., University of Illinois, Chicago, 1984.

Index

TIFFANY M. GILL is an assistant professor of history at the University of Texas at Austin.

Radical Sisters: Second-Wave Feminism and Black Liberation in Washington, D.C.
  Anne M. Valk
Feminist Coalitions: Historical Perspectives on Second-Wave Feminism in the United
  States *Edited by Stephanie Gilmore*
Breadwinners: Working Women and Economic Independence, 1865–1920
  Lara Vapnek
Beauty Shop Politics: African American Women's Activism in the Beauty Industry
  Tiffany M. Gill

The University of Illinois Press
is a founding member of the
Association of American University Presses.

University of Illinois Press
1325 South Oak Street
Champaign, IL 61820–6903
www.press.uillinois.edu